RAILWAYS RESTORED

1990/91 EDITION

EDITED BY ALAN C. BUTCHER

D1232815

LONDON

IAN ALLAN LTD

Above:
The man responsible for it all. Tom Rolt is seen in action during 1951 whilst acting as guard on the Talyllyn. For the first few years Tom Rolt and a handful of other volunteers were responsible for running the daily summer service.

Chairman's Foreword

For 1990 I have asked Peter Manisty, our Vice President and oldest Member of Council, to write the Introductory Sections of this Anniversary Year Book. It promises to be a splendid year for all of us.

À toute Vapeur — Full Steam Ahead
David Morgan

Association of Railway Preservation Societies' Yearbook

Contents

First published 1990

ISBN 0 7110 1917 7

Published by Ian Allan Ltd, Shepperton, Surrey and printed by Ian Allan Printing Ltd at their works at Coombelands in Runnymede, England

Editor's Notes

On the following pages will be found a guide to the major preserved railways, railway museums and preservation centres in the British Isles. Information for visitors has been set out in tabular form for easy reference, together with a locomotive stocklist for most centres.

Many preservation centres and operating lines provide facilities for other groups and organisations to restore locomotives and equipment on their premises. It has not been possible to include full details of these groups, but organisations which own locomotives are shown under the centres at which they operate. In addition a full list of member societies of the ARPS is given elsewhere. In the case of most operating lines their length is given but there is no guarantee that services are operated over the entire length.

Within the heading to each entry a heading block has been incorporated for easy reference as to what each site offers in the way of passenger service to visitors. These are as follows:

 Railways providing a passenger service between two or more stations with public access; eg Mid-Hants Railway.

 SC A railway or preservation site offering a passenger service on a short length of line, on a regular basis, with public access at only one point; eg Lavender Line.

M A museum or site that does *not* offer a passenger service on a regular basis, if at all; eg Science Museum, London. Some sites may however offer rides on miniature railways.

Under the the heading **References** will be found the details of articles which have appeared in the Ian Allan magazine *Railway World* during the past two years.

The after-effects of deregulation of the bus industry are still resulting in changes and the details given under **Access by public transport** should be checked beforehand to ensure services shown are still operating.

The editor would be pleased to receive good quality black and white photographs or colour transparencies for consideration for use in future editions of this title.

Alan C. Butcher

Front cover:
Pride of the East Anglian Railway Museum. Following a lengthy period of restoration No 69621 was restored to service over the August 1989 bank holiday weekend. It is seen here in action on the centre's demonstration line passing the restored signalbox.
G. D. King

The Association of Railway Preservation Societies

10th Anniversary of *Railways Restored*

1990 is being promoted by the ARPS as 'Railway Preservation Year'.

It is the 10th Anniversary of this Yearbook, *Railways Restored*, published by Ian Allan, the first issues of which included timetables. Recently however, David Wilson has launched a companion guide, *Wilson's Preserved Steam Railway Timetable*, which sits alongside *Railways Restored*.

1990 is, more importantly, the 40th anniversary of the Talyllyn Railway Preservation Society and the 30th of the Bluebell and Middleton Railway Preservation Societies. These are the three PIONEER preserved railways. It is also the 30th anniversary of the ARPS.

Through the efforts of railway preservation societies an extensive range of railway items, covering almost the whole spectrum of the age of steam railways, is being preserved. Without the efforts of those enthusiasts (mostly voluntary) steam trains would now only be known through pictures, recordings, models and memories.

Railway preservation societies have sprung up independently, through the initiative of their promoters. But all such societies have interests in common. New societies benefit from access to the know-how of established ones. Established societies, for their part, find it in their interest that new ones should be soundly organised, to minimise the possibility of physical or financial disaster, which would mar the whole movement in the public eye. All societies benefit from information about sources of equipment and material. They benefit, too, from joint publicity and from joint representation to higher national (and other) authorities and bodies.

These needs are met by the Association of Railway Preservation Societies Ltd. Most societies in the British Isles are members of the Association, which is a non-profit-distributing voluntary body, incorporated as a company limited by guarantee.

Background

The Association originated in November 1959, largely due to the efforts of the late Noel Draycott who united five preservation groups under the banner of the Railway Preservation Society and laid the keel of the ARPS.

Today it has 180 corporate members societies (full and associate) and over 500 private members.

The ARPS has always maintained very close liaison with British Railways and one of the first major events in its history occurred on 1 April 1962 with the running of the 'Blue Belle', hauled by Capt Bill Smith's GNR Class J52 0-6-0T No 1247 from London Bridge to Sheffield Park and return. Dr Richard Beeching, the Chairman of the British Transport Commission, joined the train at Three Bridges and on arrival at Sheffield Park (after opening Freshfield Halt) said: 'In order to make the whole system of British Railways more healthy and vigorous it will be necessary to displace some of the old equipment and some services. As we do that, so the desirability of preservation will become more apparent, but I would like to warn all those people who are interested in it that you must not overdo it to the point where you spoil the market for yourselves. I think in this connection, the setting up of the Association of Railway Preservation Societies is likely to be a very helpful measure because we can well afford to have a scattering of preservation societies throughout the country, but if it is done to excess, then the efforts of those who are most serious will be spoiled by those who are not prepared to put in enough effort to run societies properly.' Dr Beeching's point has, in 1990, been well proved by the ARPS.

We are most grateful to Alan C. Butcher who (with Chris Leigh in the early issues) has edited our Yearbook throughout the 10 years with consistant strength and reliability — long may he remain at the helm.

Peter Manisty
Vice Chairman ARPS

Objectives

The main objects of the ARPS are to further the mutual co-operation of railway preservation organisations, to promote publicity on their behalf and to encourage high standards of competence. It also obtains sponsorship from heritage and commercial bodies on behalf of its members.

There are three things that the Association does not do: it runs no railway preservation activities directly; and it neither raises funds nor distributes them. Subscriptions cover only running expenses. (It leaves fund raising to its colleagues in the Transport Trust.)

It is manned entirely by volunteers.

By encouraging high standards the Association safeguards the interests of the public who visit, and subscribe to, railways preservation schemes. Full corporate membership is not granted lightly and all corporate members must give an assurance that they will comply with the Association's Code of Practice.

Meetings are held three times a year, usually on member railways or depots, and enable members' representatives to meet formally and informally, and to inspect (and learn from) the preservation activities of their hosts.

The mainstay of the ARPS is its Journal. Published four times a year it is a bright and colourful publication.

Some achievements of the Association include:
● Block purchases in 1966 of steam locomotives from British Rail negotiated on behalf of member societies (13 locomotives and two coaches for £23,425!).
● The release (in 1968) from Dai Woodham's scrapyard at Barry of the first of many loco-

motives which had previously been disposed of by BR on the condition that they would not be re-sold. (Midland 4F No 43924.) Contrary to Jonah Forebodings the *last* of over 200 steam locomotives for preservation left Barry on 9 November 1989, No 3845.
● Arrangements for locomotives and other exhibits from the National Collection to be loaned to members (*Oliver Cromwell* at Bressingham was an early achievement).
● The yearly publication of the *Guide to Steam Trains in the British Isles* issued free to the public, First published by BP — The Yellow — and now by British Coal (over 500,000 copies).

● The acceptance by the more staid professional museum movement of the possibility of our members 'joining forces'. Initial discussion well under way.
● The staging in 1989 in Utrecht of the first-ever International Railway Preservation Conference.

'How long can it all go on? Surely the bubble will burst?' the Jonahs have been singing for years! To both questions the ARPS has the answer — for ever and no.

But it will require even greater strength and a united and determined effort to keep 'pressing ahead'.

Ian Allan Railway Heritage awards

The Railway Heritage Awards were born in 1979 as the Best Restored Station Competition — the brainchild of Michael Harris — and it was run by Ian Allan Ltd in association with Travel Britain.

In 1981, at the request of Ian Allan, The ARPS took over the running with Ian Allan remaining as chief sponsor and paymaster — Andrew Roberts was in charge on behalf of the ARPS.

Throughout the years British Rail has given unstinting and enthusiastic support, including several presentations by its Chairmen, Sir Peter Parker and Sir Robert Reid, with both Euston and Marylebone as venues for the ceremonies.

The 1985 awards were made by David Shepherd and the 1986 awards by Prince Michael of Kent — both at the Royal Society of Arts. In 1985 British Rail, under the baton of David Perry, mounted a splendid exhibition stand which later toured the country.

In 1986 British Rail restarted its own Best Kept Station Competition and reduced the support for the Ian Allan/ARPS project — nevertheless they still provided a major slice including a large number of BR entries, which, even then, still tended to exceed those from the private sector.

The Railway Heritage Trust and British Coal added weight to the sponsors and provided generous support.

By now Gordon Biddle had taken over on behalf of the ARPS and in 1989, to celebrate the 10th year of the awards the British Rail Community Trust sponsored a prestigious brochure which had a wide distribution — the bulk of which were distributed by English Heritage with its own Conservation Bulletin

and introduced the awards to a wide section of 'heritage-minded' people.

As a result the scope of the Awards is rapidly expanding and 1989 was a record year with continuing success forecast for 1990.

The 1989 awards were presented by Sir Robert Reid at the Royal Society of Arts on Monday 26 March 1990.

The winners for 1989 are:

Volunteer Sector *(13 entries)*
Ingrow West (K&WVR) — Premier Award
Alston (South Tynedale)
Ramsbottom (East Lancs) } Commendations
Champions Award (for previous Premier Award winners)
Oakworth (K&WVR)
Signalbox (special 1989 award — 9 entries)
Didcot Railway Centre (GWS) — Award
Llangollen Goods Jct (Llangollen) Honourable Mention, no prize

Public and Commercial Sector *(68 entries)*
Railway Heritage Trust
Gobowon Station (LMR)
Premier award
Lewes Station (SR)
First Class Awards
Brondesbury Park (LMR)
Perth (ScR)
Melrose (Private/LA)
Certificate
Thorpe Thewles (Castle Eden Country Park)

Note: Copies of the Ian Allan Railway Heritage Awards 10th Anniversary Brochure are still available from the General Administrator, Douglas Whittle on receipt of stamps to the value of 30p.

John Bartholomew's folding map of 'Railway History and Preservation Map of the British Isles', published in association with the ARPS will be available at the end of March 1990 from all major retail outlets — priced £3.95.

The ARPS Annual Award

This, the premier award made by ARPS, is made to a group or organisation making an outstanding contribution to railway preservation during the year of the award.

The Award takes the form of a Royal Train Headboard from the London, Brighton & South Coast Railway, which is on loan to ARPS from the National Railway Museum. The award is held for one year and the winning group also receives a commemorative plaque. The Award is announced and presented at the Association's Annual General Meeting which is held on the last weekend of January each year.

The ARPS Award for 1989 is made to Tenterden Railway Co Ltd (Kent & East Sussex Railway) for the professionalism of its voluntary marketing and engineering staff in construction of its extension. This culminated in the provision of facilities to make the 'Challenge Anneka' television programme about reinstating Northiam station, which meant 45min of peak viewing time television for railway preservation.

Also an ARPS Special Award 'To all whose dedication in restoring *The Great Marquess* enabled her owner, David Earl of Lindsay, to ride her footplate on the West Highland Line on 15 July 1989, a fortnight before his death'.

Previous awards have been made to:

1975—the Great Western Society Ltd
1976—the Princess Elizabeth Locomotive Society
1977—the Peterborough Railway Society Ltd (Nene Valley Railway)
1978—the Festiniog Railway Society
1979—the Severn Valley Railway Co Ltd
1980—the Scottish Railway Preservation Society Co Ltd
1981—the Great Western Society Ltd
1982—the Festiniog Railway Society Ltd
1983—the Railway Preservation Society of Ireland
1984—the Severn Valley Railway Co Ltd
1985—jointly to the A4 Locomotive Society Ltd Merchant Navy Locomotive Preservation Society Ltd and the Friends of the National Railway Museum
1986—the 71000 Duke of Gloucester Locomotive Trust Ltd
1987—the East Lancashire Railway Society
1988—staff and Friends of the National Railway Museum

Below:
The winner of the 1989 ARPS Award is the Kent & East Sussex Railway, as the citation above proclaims. Here we see ex-SECR 'P' class 0-6-0T No 1556 steaming across the A28 into the site of Northiam station on the evening of 19 May 1989. The KESR aims to reopen to the Wittersham Road-Northiam section in May 1990. *Jim Berryman*

5

1990 Railway Preservation Year List of Events

At the time of going to press the following events were planned to take place. Prospective visitors are advised to check beforehand that they are still taking place on the planned date.

March
12	John Huntley film show, Playhouse, Harlow
26	Ian Allan Railway Heritage Awards, Royal Society of Arts, London
30	John Huntley film show, Gainsborough Model Railway Society

April
9	John Huntley film show, Fairfield Halls, Croydon
21/22	Severn Valley Railway, 25th Anniversary Gala
28/29	ARPS Spring Meeting Weekend, based in Brighton

May
5-7	British Coal Steam Heritage Awards and Steam Heritage Weekend, NRM, York
5-7	Talyllyn RPS, Model Railway Exhibition, Tywyn
12	'Talyllyn Pioneer' special train from London
12/13	Transport Trust AGM weekend, Ironbridge Gorge Museum
26-28	Talyllyn RPS, Vintage Transport Rally, Tywyn
26-3 June	Great Western Society, Railway Preservation Gala, Didcot

June
10-17	Middleton Railway Gala, Middleton
16	Middleton Railway Anniversary Gala Dinner
23	'Middleton Milestone' Steam Special from London to Leeds
23/24	Talyllyn Railway, 'A Midsummer Nights Steam', round the clock steam service
30	'Blue Belle' special train from London to Bluebell Railway

July
1	Talyllyn Railway, special church service to commemorate 40 years of TRPS and 125 years of TR Co
2-8	Talyllyn Railway, week of vintage train service
5	Talyllyn Railway, special train to mark 125 anniversary of TR Co
6	Severn Valley Railway, Silver Jubilee Celebrations Banquet
16	John Huntley film show, Fairfield Halls, Croydon

August
4/5	Bluebell Railway, 30th Anniversary Weekend
4/5	Talyllyn RPS, Traction Engine Weekend, Hendy, near Tywyn
25/26	Tallyllyn RPS, Land Rover Rally, Tywyn

September
20-23	Severn Valley Railway, Silver Jubilee Autumn Steam Gala
22/23	Talyllyn RPS, Study Weekend at Snowdonia National Park Study Centre, Plas Tan-y-Bwlch

October
6/7	ARPS Autumn Meeting Weekend, hosted by Scottish RPS at Bo'ness & Kenneil Railway
TBA	Talyllyn RPS, special trains to commemorate last pre-preservation train

November
10/11	Permanent Way & Civil Engineering Seminar, hosted by Middleton Railway

Abbreviations

AEC	Associated Equipment Co	DB	German Federal Railways
AEG	Allgemeine Eletricitaets Gesellschaft	DSB	Danish State Railways
A/Porter	Aveling & Porter Ltd	MoS	Ministry of Supply
A/Whitworth	Armstrong Whitworth	NSB	Norwegian State Railways
B/Drewry	Baguley/Drewry	SJ	Swedish Railways
B/Peacock	Beyer Peacock & Co	SAR	South African Railways
B/Hawthorn	Black, Hawthorn & Co	SNCF	French National Railways
BTH	British Thomson Houston	USA TC	United States Army Transportation Corps
D/Metcalfe	Davies & Metcalfe	WD	War Department
E/Electric	English Electric Ltd		
F/Jennings	Fletcher Jennings & Co	BE	Battery electric
F/Walker	Fox Walker	DE	Diesel-electric
G/England	George England & Co	DH	Diesel-hydraulic
H/Clarke	Hudswell Clarke & Co Ltd	DM	Diesel-mechanical
H/Leslie	Hawthorn Leslie & Co	E	Overhead electric
H/Hunslet	Hudson Hunslet	F	Fireless
K/Stuart	Kerr Stuart & Co Ltd	G	Geared
M/Rail	Motor Rail Ltd	PM	Petrol-mechanical
M/Vick	Metrovick (Metropolitan-Vickers)	ParM	Paraffin-mechanical
M/Wardle	Manning Wardle & Co Ltd	PT	Pannier tank
N/British	North British Locomotive Co Ltd	R	Railcar
N/Wilson	Nasmyth Wilson & Co Ltd	ST	Saddle tank
O&K	Orenstein & Koppel	T	Side tank
RSH	Robert Stephenson & Hawthorn Ltd	VB	Vertical boiler
R/Hornsby	Ruston Hornsby	WT	Well tank
R/Proctor	Ruston Proctor	4w	4-wheel
YEC	Yorkshire Engine Co		

South East

Amberley Chalk Pits Museum   SC

Narrow Gauge and Industrial Railway Collection (incorporating the Brockham Museum of Narrow Gauge Railways)

The NG&IR Collection is part of an open air industrial museum set in 36 acres of the former Pepper & Co chalk pits. A 2ft gauge line has been constructed and this is used for carrying passengers in genuine workmen's vehicles
Location: Houghton Bridge, Amberley, West Sussex (3 miles north of Arundel). On B2139. Adjacent to Amberley BR(SR) station
OS reference: TQ 031122
Operating society/organisation: Southern Industrial History Centre Trust, Amberley Chalk Pits Museum, Houghton Bridge, Amberley, Arundel, West Sussex BN18 9LT
Telephone: Bury (0798) 831370 (Museum office)
Car park: Adjacent to Amberley Station
On site facilities: Shop, light refreshments, audio-visual show
Public opening: Wednesday to Sunday (inclusive) each week, and Bank Holiday Mondays, (open all week in school summer holidays) 10.00-last entry 17.00, 24 March-28 October
Special events: Steam & Model Engineering Day 10 September
Special Notes: The NG&IR Collection is part of an open air industrial museum set in 36 acres of the former Pepper & Co chalk pits. Displays include working potter, blacksmith, boatbuilder and printer, stationary engines, historic radio collection and newly completed vintage Southdown garage and buses. A 2ft 0in gauge industrial railway system is demonstrated when possible, and a 3ft 2¼in gauge line is under construction. In addition a 2ft 0in gauge 'main line' has been constructed and this is used for carrying passengers in genuine

Locomotives
(2ft or 60cm unless otherwise indicated)

Name	No	Builder	Type	Built
Polar Bear	—	Bagnall (1781)	2-4-0T	1905
Peter	—	Bagnall (2067)	0-4-0ST	1918
Lion	—	Baldwin (44656)	4-6-0T	1917
Townsend Hook	4	F/Jennings (172L)	0-4-0T	1880
			(3ft 2¼in gauge)	
Scaldwell	—	Peckett (1316)	0-6-0ST	1913
			(3ft 0in gauge)	
—	23†	Spence	0-4-0T	1921
			(1ft 10in gauge)	
—	—	Decauville (1126)	0-4-0T	1950
—	740	O&K (2343)	0-6-0T	1907
Monty	(6)	O&K (7269)	4wDM	1936
			(3ft 2¼in gauge)	
The Major	(7)	O&K (7741)	4wDM	1937
—	2	Ransomes & Rapier (80)	4wDM	1937
—	—	Hudson-Hunslet (3097)	4wDM	1944
—	2	R/Hornsby (166024)	4wDM	1933
—	(3041)	M/Rail (Simplex) (1320)	4wDM (ex-PM)	1918
—	3101	M/Rail (Simplex) (1381) Armoured	4wPM	1918
Peldon	—	John Fowler (21295)	4wDM	1936
Redland	—	O&K (6193)	4wDM	1937
—	—	Lister (35421)	4wPM	1949
—	(LR 2593)	M/Rail (Simplex) (872)	4wPM	1918
—	27	M/Rail (Simplex) (5863)	4wDM	1934
—	—	M/Rail (Simplex) (10161)	4wDM	1949
			(2ft 11in gauge)	
Ibstock	—	M/Rail (Simplex) (11001)	4wDM	1951
CCSW	—	Hibberd (1980)	4wDM	1936
Thakeham Tiles	No 3	Hudson-Hunslet (2208)	4wDM	1941
Thakeham Tiles	No 4	Hudson-Hunslet (3653)	4wDM	1948
—	—	H/Clarke (DM686)	0-4-0DM	1948
Star Construction	—	Hudson-Hunslet	4wDm	c1941
—	18	R/Hornsby (187081)	4wDM	1937
—	—	Hudson-Hunslet (2536)	4wDM	1941
—	—	Lister (33937)	4wDM	1949
—	—	R/Hornsby (172892)	4wDm	1934
—	WD 904	Wickham (3403)	2w+2PMR	1943

workmen's vehicles. The 500yd line, was officially opened by HRH Prince Michael of Kent on 5 June 1984. The railway is operated every day the museum is open (subject to mechanical availability), with steam locomotive haulage on certain days — for details contact the museum office. Wheelchairs can normally be accommodated on the train. A Narrow Gauge Industrial Railway Introductory Exhibition sets the scene for these and other set-piece display areas

Membership details: Amberley Chalk Pit Museum Association, c/o above address

—	2	Wingrove & Rogers (5031)	4wBE	1953
—	—	Wingrove & Rogers (5034)	4wBE	1953
—	—	Wingrove & Rogers (4998)	4wBE	1953
—	—	Wingrove & Rogers (T8033)	0-4-0BE	1979

Stock

2 Penrhyn Quarry Railway 4-wheel coaches (2ft gauge, ex-1ft 10¾in gauge)

RAF Fauld bogie coach (1940) (2ft gauge)

Rye & Camber Tramway bogie (incomplete) (1895) (3ft gauge)

2 Groudle Glen Railway 4-wheel coaches (1896 and 1905) (2ft gauge)

60 other varied pieces of rolling stock of 12 different gauges ranging from 1ft 6in to 3ft 2¼in plus numerous miscellaneous exhibits including track, signals etc

†Includes hoist and 'haulage truck' for conversion to 5ft 3in gauge

Bluebell Railway

This famous steam railway was the first standard gauge passenger line to be taken over by enthusiasts. It derives its name from bluebells which proliferate in the woodlands adjoining the line. A strong Victorian atmosphere pervades this branch line which has a large collection of Southern and pre-Grouping locomotives and coaches.

Headquarters: Bluebell Railway Preservation Society, Sheffield Park station, Uckfield, East Sussex TN22 3QL

Telephone: Newick (082 572) 2370 for travel information (24hr talking timetable); Newick 3777 for bookings etc during office hours

Main station: Sheffield Park

Other public stations: Horsted Keynes

Car parks: Sheffield Park, Horsted Keynes

OS reference:
Sheffield Park TQ 403238,
Horsted Keynes TQ 372293

Access by public transport: Haywards Heath BR and bus to Horsted Keynes village weekdays, or direct to Sheffield Park on summer and winter Sundays. Additional bus services on certain days, timetable brochure available by sending sae

Refreshment facilities: Sheffield Park, Horsted Keynes (licensed bars at both stations). The 'Regency Belle' wine and dine train runs on certain dates and is also available for private charter

Souvenir shops: Sheffield Park, Horsted Keynes

Locomotives

Name	No	Origin	Class	Type	Built
—	27	SECR	P	0-6-0T	1910
Stepney	55	LBSCR	A1X	0-6-0T	1875
Fenchurch	72	LBSCR	A1X	0-6-0T	1872
Pioneer II	1178	SECR	P	0-6-0T	1910
Bluebell	323	SECR	P	0-6-0T	1910
—	263	SECR	H	0-4-4T	1905
Birch Grove	473	LBSCR	E4	0-6-2T	1898
—	488	LSWR	0415	4-4-2T	1885
—	592	SECR	C	0-6-0	1901
—	58850	NLR		0-6-0T	1880
Earl of Berkeley	3217	GWR	9000	4-4-0	1938
—	30064	SR	USA	0-6-0T	1943
—	541	SR	Q	0-6-0	1939
—	830*	SR	S15	4-6-0	1927
—	847	SR	S15	4-6-0	1937
Stowe	928	SR	V	4-4-0	1934
—	1618	SR	U	2-6-0	1928
—	31638	SR	U	2-6-0	1931
—	96	LSWR	B4	0-4-0T	1905
—	C1	SR	Q1	0-6-0	1942
Sir Archibald Sinclair	34059	SR	BB	4-6-2	1947
Port Line	35027	SR	MN	4-6-2	1948
Camelot	73082	BR	5MT	4-6-0	1955
—	75027	BR	4MT	4-6-0	1954
—	78059†	BR	2MT	2-6-0	1956
—	80064	BR	4MT	2-6-4T	1953
—	80100	BR	4MT	2-6-4T	1954
—	92240	BR	9F	2-10-0	1959
Blackmore Vale	21C123	SR	WC	4-6-2	1946

Industrial locomotives

Name	No	Builder	Type	Built
Blue Circle	—	A/Porter (9449)	2-2-0TG	1926
Baxter	—	F/Jennings (158)	0-4-0T	1877
Stamford	—	Avonside (1972)	0-6-0ST	1927
Sharpthorn	—	M/Wardle (641)	0-6-0ST	1877

*Purchased without tender

†Purchased without tender, for conversion to tank engine

Museum: Sheffield Park
Depots: Sheffield Park (locomotives), Horsted Keynes (stock)
Length of line: 5 miles — plus first section of extension of route to East Grinstead due to open from Easter 1990, with shuttle service at weekends and some weekdays as notified
Passenger trains: Sheffield Park-Horsted Keynes
Period of public operation: Sundays in January, February and December, also Boxing and New Year's Day. Saturdays and Sundays in March, April and November. Wednesdays, Saturdays and Sundays in May and October. Daily June-September inclusive. Daily for October schools half term week. Museum and locomotive sheds at Sheffield Park open daily except Christmas Day
Special events: Bluebell on Parade in May; Anniversary weekend in August; Vintage Sunday, in September
Facilities for disabled: All station facilities are on the level and ramps available for placing wheelchair visitors into trains. Special toilet in Buffet at Sheffield Park
Special notes: Special 30th anniversary events in 1990
Membership details: Membership Secretary c/o above address
Feature article references: RW May 1988 p275 (northern extension)

Right:
Southern Railway 'Schools' class 4-4-0 No 928 *Stowe* is seen here bound for Horsted Keynes. *Stowe* returned to service during 1989 following an overhaul.
R. Bamberough

Stock
Substantial collection of pre-Nationalisation coaches including SECR, LSWR, Bulleid, Maunsell and Chesham vehicles. Also freight stock and engineers' vehicles plus 45ton steam crane

Owners
592 (the Wainwright C Class Preservation Society)
541, 830, 847 and 1618 (the Maunsell Locomotive Society Ltd)
96 and 21C123 (the Bulleid Society Ltd)
263 (the H Class Trust)
73082 (the Camelot Locomotive Society)
C1 (on loan from the National Railway Museum)
928 (on loan from Montagu Venturers Ltd)
80064 (80064 Group)
35027, 1178 (the *Port Line* Project)

Kent & East Sussex Steam Railway

The epitome of the early Edwardian light railways that were developed on shoestring budgets to open up less populated areas of the countryside. The line is now being extended towards Bodiam Castle which will become the terminus at the south-western end while the picturesque town of Tenterden remains the headquarters of the railway at the other.
Headquarters: Tenterden Railway Co Ltd, Tenterden Town station, Tenterden, Kent TN30 6HE
Telephone: Tenterden (058 06) 2943 (24 hour talking timetable); Tenterden (058 06) 5155 (office)
Main station: Tenterden Town

Locomotives

Name	No	Origin	Class	Type	Built
—	32670	LBSCR	A1X	0-6-0T	1872
Sutton	10 (32650)	LBSCR	A1X	0-6-0T	1876
Knowle	32678	LBSCR	A1X	0-6-0T	1880
—	1556	SECR	P	0-6-0T	1909
Wainwright	21 (30070)	SR	USA	0-6-0T	1943
Maunsell	30065	SR	USA	0-6-0T	1943
—	20	GWR	AEC	diesel railcar	1940
—	19	NSB	21c	2-6-0	1919
—	44 (D2023)	BR	03	0-6-0DM	1958
—	45 (D2024)	BR	03	0-6-0DM	1958
—	46 (D2205)	BR	04	0-6-0DM	1958
—	D9504	BR	14	0-6-0DH	1964
—	49 (D9525)	BR	14	0-6-0DH	1965

Other public stations: Rolvenden, Wittersham Road, Northiam (opens May 1990)
Car parks: Tenterden, Wittersham Road, Northiam
OS reference:
Tenterden TQ 882336,
Rolvenden TQ 865328,
Northiam TQ 834266
Access by public transport:
Maidstone & District bus service No 400 from Ashford (Kent) BR station
Refreshment facilities: Tenterden Town. Also on train facilities. Lunch and afternoon teas on trains by prior arrangement
Souvenir shop: Tenterden Town station
Museum: Station Road, Tenterden
Depot: Rolvenden
Length of line: 4 miles — 3-mile extension to Northiam opens May 1990
Passenger trains: Tenterden-Wittersham Road, weekends and bank holidays 1 April-20 May, 11.15-16.15.

Tenterden-Northiam, weekends 26 May-28 October; daily 23 July-2 September; Wednesdays June and September; Tuesdays-Thursdays July; Sundays only November, 11.15-16.15
Special events: Please see press or phone for details
Facilities for disabled: A special coach for disabled people, 'Petros', is allocated to most trains (telephone for confirmation of availability), reserved parking at Tenterden.
Toilets with disabled access at Tenterden, and in coach 'Petros'
Special notes: 'Wealden Pullman'

Industrial locomotives

Name	No	Builder	Type	Built
Marcia	12	Peckett (1631)	0-4-0T	1923
Charwelton	14	M/Wardle (1955)	0-6-0ST	1917
Holman F. Stephens	23	Hunslet (3791)	0-6-0ST	1952
William H. Austen	24	Hunslet (3800)	0-6-0ST	1953
Northiam	25	Hunslet (3797)	0-6-0ST	1953
Linda	26	Hunslet (3781)	0-6-0ST	1952
Rolvenden	27	RSH (7086)	0-6-0ST	1943
—	40	BTH	Bo-Bo	1932
—	42	Hunslet (4208)	0-6-0DM	1948
—	—	R/Hornsby (423661)	0-4-0DM	1958

Stock
3 ex-SECR 'Birdcage' coaches
1 ex-LSWR coach
5 4-wheel coaches of NLR, GER, SECR and LC&DR origins
1 LNWR Director's saloon
1 GER observation car
SECR and LSWR Family saloons
3 Pullman cars
8 ex-BR Mk 1 coaches
1 ex-BR Mk 1 RU 'Diana'
9 ex-SR Maunsell coaches
3 steam cranes
Large interesting collection of freight vehicles, totalling 51 vehicles

Owners
10 (London Borough of Sutton)
21 and 22 (Kent & East Sussex Loco Trust)
19 (Norwegian Locomotive Trust)

dining car service operates on most Saturday evenings in season. Advance booking is essential for this train. Santa special services operate on each Saturday and Sunday in December. Advanced booking recommended

Membership details: New Members Secretary c/o above address
Feature article reference: RW January 1988, p23; RW August 1989, p460 (Northiam extension); RW October 1989, p629 (diesels)

Lavender Line   SC

The neat appearance of the station and line at Isfield is largely due to the care lavished on it by its owner, David Milham and his family.
Location: Isfield Station, Isfield, near Uckfield, East Sussex TN22 5XB
OS reference: TQ 452171
Operating society/organisation: The Lavender Line Steam Museum
Telephone: Isfield (082 575) 515
Car park: On site
Access by public transport: Train to Uckfield or Lewes, then bus to Isfield. Buses run every two hours
On site facilities: Refreshments, licensed bar, wine & dine trains (advanced booking essential), souvenir shop, museum
Length of line: 1½ miles
Public opening: Every Sunday and

Locomotives

Name	No	Origin	Class	Type	Built
—	15224	BR	12	0-6-0DE	1949

Industrial locomotives

Name	No	Builder	Type	Built
Annie	945	A/Barclay (945)	0-4-0ST	1904
—	68012	Hunslet (3193)	0-6-0ST	1944
Ugly	62	RSH (7673)	0-6-0ST	1950
—	2591	Drewry	0-4-0DM	1961

Stock
4 ex-BR Mk 1 coaches   1 ex-GWR 'Toad' brake van

Bank Holiday Monday, March-November, 10.30-17.00
Facilities for disabled: Yes
Special events: Santa specials in

December
Special notes: Luxury wine & dine trains every Friday, all year except Feb 19.30-20.00, booking essential

London Transport Museum `M`

The museum was opened in the converted Flower Market in March 1980. The displays cover nearly two centuries of public transport in London
Location: Covent Garden, London WC2E 7BB
OS reference: TQ 303809
Operating society/organisation: London Regional Transport
Telephone: 01-379 6344
Access by public transport: Underground to Covent Garden, Leicester Square or Charing Cross. Buses to Strand or Aldwych
On site facilities: Museum shop, lecture theatre, photo and research libraries (by appointment)
Public opening: Daily 10.00-18.00 (last admissions 17.15). Closed 24/25/26 December. Reduced admission prices for children, students, senior citizens, UB40 holders and pre-booked parties. Free admission for registered disabled
Facilities for disabled: Disabled toilets available, wheelchair access to most of the displays. Also taped guide for visually handicapped visitors. Free admission for registered disabled visitors and person accompanying them. Please advise in advance if a party of disabled visitors would like to visit
Special notes: Visitors can operate

the controls of a tram, a bus, an Underground train, signals and points. In addition to the vehicles and rolling stock there are models, signs, posters, paintings, audio-visual displays and a 1906 Otis lift car. At certain times there will be films and temporary exhibitions. In addition to the vehicles

on display there is a growing reserve collection
Membership details: There is a Friends of the London Transport Museum, please contact above address for details
Feature article reference: RW March 1989, p150

Locomotives

Name	No	Origin	Class	Type	Built
—	23	Met Rly	A	4-4-0T	1866
John Hampden	5	Met Rly		Bo-Bo	1922

Industrial locomotives

Origin	Builder	Type	Built
Wotton Tramway	A/Porter (807)	0-4-0TG	1872

Electric stock
4248 District Rly Q23 stock driving motor coach 1923
11182 LPTB 1938 stock driving motor coach
400 Met Rly bogie stock coach 1899
30 City & South London Rly 'Padded Cell' coach 1890
Great Northern Piccadilly & Brompton Railway 'Gate stock' car 1906

Stock
1 Met Rly milk van
1 horse tram
3 electric trams
3 horse buses
8 motor buses
2 trolleybuses

North Downs Steam Railway `SC`

The North Downs Steam Railway is a rapidly developing society, establishing a museum and working railway, on a greenfield site at Stone Lodge, Dartford
Location: Stone Lodge Centre, Dartford, Kent
Operating society: North Downs Steam Railway
Telephone: Dartford (0322) 28260
Main station: Cotton Lane — free car parking available
Other station: London Road — (new station to open during 1990)
Directions: By car — leave M25 Junction 1a (Dartford Tunnel). Follow Stone Lodge/Historic Dartford signs up Cotton Lane (2min).
By train — Network SouthEast to Dartford. Then Kentish Bus to Stone

Industrial locomotives

Name	No	Builder	Type	Built
Scottie	1	R/Hornsby (412427)	4wDM	1957
Burt	2	M/Rail (9019)	4wDM	1951
North Downs	3	RSH (7846)	0-6-0T	1955
—	4	Fowler (4220008)	0-4-0DH	1959
Crabtree	5	R/Hornsby (338416)	4wDM	1953
Princess Margaret	6	Barclay (376)	0-4-0DM	1948
Telemon	7	Drewry/Vulcan (D295)	0-4-0DM	1955
Octane	8	YEC (2686)	0-4-0DE	1960
—	9	R/Hornsby (512572)	4wDM	1965
Topham	10	Bagnal (2193)	0-6-0ST	1922
Thalia	—	Drewry/RSH (7816)	0-4-0DM	1954

Stock
2 ex-LT T stock DMB cars, 2758 and 2749
1 ex-LCDR 4-wheel carriage (body only)
1 ex SECR carriage (body only)
2 ex-BP oil tanks

Lodge Farm entrance (routes 480 and 481), 5min walk
Length of line: Demonstration line open (300yd). 'Main line' due to open during early 1990 (½-mile). Journey time on demonstration line 15min, (three trips)
Public opening: Every Sunday and bank holiday all year round. Saturdays 14 July-22 September. Passenger trains at least every ½hr from 11.00 to 17.00
Special events: NDSR 10th Birthday Gala 30 June, 1 July; Children's Weekend 1/2 September; Industrial Weekends 14/15 April and 22/23 September. Santa Trains every weekend in December
Facilities for disabled: Special compartment in train for wheelchairs and special toilet facilities
Membership and service details: North Downs Steam Railway, 29 Southbourne, Washford Farm, Ashford, Kent TN23 2UB
Tel: Ashford (0233) 46170

Stock (continued)
1 ex-Blue Circle open cement wagon
1 ex-LT brake van chassis
1 ex-SR Bogie van
1 ex-SR PMV
1 ex-LT brake van
1 Grafton 5-ton diesel-hydraulic crane
1 ex-Esso oil tank

Below:
This unusual machine was built by Motor Rail in 1951. Named *Burt,* **it is seen in action during an Industrial Diesel Weekend, 16 September 1989.** *A. Cottenham*

North Woolwich Old Station Museum M

No expense has been spared in the very imaginative restoration of this attractive Victorian terminus building overlooking the Thames. Railway artefacts, documents, drawings, etc are well displayed in glass cases or on the walls, the stock being stabled in the platform area. Convenient for the new City airport and connections for the Docklands Railway
Location: North Woolwich Old Station Museum, Pier Road, North Woolwich, London E16 2JJ
OS reference: TQ 433798
Organisation: Passmore Edwards Museum Governors
Telephone: 01-474 7244
Car park: Only in adjoining streets

Locomotives

Name	No	Origin	Class	Type	Built
—	229	GER	209	0-4-0ST	1876

Industrial locomotives

Name	No	Builder	Type	Built
—	—	Hibberd (3294)	4wDM	1948
—	—	Peckett (2000)	0-6-0ST	1942
—	—	RSH (7667)	0-6-0ST	1950

Stock
1 ex-LNER coach
2 compartment sections of LTSR coach

Public transport: BR North London Link. Buses: 101, 69 and 58
Facilities: Museum shop

Public opening: Monday to Saturday, 10.00-17.00. Sunday and Bank Holidays, 14.00-17.00

Romney, Hythe & Dymchurch Railway

This line was built in 1926/27 as a one-third size miniature main line, and is by far the longest and most fully-equipped 15in gauge railway in the world. It carries not only daytrippers and holidaymakers but also children to and from the local school at New Romney.

Locomotives

Name	No	Builder	Type	Built
Green Goddess	1	Davey Paxman	4-6-2	1925
Northern Chief	2	Davey Paxman	4-6-2	1925
Southern Maid	3	Davey Paxman	4-6-2	1926
The Bug	4	Krauss (8378)	0-4-0TT	1926
Hercules	5	Davey Paxman	4-8-2	1926
Samson	6	Davey Paxman	4-8-2	1926

Headquarters: Romney, Hythe & Dymchurch Railway, New Romney station, Kent TN28 8PL
Telephone: New Romney (0679) 62353/63256
OS reference: TR 074249
Main station: Hythe
Other public stations: Dymchurch, Jefferstone Lane, New Romney, Romney Sands, Dungeness
Car parks: Hythe, Dymchurch, New Romney, Dungeness
Access by public transport: Sandling Junction BR station (1½ miles), Folkestone Central BR station — 4 miles: bus connection from Folkestone bus station to Hythe
Refreshment facilities: New Romney, Dungeness. Also an observation coach on certain trains
Souvenir shops: Hythe, New Romney
Museum: New Romney
Depot: New Romney
Length of line: 13½ miles, 15in gauge
Passenger trains: Train frequency depends on the time of year: maximum frequency is 45 minutes
Period of public operation: Daily from Easter until end of September, and at weekends in March and October
Special events: Enthusiasts' Days 20 May, 23 September 1990
Special notes: Senior citizen concession Fridays, Saturdays, Sunday, (return journey for single fare). Model railway and exhibition at New Romney. Parties can be catered for at New Romney
Membership details: RH&DR Association, 26 Norman Close, Battle, East Sussex TN33 0BD

Name	No	Builder	Type	Built
Typhoon	7	Davey Paxman	4-6-2	1926
Hurricane	8	Davey Paxman	4-6-2	1926
Winston Churchill	9	YEC (2294)	4-6-2	1931
Doctor Syn	10	YEC (2295)	4-6-2	1931
Black Prince	11	Krupp (1664)	4-6-2	1937
John Southland	12	TMA Birmingham	Bo-Bo	1983
—	14	TMA Birmingham	Bo-Bo	1989
—	PW1	M/Rail (7059)	4wDM	1938
—	PW2	RH&DR	4wPM	1965
Redgauntlet	PW3	RH&DR	4wPM	1975

Stock
42 saloon bogie coaches
12 open bogie coaches
3 semi-open coaches
5 luggage/brake saloons
1 Parlour car
1 mess coach
40 assorted wagons

Below:
On 14 May 1989 the RH&DR put 11 locomotives in steam for an enthusiasts' weekend and Nos 1 to 11 are in this view. No 11, fourth from left, was returned to service following an extensive rebuild, with amongst other changes the addition of German-type smoke deflectors and snowplough.

Ruislip Lido Railway

SC

The 12in gauge line is operated by enthusiasts as an attraction within Ruislip Lido, a country park which is maintained by the London Borough of Hillingdon
Location: Ruislip Lido, Reservoir Road, Ruislip, Middlesex
Operating society/organisation: Ruislip Lido Railway Society Ltd, Membership Secretary, 12 Croft Gardens, Ruislip HA4 8EY
Telephone: Ruislip 34081
Car park: Available at Lido
Access by public transport: Ruislip Underground station (Metropolitan and Piccadilly lines) then by bus H13 (Monday-Saturday), 114 (Sundays) or E2 (Summer Sundays). Lido is off A4180

Locomotives

Name	No	Builder	Type	Built
Robert	3	Severn-Lamb	B-2 PH	1973
Lady of the Lakes	5	Ravenglass & Eskdale Railway Co Ltd	B-B DH	1985

Locomotive notes: Both locomotives are available for service, and a further diesel is to be delivered by spring 1990. A steam locomotive is under construction

Stock
4 open coaches
5 closed coaches
Miscellaneous service stock

Refreshment facilities: Available at Lido site
Length of line: 1½ miles, with planned extension in progress round the Lido. The first stage of which is now in operation, second stage planned for operation in summer 1990
Public opening: The line is open Sundays throughout the year, Saturdays Easter to end of October, and daily in all school holidays and in June, July and August, Mondays, Wednesdays and Fridays in April, May, September and October. Trains run from 12.00-17.00 (14.00-17.00 on Saturdays)

Journey time: Single 6min, return 15min
Facilities for disabled: Limited number of wheelchair passengers can be accepted for travel
Membership details: c/o above address

Science Museum M

Built on land acquired with the profits from the Great Exhibition of 1851, the Science Museum was one of the first to include industrial archaeology. Here you will find the originals featured in the history books, such as Robert Stephenson's *Rocket*.
Location: South Kensington
OS reference: TQ 268793
Operating society/organisation: Science Museum, Exhibition Road, South Kensington, London SW7
Telephone: 01-938 8000
Access by public transport: South Kensington Underground station
Catering facilities: Coffee shop on 3rd floor, tea, coffee, sandwiches etc
On site facilities: Book shop
Public opening: Weekdays 10.00-18.00, Sundays 11.00-18.00. Closed 1 January, Good Friday, May Day Monday, 24-26 December
Special events: All organised by the National Railway Museum, York, which is part of the Science Museum. Telephone (0904) 621261 for details

Locomotives

Name	No	Origin	Class	Type	Built
Caerphilly Castle	4073	GWR	'Castle'	4-6-0	1923
Deltic	—	E/Electric	—	Co-Co	1955
Rocket	—	L&MR	—	0-2-2	1829
Rocket	—	(Replica)	—	0-2-2	1935
Sans Pareil	—	L&MR	—	0-4-0	1829
	1	C&SLR	—	4wE	1890
Puffing Billy	—	Wylam Colliery	—	0-4-0	1813

Industrial locomotives

Name	No	Builder	Type	Built
Agenoria	—	Foster Raistrick	0-4-0	1829
Bauxite	2	B/Hawthorn (305)	0-4-0ST	1874

Stock
LPTB Underground coach, 3327 (built 1927)

Locomotive notes: All restored to static display condition

Facilities for disabled: Toilets on ground floor, ramp and lifts to all floors (except basement). Parties should contact before arrival if extra assistance is required
Special notes: Static exhibits only

Sittingbourne & Kemsley Light Railway SC

The Sittingbourne & Kemsley Light Railway is part of the 2ft 6in gauge railway built to convey paper and other materials between mills at Sittingbourne and Kemsley and the Dock at Ridham on the banks of the Swale. The first section of the line opened in 1906 and two of the engines then in use remain on the line today.

The railway is now leased from U.K. Paper Group and is operated as a tourist attraction. Passenger trains are normally steam-hauled and are formed of a varied selection of open and covered coaches. For the first half mile of the journey the train twists and turns through Milton Regis on a concrete viaduct which was one of the

Locomotives

Name	No	Builder	Type	Built
Alpha	—	Bagnall (2472)	0-6-2T	1932
Triumph	—	Bagnall (2511)	0-6-2T	1934
Superb	—	Bagnall (2624)	0-6-2T	1940
Unique	—	Bagnall (2216)	2-4-0F	1924
Premier	—	K/Stuart (886)	0-4-2ST	1905
Leader	—	K/Stuart (926)	0-4-2ST	1905
Melior	—	K/Stuart (4219)	0-4-2ST	1924
Edward Lloyd	—	R/Hornsby (435403)	4wDM	1961
Victor	—	Hunslet (4182)	4wDM	1953

Industrial standard gauge locomotives

Name	No	Builder	Type	Built
—	4	H/Leslie (3718)	0-4-0ST	1928
Bear	—	Peckett (614)	0-4-0ST	1896
—	1	Barclay (1876)	0-4-0F	1925

first reinforced concrete structures to be built

Headquarters: Sittingbourne & Kemsley Light Railway Ltd, The Wall, Milton Regis, Sittingbourne, Kent

Telephone: Sittingbourne (0795) 424899 (talking timetable)

Main station: Sittingbourne

Car park: Sittingbourne

Access by public transport: Sittingbourne BR station, A2 and M2 roads

OS reference: Sittingbourne 905643, Kemsley Down 920662

Refreshment facilities: Kemsley Down

Souvenir shop: Sittingbourne

Depot: Kemsley Down (access by rail only)

Length of line: 2 miles, 2ft 6in gauge

Locomotive notes: In service: *Triumph, Superb, Premier*. Under repair: *Leader, Melior, Victor*. On static display *Alpha, Unique* and standard gauge exhibits

Stock
10 bogie coaches (4 ex-Chattenden & Upnor Railway)
2 open coaches
Various wagons

Passenger trains: Ex-industrial line Sittingbourne-Kemsley Down

Journey time: 15min each way

Period of public operation: Please contact for details

Special events: Please contact for details

Special notes: There is no public access to Kemsley Down other than by the railway on operating dates. When the line is closed all stock is stored in security compounds, on the mill premises. Family ticket available, special rates for parties and senior citizens

Membership details: Mrs Stickler, Lite Hjem, Woodlands Estate, Blean, Canterbury, Kent CT2 9JN

Southall Railway Centre   SC

During the autumn of 1988 the GWRPG moved all their stock into the former BR diesel depot adjacent to their old site. At the time of writing the area was being up-graded to allow the general public into the site, this involves fencing the centre off from the adjacent BR tracks. Please see press for details of open days etc

Location: The former BR diesel depot, approximately 10min from BR station. Access is only possible via the footbridge at the London end of the station, during opening times only

Operating society/organisation: GWR Preservation Group

Telephone: 01-574-1529 R. A. Gorringe (evening and weekend only)

Facilities for disabled: Access to the site is not possible, involving two flights of steps, those wishing to visit are advised to make contact before their visit and alternative arrangements will be made

Locomotives

Name	No	Origin	Class	Type	Built
—	2885	GWR	2884	2-8-0	1938
—	4110	GWR	5101	2-6-2T	1936
—	9682	GWR	5700	0-6-0PT	1949
—	68078*	LNER	J94	0-6-0ST	1946

*Not on site

Industrial locomotives

Name	No	Builder	Type	Built
—	—	AEC Southall	4wDM	1938
—	2100	Peckett (2100)	0-4-0ST	1949
Birkenhead	7386	RSH (7386)	0-4-0ST	1948
Francis Baily of Thatcham	AD251	R/Hornsby (390772)	0-4-0DM	1957

Stock
1 BR 'Gane' wagon
1 BR 'Tunny' wagon
1 BR 'Rectank' wagon
1 BR Weltrol
1 BR Brake van
1 BR Generator van
1 BR Goods van
1 GWR 'Mink' van
1 GWR brake van
2 BP oil tank wagons
1 GWR bogie bolster wagon
1 LMS parcels van
1 LMS goods van
1 LMS stores van
1 Staff coach, former LMS BCK
1 Wagons Lits coach

Owners
2100 (the City of Portsmouth Museum)

Central Southern

Buckinghamshire Railway Centre   SC

Formerly known as Quainton Road, the name of the station, the Centre has been improved considerably during recent years. Its true potential could, however, be realised by an enlightened approach allowing operation of steam trains to and from Marylebone

Location: Adjacent to BR goods only line to Aylesbury. Turn off A41 at Waddesdon 6 miles NW of Aylesbury, Bucks

OS reference: SP 738190

Operating society/organisation: Quainton Railway Society Ltd, The Railway Station, Quainton, near Aylesbury, Bucks HP22 4BY

Telephone: Quainton (029675) 450

Car park: Quainton Road — Free parking

Access by public transport: BR Aylesbury station. Special bus on Bank Holidays connects Centre with BR trains

On site facilities: Souvenir bookshop, light refreshments, toilets, steam-hauled train rides. Museum of small relics, secondhand bookshop

Catering facilities: Victorian Tea specials. Afternoon tea in LNWR dining car, write for details to catering manager. Lunches and afternoon teas by arrangement

Length of line: Two ½-mile demonstration lines

Public opening: Sundays and Bank Holidays: Easter-end October. Wednesdays in June, July and August. Limited opening (no engines in steam) Thursdays to Saturdays, June to September

Special events: Santa Specials in December (please write for details), others throughout the year. Write for details

Facilities for disabled: Access to most of site, but not toilets. No advance notice required

Special notes: One of the largest collection of standard gauge

Locomotives

Name	No	Origin	Class	Type	Built
—	1	Met Rly	E	0-4-4T	1898
—	0314	LSWR	0298	2-4-0WT	1874
Wightwick Hall	6989	GWR	'Hall'	4-6-0	1948
—	7200	GWR	7200	2-8-2T	1934
—	7715	GWR	5700	0-6-0PT	1930
—	9466	GWR	9400	0-6-0PT	1952
—	41298	LMS	2MT	2-6-2T	1951
—	41313	LMS	2MT	2-6-2T	1952
—	46447	LMS	2MT	2-6-0	1950
—	D2298	BR	04	0-6-0DM	1960
—	25057	BR	25	Bo-Bo	1963

Industrial locomotives

Name	No	Builder	Type	Built
Sydenham	—	A/Porter (3567)	4wTG	1895
Scott	—	Bagnall (2469)	0-4-0ST	1932
—	—	Baguley (2161)	0-4-0DM	1941
Swanscombe	—	Barclay (699)	0-4-0ST	1891
—	GF3	Barclay (1477)	0-4-0F	1916
Tom Parry	—	Barclay (2015)	0-4-0ST	1935
—	—	Barclay (2243)	0-4-0F	1948
Osram	—	Fowler (20067)	0-4-0DM	1933
—	3	H/Leslie (3717)	0-4-0ST	1928
Sir Thomas	—	H/Clarke (1334)	0-6-0T	1918
—	—	H/Clarke (1742)	0-4-0ST	1946
—	—	Hunslet (2067)	0-4-0DM	1940
Arthur	—	Hunslet (3782)	0-6-0ST	1953
Juno	—	Hunslet (3850)	0-6-0ST	1958
—	65	Hunslet (3889)	0-6-0ST	1964
—	66	Hunslet (3890)	0-6-0ST	1964
—	26	Hunslet (7016)	0-6-0DH	1971
Redland	—	K/Stuart (K4428)	0-4-0DM	1929
Coventry No 1	—	NBL (24564)	0-6-0ST	1939
—	—	Peckett (1900)	0-4-0T	1936
Gibraltar	—	Peckett (2087)	0-4-0ST	1948
—	—	Peckett (2104)	0-4-0ST	1948
—	—	Peckett (2105)	0-4-0ST	1948
—	T1	Hibberd (2102)	4wD	1937
Tarmac	—	Hibberd (3765)	0-4-0DM	1955
—	—	Sentinel (6515)	4wVBTG	1926
—	11	Sentinel (9366)	4wVBTG	1945
—	7	Sentinel (9376)	4wVBTG	1947
—	—	Sentinel (9537)	4wVBTG	1947
Chislet	9	Yorkshire (2498)	0-6-0ST	1951

locomotives, together with a most interesting collection of vintage coaching stock, much of which was built in the last century

Feature article reference: RW June 1989, p333 (locomotive 6024)

Stock

1 LCDR 1st Class 4 wheeler	
1 MSLR 3rd Class 6 wheeler	1 LNWR full brake 6 wheeler
4 LNWR coach bodies	1 LNWR combination truck
2 GNR 6 wheelers	1 LSWR ventilated fruit van
3 LNWR coaches	1 SR PMV
3 LMSR coaches	1 LMSR passenger brake van
1 BR(W) Hawksworth brake 3rd	1 GWR passenger brake van
2 BR Mk 1s	1 BR(W) 'Siphon G'
1 BR Suburban brake	1 BR horse box
3 LNER coaches	1 BR CCT

3 ex-London Underground coaches
1 2ft gauge post office mailbag car 803
Sentinel/Cammell 3-car steam railcar unit 5208 (ex-Egyptian National)
Numerous goods vehicles/wagons/vans

Owners

41298, 41313 and 46447, *Juno* (the Ivatt Locomotive Trust)
9466 (the 9466 Group)

Cholsey & Wallingford Railway   SC

Location: Hithercroft Industrial Estate, Wallingford, Oxfordshire
Operating Society: Cholsey & Wallingford Railway Preservation Society, PO Box 16, Wallingford, Oxon OX10 0NF
Telephone: 0491 35067 (weekends and Bank Holidays only)
Car park: Habitat adjacent to Wallingford station
Access by public transport: South Midland Bus Company, BR Didcot Parkway or Cholsey
Public Opening: Every Saturday and Sunday Easter-end September

Locomotives

Name	No	Origin	Class	Type	Built
—	4247	GWR	4200	2-8-0T	1916
George Mason	08 123	BR	08	0-6-0	1955

Industrial locomotives

Name	No	Builder	Type	Built
Walrus	3271	Planet (3271)	0-4-0	1949
—	304470	R/Hornsby	0-4-0	—

10.00-16.30. Trains run last Sunday and bank holidays 12.00-16.30
Length of line: ¾-mile
Journey time: Approximately 15min
On site facilities: Souvenir and coffee shops. Museum, model railway. Children's mini railway.
Special events: Railfair 17 June; Cholsey Flower Festival 11 August.
Special notes: Light Railway Order now granted and work is proceeding to return to Cholsey (BR) bay platform
Feature article references: RW June 1988, p362 ('The Branch in 1958')
Membership details: Bob Morrison, at above address

Didcot Railway Centre   SC

Based around the GWR engine shed and depot, the Centre now has a typical GWR small country station with signalbox (from Radstock), re-creation of Brunel's broad gauge railway, two demonstration lines, and a small relics museum
Location: Adjacent to BR station, Didcot, Oxfordshire. Access via station subway
OS reference: SU 525907
Operating society/organisation: Great Western Society Ltd, Didcot Railway Centre, Didcot, Oxon OX11 7NJ
Telephone: Didcot (0235) 817200
Car park: Didcot BR station
Access by public transport: Didcot Parkway BR station
Refreshment facilities: Refreshment room open all days centre is open (lunches, snacks)
On site facilities: GWR locomotive depot, replica GWR station, museum and broad gauge demonstration. Souvenir sales. Rides are available on the demonstration lines on steamdays
Length of line: 1,000yd
Public opening: Saturdays and Sundays all year. Tuesdays to Fridays (and Bank Holidays) 3 April-28 September. Steamdays first and last Sunday each month from March, Bank Holidays, all Sundays June-August and all Wednesdays in August. Open 11.00-17.00
Train rides: On Steamdays there is normally continuous operation of the passenger train, interrupted by freight train demonstrations and turning of the locomotives on some days
Special events: Spring Steam Gala daily 26 May-3 June; Disabled Day 8 July; Autumn Steam Gala

Locomotives

Name	No	Origin	Class/builder	Type	Built
—	22	GWR	Diesel Railcar	1A-A1	1940
—	1338	GWR	Kitson (3799) Cardiff Rly	0-4-0ST	1898
Trojan	1340	GWR	Avonside (1380)	0-4-0ST	1897
—	1363	GWR	1361	0-6-0ST	1910
—	1466	GWR	1400	0-4-2T	1936
—	3650	GWR	5700	0-6-0PT	1939
—	3738	GWR	5700	0-6-0PT	1937
—	3822	GWR	2884	2-8-0	1940
—	4144	GWR	5101	2-6-2T	1946
Maindy Hall	4942	GWR	'Hall'	4-6-0	1929
Nunney Castle	5029	GWR	'Castle'	4-6-0	1934
Drysllwyn Castle/ Earl Bathurst	5051	GWR	'Castle'	4-6-0	1936
—	5322	GWR	4300	2-6-0	1917
—	5572	GWR	4575	2-6-2T	1927
Hinderton Hall	5900	GWR	'Hall'	4-6-0	1931
King Edward II	6023	GWR	'King'	4-6-0	1930
—	6106	GWR	6100	2-6-2T	1931
—	6697	GWR	5600	0-6-2T	1928
Burton Agnes Hall	6998	GWR	'Hall'	4-6-0	1949
—	7202	GWR	7200	2-8-2T	1934
Cookham Manor	7808	GWR	'Manor'	4-6-0	1938
Duke of Gloucester	71000	BR	8P	4-6-2	1954
Western Yeoman	D1035	BR	52	C-C	1962
—	D7018	BR	35	B-B	1962
Pontyberem	2	Burry Port & Gwendraeth Valley Rly		0-6-0ST	1900
Shannon	5	Wantage Tramway		0-4-0WT	1857

Industrial locomotives

Name	No	Builder	Type	Built
Bonnie Prince Charlie	1	RSH (7544)	0-4-0ST	1949
—	26	Hunslet (5238)	0-6-0DH	1962

Locomotive notes: Locomotives available in 1990 should be: 3822, 5572, 6106, 6998 *Burton Agnes Hall*, D1035 and D7018. Locomotives under restoration include: 3650, 5029 *Nunney Castle*, 7202. Construction of the Firefly Trust's reproduction broad gauge locomotive *Firefly* is being undertaken

29/30 September; Photographers Evening 27 October; Santa Steamings 2, 9, 16, 23 December; New Year Steamings 30 December-1 January 1991
Facilities for disabled: Steps at access from BR subway may cause

Below:
For a period during 1989 two GWR 4-4-0s could be seen in action at the Didcot Railway Centre. Nos 3440 *City of Truro* **and 3217** *Earl of Berkeley* **are seen here alongside No 6998** *Burton Agnes Hall,* **12 May 1989.** *P. Q. Treloar*

Stock
Over 40 ex-GWR coaches are preserved along with numerous ex-GWR freight wagons

Owners
5 (on loan from the National Railway Museum)
D1035 (Foster Yeoman — actually D1010)
D7018 (Diesel & Electric Group)

problems but assistance can normally be provided (advance notification is useful)
Membership details: Brian Phillips, at above address
Feature article references: RW February 1988 (diesel day); RW December 1989, p717 (No 71000)

Gloucestershire Warwickshire Railway

Part of an ambitious project to link Cheltenham racecourse with Stratford racecourse, much has been done to recreate the railway and buildings that made up this cross-country route. The railway is home to many owners of private locomotives and rolling stock, so from time to time the items on display may vary
Location: Toddington Station, Toddington
OS reference: SO 050322
Operating society/organisation: Gloucestershire Warwickshire Steam Railway PLC, The Station, Toddington, Cheltenham, Glos GL54 5DT

Locomotives

Name	No	Origin	Class	Type	Built
—	2807*	GWR	2800	2-8-0	1905
—	4277	GWR	4200	2-8-0T	1920
Kinlet Hall	4936	GWR	'Hall'	4-6-0	1929
Peninsular and Oriental SNCo	35006	SR	MN	4-6-2	1941
—	76077	BR	4MT	2-6-0	1956
—	D9537	BR	14	0-6-0DH	1965
—	D9539	BR	14	0-6-0DH	1965
—	D9553	BR	14	0-6-0DH	1965

*Transferred to Birmingham Railway Museum, Tyseley for restoration

Telephone: Toddington (024269) 405
Access by public transport: Public transport is very limited with occasional buses from Cheltenham, Stratford on Avon and Evesham only. Local bus service Castleways will answer timetable queries on (0242) 602949
Car park: On site
On site facilities: Sales, catering, museum, narrow gauge rides, toilets
Length of line: 4 miles
Public opening: During the week the station is unmanned but visitors are welcome. Public services on Sundays, Bank Holiday Mondays, plus some Saturdays between March and October
Special events: Santa Specials in December; Mince Pie Specials and New Year specials on 1 January 1991
Special notes: The site is being developed as the headquarters of the railway between Cheltenham and Stratford. The GWR owns the railway land between Cheltenham and Honeybourne, and has been operating over 2½-miles from Toddington to Winchcombe. 1988 saw the track relaid all the way to Gretton and trains are due to start running there from Easter 1990

Below:
The Gloucestershire Warwickshire Railway offers steam or diesel traction between Toddington and Winchcombe. On 23 July 1989 *Robert Nelson No 4* is prepared to operate the afternoon's service. This Hunslet 0-6-0ST was acquired from the Great Central Railway.
Mervyn Turvey

Industrial locomotives

Name	No	Builder	Type	Built
Huntsman	—	Bagnall (2655)	0-6-0ST	1941
John	—	Peckett (1976)	0-4-0ST	1939
Robert Nelson No 4	—	Hunslet (1800)	0-6-0ST	1936
King George	—	Hunslet (2409)	0-6-0ST	1942
—	19	Fowler (4240016)	0-6-0DH	1964
—	21	Fowler (4210130)	0-4-0DM	1957
—	—	H/Clarke (D615)	0-6-0DM	1938
—	—	Hibberd (2893)	4wPM	1943

Stock
3 ex-GWR coaches
13 ex-BR coaches
1 ex-LMS coach
Numerous plus wagons

Owners
2807 and 4277 (the Cotswold Steam Preservation Ltd)
35006, 76077 (the P and O Locomotive Society)
D9537, D9539 and D9553 (Cotswold Diesel Preservation Group)

Industrial narrow gauge locomotives (2ft gauge)

Name	No	Builder	Type	Built
Isibutu	5	Bagnall (2820)	4-4-0T	1946
George B	—	Hunslet (680)	0-4-0ST	1898
Chaka	—	Hunslet (2075)	0-4-2T	1940
Justine	—	Jung (939)	0-4-0WT	1906
—	—	Henschel (15968)	0-8-0T	1918
—	2	Lister (34523)	4wDM	1949
—	3	M/Rail (4565)	4wPM	1928
Spitfire	—	M/Rail (7053)	4wPM	1937
—	1	R/Hornsby (166010)	4wDM	1932
—	L5	R/Hornsby (181820)	4wDM	1936
—	—	R/Hornsby (354028)	4wDM	1953

Stock
1 coach
11 wagons

Hampshire Narrow Gauge Railway Society

SC

Location: Close to Southampton and Winchester, on private property. The site is only open to the public on advertised dates, other times by application (with SAE) to address below
OS reference: SU 522173
Operating society/organisation: Hampshire Narrow Gauge Railway Society, c/o 4 Holmdale Road, Gosport, Hants PO12 4PJ
Car park: On site but very limited
On site facilities: 2ft gauge line, light refreshments and souvenir shop. Toilets (not yet suitable for disabled). Visitors can visit workshops on request
Public opening: Please send SAE to Secretary

Locomotives

Name	No	Builder	Type	Built
Wendy	1	Bagnall (2091)	0-4-0ST	1919
AGWI Pet	2	M/Rail (4724)	4wP	1939
Cloister	3	Hunslet (542)	0-4-0ST	1891
Brambridge Hall	4	M/Rail (5226)	4wP	1936
—	5	R/Hornsby (392117)	4wD	1956
Josephine	6	Hunslet (1842)	0-4-2ST	1936
—	7	Hanomag (8310)	0-8-0T	1918
—	8	O/Koppel (4013)	4wD	1933
Norden	9	O/Koppel (20777)	0-4-0D	1936

Stock
1 bogie coach
Various freight stock
Carriage portion of ex-LSWR 4-2-4T *The Bug* (standard gauge)

Hollycombe Steam Collection

SC

An unusual collection of traction engines, Bioscope, organs, steam gallopers, Mighty Emperor Burrell Steam Engine, sawmill and paddle steamer engine which also includes a 7¼in gauge steam railway which climbs some fair gradients through the woodlands and gardens
Location: Iron Hill, Hollycombe, near Liphook, Hants
OS reference: SU 852295
Operating society/organisation: Hollycombe Steam & Woodland Garden Society, Iron Hill, Liphook, Hants GU30 7LP
Telephone: Liphook (0428) 724900 (opening days only); otherwise (04203) 4740
Car park: On site
Access by public transport: Liphook BR station (1½ miles)
On site facilities: Shop and refreshments.
Public opening: Please see press for details
Special events: Please see press for details

Industrial locomotives

Name	No	Builder	Type	Built
Excelsior	—	A/Porter (1607)	2-2-0WTG	1880†
Caledonia	70	Barclay (1995)	0-4-0WT	1931*
Jerry M	38	Hunslet (638)	0-4-0ST	1895*
Newcastle	—	H/Leslie (2450)	0-4-0ST	1899
—	16	R/Hornsby	4wDM	1941*

*2ft gauge †3ft gauge

Right:
Two of Hollycombe's attractions are seen here; *Emperor*, a Burrell Showmans Engine, and a set of steam gallopers, October 1989.

Isle of Wight Steam Railway

Separated from the mainland by the Solent, the line's isolation encouraged the maintenance and retention of Victorian locomotives and coaching stock which still operate the line today. Its rural charm enhances its attraction for the island's holidaymakers during the summer season

Headquarters: Isle of Wight Steam Railway, Haven Street station, Ryde, Isle of Wight PO33 4DS
Telephone: Station: Isle of Wight (0983) 882204
Main station: Haven Street
OS reference: SZ 556898
Other public stations: Wootton
Car park: Haven Street
Access by public transport: Service 1a bus from Ryde or Newport to Wootton, also seasonal services 3 and 43 to Havenstreet
Refreshment facilities: Light refreshments available
Souvenir shop: Haven Street
Museum: Small exhibits museum at Haven Street
Depot: Haven Street
Length of line: 2 miles
Passenger trains: Haven Street-Wootton
Period of public operation: 15-29 April — Thursdays, Sundays and Bank Holidays; May — Wednesdays, Thursdays, Sundays and Bank Holidays; June-August — Tuesdays, Wednesdays, Thursdays and Bank Holidays; September — Wednesdays, Thursdays and Sundays; October — Sundays
Special events: Summer Steam Extravaganza, 24-27 August; Santa Specials, in December until Xmas (please write for details)
Facilities for disabled: Limited facilities but can be catered for singly, or in groups (by prior arrangement), toilets available
Special notes: Summer Steam Show, August Bank Holiday Friday, Saturday, Sunday and Monday. Traction engines, fairground organs, vintage cars etc.
Membership details: Mr J. Price at above address
Feature article reference: RW October 1989, p621 (including BR)

Locomotives

Name	No	Origin	Class	Type	Built
Freshwater	W8 (32646)	LBSCR	A1X	0-6-0T	1876
—*	11 (32640)	LBSCR	A1X	0-6-0T	1878
Calbourne	W24	LSWR	02	0-4-4T	1891
—	D2554	BR	05	0-6-0DM	1956
—	D2059	BR	03	0-6-0DM	1959

*depicted as IWCR No 11

Industrial locomotives

Name	No	Builder	Type	Built
Invincible	37	H/Leslie (3135)	0-4-0ST	1915
Ajax	38	Barclay (1605)	0-6-0T	1918
Tiger	—	N/British (27415)	0-4-0DH	1954

Locomotive notes: *Ajax* is not on public display.

Stock
4 IWR coaches (bodies only)
1 IWR coach
3 LBSCR coaches
3 SECR coaches
1 LCDR coach
5 LCDR coaches (bodies only)
1 LBSCR coach (body only)
1 crane
1 ex-BR ballast tamper
1 Wickham trolley
30 wagons
6 parcels vans
2 ex-LT hoppers
1 ex-BR Lowmac

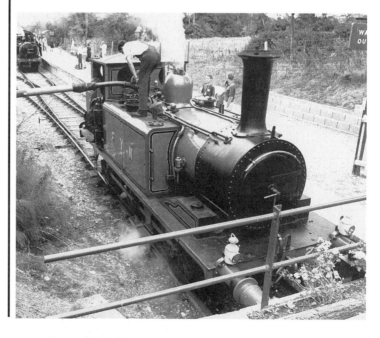

Below:
In this unusual view both of the Isle of Wight Steam Railway's 'Terrier' tanks can be seen. No W8 has been restored as Freshwater, Yarmouth & Newport Railway No 2 whilst No 11 sports the livery of the Isle of Wight Central Railway. The location is Wootton on 26 August 1989.
John H. Bird

Mid-Hants Railway

The Mid-Hants line was often used by the Bournemouth expresses on diversions during steam days and was therefore built to main line standards. This has enabled the line's new owners to operate large and powerful locomotives over the line which now has a direct connection with BR

Headquarters: Mid-Hants Railway PLC, Alresford station, Alresford, Hants SO24 9JG

Telephone: Alresford (0962) 733810/734200

Main station: Alresford

Other public stations: Ropley, Medstead & Four Marks, Alton

OS reference: Alresford SU 588325, Ropley SU 629324

Car park: Alresford, BR car park Alton

Access by public transport:
BR train services — just over 1hr from London. Through ticketing arrangements available from Waterloo and all BR stations. Alternatively, travel to Winchester station and take the bus to Alresford.

Bus services — are operated by Alder Valley.

On weekdays and Saturdays use route 215 (hourly, Guildford-Alton-Alresford-Winchester-Southampton), 214 (hourly, Alresford-Winchester).

On Sundays, use route 453 (two-hourly, Guildford-Aldershot-Alton-Alresford-Winchester).

Routes 215 and 453 call at Alton BR station, pass close to Ropley and Alresford stations. Routes 214 and 453 stop in City Road, Winchester, near Winchester BR station.

On Tuesdays, Thursdays and Saturdays, Oakley Services operate to Alresford from Basingstoke.

For more information contact: Alder Valley enquiry offices, telephone Guildford 575226 or Aldershot 23322. Oakley Services telephone Basingstoke 780731

Refreshment facilities: Buffet service on most trains

Catering facilities: The 'Watercress Belle' operates on the 1st and 3rd Saturdays April-October. Early booking is essential, please telephone to confirm seat availability

Souvenir shops: Alresford, Ropley

Depot: Ropley

Length of line: 10 miles

Passenger trains: Alton-Alresford. Sundays 7 January-28 October; Saturdays and Bank Holidays 7 April-

Locomotives

Name	No	Origin	Class	Type	Built
—	120	LSWR	T9	4-4-0	1899
—	30499	LSWR	S15	4-6-0	1920
—	506	LSWR	S15	4-6-0	1920
—	31625	SR	U	2-6-0	1929
—	31806	SR	U	2-6-0	1926
—	31874	SR	N	2-6-0	1925
Bodmin	34016	SR	WC	4-6-2	1945
Tangmere	34067	SR	BB	4-6-2	1947
Swanage	34105	SR	WC	4-6-2	1950
British India Line	35018	SR	MN	4-6-2	1945
—	73096	BR	5MT	4-6-0	1956
—	76017	BR	4MT	2-6-0	1954
Sturdee	601	MoS	WD	2-10-0	1943
Franklin D. Roosevelt	70340	USATC	S160	2-8-0	1944
—	D3358	BR	08	0-6-0DE	1957
—	D5217	BR	25	Bo-Bo	1961
—	D5353	BR	27	Bo-Bo	1961

Industrial locomotives

Name	No	Builder	Type	Built
—	4	Fowler (22889)	0-4-0DM	1939
Errol Lonsdale	196	Hunslet (3796)	0-6-0ST	1953

Stock
2 steam cranes
1 'Plassermatic' tamping/levelling machine
1 Plasser & Theurer AL250 lining machine
36 ex-BR Mk 1 coaches
8 ex-SR coaches
3 ex-LSWR coaches
Numerous goods vehicles

Owners
120 (on loan from the National Railway Museum)
30499 and 506 (the Urie Locomotive Society)
34105 (the 34105 Light Pacific Group)
76017 (the Standard 4 Locomotive Group)

Below:
The NRM's Class M7 0-4-4T was on short term loan to the MHR during 1989 and will be one of the exhibits at York during 1990. *R. E. Ruffell*

27 October; Tuesdays, Wednesdays & Thursdays 29 May-19 July; Daily 23 July-9 September. Santa Specials 24/25 November, 1/2, 8/9, 15/16, 22/23 December (bookings commence end of August)
Journey time: Round trip 1hr 40min max
Special events: Valentine Luncheon 11 February; Mothers' Day Specials 24/25 March; Easter Bunny Runs 13-16 April; Gardening Weekend 5-7 May; Toys of Yesteryear 27-29 May; Watercress Williams' Birthday

10 June; Mid-Hants Railways 125th Anniversary Celebration 30 June/1 July; MG Sports Car Rally 15 July; Taste of Hampshire 21/22 July; War on the Line 16 September; Teddy Bear Specials 13/14 October; Halloween 27 October (bookings commence end of August)
Period of public operation: Weekends and Bank Holidays from mid March-end October
Facilities for disabled: Toilets at Ropley, special facilities for disabled passengers on selected trains

Membership details: Membership Secretary, c/o above address

Below:
Urie 'S15' No 506 climbs the Alps as it heads for Medstead & Four Marks station on the Mid-Hants Railway on a fine winter's day, 22 January 1989. 1989 was the first year that the railway ran a Sunday service during the early spring.
A. R. Butcher

Swindon & Cricklade Railway SC

This is the only preserved section of the former Midland & South Western Junction Railway, the society having had to relay track and associated works
Location: Tadpole Lane, Blunsdon (approximately mid way between Blunsdon St Andrew and Purton)
Operating society/organisation: Swindon & Cricklade Railway, Blunsdon Station, Blunsdon, Swindon, Wiltshire SN2 4DZ
Telephone: Swindon (0793) 771615 (weekends only)
Station: Blunsdon
OS reference: SU 110897
Length of line: 1-mile
Car park: Tadpole Lane, Blunsdon
Refreshment facilities: Blunsdon station amenities building

Locomotives

Name	No	Origin	Class	Type	Built
Foremarke Hall	7903	GWR	'Hall'	4-6-0	1949
—	5637	GWR	56xx	0-6-2T	1924
—	D2022	BR	03	0-6-0DM	1958
—	08114	BR	08	0-6-0DE	1955
—	D5222	BR	25	Bo-Bo	1965

Industrial locomotives

Name	No	Builder	Type	Built
—	—	Fowler (4210105)	0-4-0DM	1955
Gnundraclese	—	Fowler (4210137)	0-4-0DM	1958
—	—	Fowler (21442)	0-4-0DM	1936
Richard Trevithick	—	Barclay (2354)	0-4-0ST	1955
Merlin	1967	Peckett (1967)	0-4-0ST	1939

Souvenir shop: Blunsdon station amenities building. Museum in converted coach
Depot: Blunsdon
Public opening: Saturdays and Sundays throughout the year.
Passenger trains: Passenger services operate 15/16 April; 27/28 May; 17 June; 15 July; 26/27 August; 16 September; 31 October (evening). Details from Public Relations Manager c/o above address
Special events: Santa Specials 8/9, 15/16, 22/23 December
Facilities for disabled: Access to shop and refreshments
Membership details: Membership Secretary c/o above address

Stock
5 BR Mk 1 coaches
2 GWR coaches
Selection of goods rolling stock
20-ton steam crane
3-ton steam crane
Wickham railcar

Owners
7903 (the Foremarke Hall Locomotive Group)
5637 (the 5637 Locomotive Group)

Swindon GWR Museum M

The Great Western Railway Museum began life as a lodging house for railway workers, and was then a Wesleyan Methodist Chapel for 90 years before being acquired by Swindon Borough Council and converted into a museum. Alongside the museum, in the heart of the railway village, visitors can glimpse the living conditions of the railworkers at the turn of the century, in the carefully restored workman's house
Location: Faringdon Road, Swindon, Wiltshire
OS reference: SU 145846
Operating society/organisation: Borough of Thamesdown, GWR Museum, Faringdon Road, Swindon, Wiltshire
Telephone: Swindon (0793) 26161 ext 3131
Car park: Swindon BR station and street parking
Access by public transport:

Locomotives

Name	No	Origin	Class	Type	Built
—	2516	GWR	2301	0-6-0	1887
Lode Star	4003	GWR	'Star'	4-6-0	1907
—	9400	GWR	9400	0-6-0PT	1947
North Star*	—	GWR	—	2-2-2	1837
—	4	GWR	Diesel railcar	Bo-Bo	1934

*Broad gauge replica

Owners
All locomotives are part of the National Railway Museum Collection

Swindon BR (10 minutes)
On site facilities: A selection of souvenirs is available
Public opening: Weekdays 10.00-17.00, Sundays 14.00-17.00. Closed Good Friday, Christmas Day, Boxing Day and New Year's Day
Special Notes: The Museum also houses a considerable number of photographs depicting scenes of the GWR along with nameplates, models, posters, tickets, etc. *New for 1990:* Return to Swindon Special Exhibition — opening 10 April to coincide with National Railway Museum Special 'On Tour' exhibition during this period

Winchcombe Railway Museum M

Three miles from the Gloucestershire-Warwickshire railway, the diverse collection includes signalling equipment, lineside fixtures, horse-drawn road vehicles, tickets, lamps, etc. Indoor and outdoor displays set in ½ acre of traditional Victorian Cotswold Garden. Visitors are encouraged to touch exhibits
Location: 23 Gloucester Street, Winchcombe, Gloucestershire

OS reference: SP 023283
Operating society/organisation: Winchcombe Railway Museum Association, 23 Gloucester Street, Winchcombe, Gloucestershire
Telephone: Winchcombe (0242) 602257/62641
Car park: On street at entrance
Access by public transport: Bus service from Cheltenham operated by Castleways Ltd

On site facilities: Relic, refreshments and souvenir shop
Public opening: Daily Easter to October 13.30-18.00. Weekends and holidays only November to March 13.30-dusk
Facilities for disabled: Access to all parts except toilets
Special notes: Many visitor-operated exhibits

South West

Avon Valley Railway · SC

Formerly the Bristol Suburban Railway, services re-commenced over the Bitton-School Road Halt section in August 1983

Headquarters: Bitton Railway Co Ltd, Bitton Station, Bristol, Avon

Main station: Bitton

OS reference: ST 670705

Car park: Bitton

Access by public transport: Badgerline service No 332 (Bristol-Bath), No 558 (Bristol-North Common) or 632 (Bristol-Bath)

Catering facilities: Refreshment room is able to supply hot snacks. Restaurant coach is available for private party catering

On site facilities: Toilets, snack bar

Length of line: 1½ miles

Public opening: Please contact for details, available on pre-recorded message on Bitton (0272) 327296

Special events: Diesel days 22 July and 19 August. Santa Specials 1/2, 8/9, 15/16, 21-24, 26 December

Facilities for disabled: Coach converted to disabled vehicle

Membership details: Mrs V. Baldwin, 18 Gays Road, Hanham, Bristol

Locomotives

Name	No	Origin	Class	Type	Built
Sir Frederick Pile	34058	SR	BB	4-6-2	1947
—	44123	LMS	4F	0-6-0	1925
—	45379	LMS	5MT	4-6-0	1937
—	47324	LMS	3F	0-6-0T	1926
—	48173	LMS	8F	2-8-0	1943

Locomotive notes: All locomotives undergoing restoration.

Industrial locomotives

Name	No	Builder	Type	Built
Edwin Hulse	2	Avonside (1798)	0-6-0ST	1918
Littleton No 5	—	M/Wardle (2018)	0-6-0ST	1922
Fonmon	—	Peckett (1936)	0-6-0ST	1924
—	—	RSH (7151)	0-6-0T	1944
—	—	R/Hornsby (235519)	4wDM	1945
—	—	Baguley/Drewry (2153)	0-4-0	1941
—	2	Bagnall (2842)	0-4-0ST	1946
General Lord Robertson	610	Sentinel (10143)	0-8-0DH	1961
Kingswood	—	Barclay (446)	0-4-0DM	1959
—	10128	Sentinel (10128)	0-4-0DM	1963

Locomotive notes: R/Hornsby (235519) and Bagnall (2842) undergoing restoration.

Stock
9 ex-BR Mk1 coaches (2 stored off-site)
1 ex-BR Mk 1 Restaurant Coach
1 ex-BR Mk 1 sleeper
1 ex-GER coach chassis
1 ex-LMS 'Royal Scot' corridor 3rd
1 ex-LMS brake composite corridor
3 open wagons
3 box vans
3 refrigerated box vans
1 ex-GWR Fruit 'C'
1 ex-GWR ballast wagon
1 ex-GWR hand crane and match truck
1 ex-GCR box van
1 ex-BR Lowmac
1 ex-BR ballast wagon
1 ex-LMS 12-ton box van
1 ex-LMS 5½-ton handcrane and runner

Owners
44123 and 47324 (the London Midland Society)

Bicton Woodland Railway

A passenger-carrying line of 18in gauge with stock mainly from the Woolwich Arsenal Railway and of World War 1 vintage
Location: Bicton Park, near Sidmouth
OS reference: SY 074862
Operating society/organisation: Bicton Woodland Railway, Bicton Gardens, East Budleigh, Budleigh Salterton, Devon
Telephone: Colaton Raleigh (0395) 68465
Car park: On site
Access by public transport: Buses pass half-hourly from Exeter, Exmouth, Sidmouth in season
On site facilities: Refreshments, shop, one museum, toilets, 18in gauge railway

Locomotives

Name	No	Builder	Type	Built
Woolwich	1	Avonside (1748)	0-4-0T	1916
Bicton	2	R/Hornsby (213839)	4wDM	1942
Carnegie	3	Hunslet (4524)	0-4-4-0DM	1954
Clinton	4	H/Hunslet (2290)	0-4-0	1941
Budley*	—	R/Hornsby (235624)	4wDM	1945

*Static exhibit

Stock
4 open bogie coaches
5 closed bogie coaches

Length of line: 3,250yd
Public opening: Please contact for details

Facilities for disabled: Toilets, wheelchairs available. Special carriage for wheelchairs

---

Bodmin & Wenford Railway

The Bodmin & Wenford typifies the bygone branch railways of Cornwall. The terminus, close to Bodmin town centre, has an interesting collection of small standard gauge locomotives and rolling stock; and the operating line winds down to a junction with British Rail at Bodmin Parkway. From the track there are glimpses of Bodmin Moor, and scenic views across the beautiful valley of the River Fowey
Location: Bodmin General station, on B3269
Operating society/organisation: Bodmin & Wenford Railway, Bodmin General Station, Bodmin, Cornwall PL31 1AQ
Telephone: Timetable enquiries (0208) 73666, other enquiries (0208) 75611
Car park: On site
Access by public transport: Interchange with BR at Bodmin Parkway (arrivals by BR train only). Local bus to Bodmin
Refreshment facilities: Light refreshments only
On site facilities: Museum, toilets
Length of line: 3½ miles General-Parkway (track to Boscarne is *in situ* but not useable)
Public opening: Museum open daily Easter-end September, 10.30-17.00
Passenger trains: 13-17 April; 5-7, 13, 20, 26-31 May; 1-3, 10, 17 June; daily

Locomotives

Name	No	Origin	Class	Type	Built
—	3802	GWR	2884	2-8-0	1938
—	5552	GWR	4575	2-6-2T	1928
Western Lady	D1048	BR	52	C-C	1962
—	W79976	BR (AC Cars)	—	4wDM	1958
—	D3452	BR	10	0-6-0DE	1957
—	D3559	BR	08	0-6-0DE	1958

Industrial locomotives

Name	No	Builder	Type	Built
—	19	Bagnall (2962)	0-4-0ST	1950
Alfred	—	Bagnall (3058)	0-4-0ST	1953
—	—	Bagnall (3121)	0-4-0F	1957
Peter	—	Fowler (22928)	0-4-0DM	1940
Progress	—	Fowler (4000001)	0-4-0DM	1945
Swiftsure	—	Hunslet (2857)	0-6-0ST	1943
—	—	Hunslet (3133)	0-4-0DM	1949
—	—	Peckett (1611)	0-4-0ST	1923
Corrall	—	R/Hornsby (304470)	0-4-0DM	1946
Lec	—	R/Hornsby (443642)	4wDM	1960

Stock
8 BR Mk 1 coaches
Various freight wagons

Owners
D1048 (the Western Lady Ltd)

18 June-30 September; 2, 9, 16, 23 December (Santa Steaming)
Facilities for disabled: Yes

Membership details: C/o above address

Bristol Industrial Museum SC

The Museum houses machinery and vehicles associated with Bristol's industrial past, from horse-drawn vehicles to aircraft
Location: Princes Wharf, Bristol
OS reference: ST 585722
Operating society/organisation: Bristol Industrial Museum, Princes Wharf, Bristol, Avon BS1 4RN
Telephone: Bristol (0272) 251470
Car parks: Available nearby
Access by public transport: Buses to centre of town
On site facilities: Shop

Industrial locomotives

Name	No	Builder	Type	Built
Portbury	S3	Avonside (1764)	0-6-0ST	1917
Henbury	S9	Peckett (1940)	0-6-0ST	1937
—	3	F/Walker	0-6-0ST	1874
—	—	R/Hornsby	0-4-0DM	1958

Length of line: ½-mile
Public opening: Saturday-Wednesday 10.00-13.00; 14.00-17.00
Facilities for disabled: Reasonable access
Special notes: Operation of railway on advertised weekends only
Membership details: Officer in charge D. Martin, Bristol Harbour Railway c/o above address

Dart Valley Railway (Buckfastleigh section)

A typical West Country branch line meandering up the steep Dart Valley to Buckfastleigh which is home to the railway's workshops, a butterfly and otter farm and several other attractions
Headquarters: Dart Valley Railway, Buckfastleigh station, Buckfastleigh, Devon
Telephone: Buckfastleigh (0364) 42338
Main station: Buckfastleigh
Other public stations: Staverton Bridge
OS reference: Buckfastleigh SX 747663, Staverton Road SX 785638
Car park: Buckfastleigh
Access by public transport: Bus, X 38/9 Exeter-Plymouth; 188 Newton Abbot-Buckfastleigh
Refreshment facilities: Buckfastleigh
Souvenir shop: Buckfastleigh
Museum: Buckfastleigh
Depot: Buckfastleigh
Length of line: 7 miles
Passenger trains: Buckfastleigh-Littlehempston Riverside alongside the River Dart
Period of public operation: Telephone above for details
Facilities for disabled: Limited
Membership details: Mr A. Bissett, Dart Valley Railway Association, 98 Union Road, Shirley, Solihull, West Midlands B90 3DG

Locomotives

Name	No	Origin	Class	Type	Built
Bulliver	1420	GWR	1400	0-4-2T	1933
Ashburton	1450	GWR	1400	0-4-2T	1935
—	1369	GWR	1366	0-6-0PT	1934
Dartington	1638	GWR	1600	0-6-0PT	1951
—	3803*	GWR	2884	2-8-0	1939
—	4588	GWR	4575	2-6-2T	1927
Dumbleton Hall	4920	GWR	'Hall'	4-6-0	1929
—	6435	GWR	6400	0-6-0PT	1937
Thornbury Castle	7027	GWR	'Castle'	4-6-0	1949
Ardent	D2192	BR	03	0-6-0DM	1961
Western Fusilier	D1023	BR	52	C-C	1963
Tiny†	—	SDR	—	0-4-0VBT	1868

*Undergoing restoration at the Birmingham Railway Museum, Tyseley
†Broad gauge (7ft 0¼in)

Industrial locomotives

Name	No	Builder	Type	Built
Ashley	1	Peckett (2031)	0-4-0ST	1942
Lady Angela	1690	Peckett (1690)	0-4-0ST	1926
—	—	Bagnall (2766)	0-6-0ST	1944
Barbara	—	Hunslet (2890)	0-6-0ST	1943
Glendower	—	Hunslet (3810)	0-6-0ST	1954
—	—	Fowler (421014)	0-4-0DM	1958
Enterprise	—	H/Clarke (D810)	0-6-0DM	1953

Stock
DMU vehicles, Class 116 Nos 59003 and 59004 and Class 127 Nos 51592 and 51604.   6 ex-BR Mk 1 coaches.   12 ex-GWR coaches

Owners
0298 (30587) (on loan from the National Railway Museum)
Tiny, 7ft 0¼in gauge, part of the National Collection
3803 and 4920 (the Dumbleton Hall Society)
Glendower, Barbara and Bagnall 2766 (the Glendower Group)
7027 (the Birmingham Railway Museum, being restored by Dumbleton Hall Preservation Society)
D1023 (the National Railway Museum)

Dart Valley Railway (Torbay section)

A line that succeeds in imparting the feeling of running from A to B, linking, as it does, the Dartmouth ferry at Kingswear to Paignton and BR. A trip in the observation car is well worth the supplement for the views of the sea, the climb through the tunnel, and the descent through the wooded hillside to Brunel's terminus at Kingswear on the banks of the River Dart

Headquarters: Paignton Queen's Park station, Paignton, Devon
Telephone: Paignton (0803) 555872
Main station: Paignton Queen's Park
Other public stations: Goodrington, Churston, Kingswear (for Dartmouth)
OS reference: SX 889606
Car parks: Paignton municipal car

Below:
The DVR's Torbay line provides views over both Torbay and the River Dart during the course of its route from Paignton to Kingswear. GWR Prairie tank No 4555 is seen here climbing away from the bay with a morning service to Kingswear. *Mark S. Wilkins*

Locomotives

Name	No	Origin	Class	Type	Built
—	4555	GWR	4500	2-6-2T	1924
Goliath	5239	GWR	5205	2-8-0T	1924
Lydham Manor	7827	GWR	7800	4-6-0	1950
Ardent	D2192	BR	03	0-6-0DM	1961
Mercury	D7535	BR	25	Bo-Bo	1965

Stock
9 ex-BR Mk 1 coaches
1 ER Suburban coaches (ex-King's Cross)
1 Pullman observation coach
1 auto-coach
Stock is sometimes transferred to and from the Buckfastleigh line

park, Goodrington, Dartmouth (ferry to Kingswear)
Access by public transport: Adjacent to both BR station and Devon General bus station
Refreshment facilities: Kingswear
Museum: Buckfastleigh (Dart Valley line)
Depot: Buckfastleigh (Dart Valley line)
Length of line: 7 miles

Passenger trains: Paignton-Kingswear, views of Torbay and Dart estuary, 495yd tunnel
Period of public operation: Easter to October
Facilities for disabled: Limited
Special events: Santa Specials — please see press for details
Membership details: Mr M. Bellamy, Renewals Officer, 66 Main Avenue, Torquay, Devon TQ1 9EG

East Somerset Railway

Set up by the artist, David Shepherd, 'the man who loves giants', the railway line is home to *Black Prince* and *The Green Knight* housed in their 'traditional' shed. As one might expect, Cranmore station is well laid out and aesthetically pleasing. The signalbox serves as an ideal art gallery where his paintings and prints can be bought
Headquarters: East Somerset Railway, (Cranmore Railway Station) Shepton Mallet, Somerset
OS reference: ST 664429
Telephone: Cranmore (074 988) 417
Main station: Cranmore
Car park: Cranmore — free
Refreshment facilities: Restaurant car at depot offering lunches, snacks, teas, etc. Group catering by arrangement. Picnic areas at Cranmore, Merryfield Lane stations and depot
Souvenir shop: Cranmore
On site facilities: Museum and signalbox art gallery, new childrens' play area, wildlife information centre
Depot: Cranmore West
Length of line: 2 miles
Passenger trains: Cranmore West to Mendip Vale. Stations at Cranmore West, Merryfield Lane and Mendip Vale, unlimited train travel
Period of public operation: Depot open daily 27 March-30 October, with trains running each Sunday, Public Holidays; Wednesdays, Thursdays

Locomotives

Name	No	Origin	Class	Type	Built
—	6634	GWR	5600	0-6-2T	1928
—	32110	LBSCR	E1	0-6-0T	1877
—	47493	LMS	3F	0-6-0T	1927
The Green Knight	75029	BR	4MT	4-6-0	1954
Black Prince	92203	BR	9F	2-10-0	1959

Industrial locomotives

Name	No	Builder	Type	Built
Lord Fisher	1398	Barclay (1398)	0-4-0ST	1915
Lady Nan	1719	Barclay (1719)	0-4-0ST	1920
—	4101	Dubs (4101)	0-4-0CT	1901

Stock
6 ex-BR Mk 1 coaches
1 ex-LMS coach
1 ex-LNER (design) sleeping car
25 assorted wagons, mostly LMS and SR

Owner
6634 (the 6634 Locomotive Co)

and Saturdays in peak season and on certain other days. Closed January and February (except 1 January). Depot open weekends only November, December and March 10.00-16.00. Last admission 30min before closing time. Each day ticket allows unlimited travel on all timetabled trains
Special events: 7 May — Teddy Bears Day; 21 July — Jazz Night in the Engine Shed; 22 July — Vintage Vehicle Rally; 27 August — Cranmore Village Fayre; 6-7 October — Enthusiasts Weekend; 1-2, 8-9, 15-16, 22-23 December — Santa Specials
Facilities for disabled: Limited, advance notice required
Special Notes: Santa special steam trains on Saturday and Sundays in December
Membership details: Please apply to above address, SAE for brochure

Launceston Steam Railway

The railway runs through the beautiful Kensey Valley on a track gauge of 1ft 11½in, following the trackbed of the old North Cornwall line. The locomotives formerly worked on the Dinorwic and Penrhyn railways in North Wales. Launceston station contains a museum of vintage cars and motorcycles and there is also a collection of stationary steam engines which are demonstrated at work. There are catering and gift shop facilities and an exhibition of model railways, together with a very well stocked model shop. At the far end of the line there are pleasant walks and a picnic area. The covered rolling stock ensures an enjoyable visit whatever the weather

Industrial locomotives

Name	No	Builder	Type	Built
Lilian	—	Hunslet (317)	0-4-0ST	1883
Velinheli	—	Hunslet (409)	0-4-0ST	1886
Covertcoat	—	Hunslet (679)	0-4-0ST	1898
Sybil	—	Bagnall (1760)	0-4-0ST	1906
Dorothea	—	Hunslet (763)	0-4-0ST	1901
—	—	M/Rail (5646)	4wDM	1933
—	—	M/Rail (9546)	4wDM	1950

Locomotive notes: The three Hunslet locomotives (317/409/679) are expected to be in use during 1989.

Stock
1 electric inspection trolley
Bogie and 4-wheel coaches

Right:
Lilian waits patiently on the Launceston Steam Railway whilst operating the day's services.
Paul Fletcher

Location: Newport Industrial Estate, Launceston, Cornwall
OS reference: SX 328850
Operating Society/organisation: The Spice Settlement Trust Co Ltd, trading as the Launceston Steam Railway, Newport, Launceston
Telephone: (0566) 5665
Stations: Launceston-Hunts Crossing-New Mills. Note: the line now terminates ½-mile from the hamlet of New Mills and refreshments are available at the temporary terminus
Car park: Newport Industrial Estate, Launceston
Length of line: 2 miles, but 2½ miles when New Mills extension opens
Gauge: 1ft 11½in
Access by public transport: BR Gunnislake 13 miles, Plymouth or Bodmin 25 miles
On site facilities: Cafe and restaurant, transport museum, workshop tours, gift and bookshop, and model railway display with model shop, all situated at Launceston
Period of public operation: Easter holiday, then Tuesdays and Sundays until Whitsun. Daily Whitsun until end of September. Tuesdays and Sundays in October. Santa Specials every Saturday and Sunday in December, also Christmas Eve and Boxing Day
Public opening: Trains run from 11.00-17.00. Departures every 40min and more frequently if required. Unlimited riding on date of issue of ticket
Journey time: Return 35min, no single tickets available
Facilities for disabled: Easy access to all areas except bookshop and motorcycle museum. No toilet facilities for disabled
Special events: Double-headed trains on Wednesdays in July and August (whenever possible)

Plym Valley Railway   M

A scheme dedicated to the restoration of services over the former GWR Marsh Mills-Plym Bridge line, a distance of 1½ miles. The stock includes a former South African Railways Garratt-type locomotive of 3ft 6in gauge.
Location: 5 miles from centre of Plymouth, Devon, north of A38. From Marsh Mills roundabout, take B3416 to Plympton, follow signs
OS reference: SX 517564
Operating society/organisation: Plym Valley Railway Co Ltd, Marsh Mills Station, Coypool Road, Marsh Mills, Plymouth, Devon PL7 4NL
Telephone: Plymouth (0752) 330478
Access by public transport: Buses from Plymouth, Nos 20, 20A, 21, 22A, 51. Stop close to site
On site facilities: Shop and refreshments at Marsh Mills, Coypool (weekends only)
Public opening: Site open most days from 10.00
Special events: Please see press for details
Special notes: Visitors are advised

Locomotives

Name	No	Origin	Class	Type	Built
—	7229	GWR	7200	2-8-2T	1935
—	4160	GWR	5101	2-6-2T	1948
Wadebridge	34007	SR	WC	4-6-2	1945
—	75079	BR	4MT	4-6-0	1956
—	D3002	BR	08	0-6-0DE	1953
Springbok*	4112	SAR	GMAM	4-8-2+2-8-4	1957

Industrial locomotives

Name	No	Builder	Type	Built
—	3	H/Leslie (3597)	0-4-0ST	1926
—	—	T/Hill (125V)	4wDH	1963

*Ex-South African Railways 3ft 6in gauge

Owners
4160 and 4112 (the 4160 Ltd)

that, at the moment, the railway and its locomotives are still under restoration. Prospective visitors are advised to take the advice of their guides. Steam and diesel operating on various weekends
Membership details: Marsh Mills Station, Coypool Road, Marsh Mills, Plymouth PL7 4NL

Seaton & District Electric Tramway

A passenger-carrying 2ft 9in gauge electric tramway, operating on the trackbed of the former LSWR Seaton branch
Location: Seaton, Devon
OS reference: SY 252904
Operating society/organisation: Seaton & District Electric Tramway Co, Riverside Depot, Harbour Road, Seaton, Devon EX12 2NQ
Telephone: Seaton (0297) 21702/20375

Locomotives

Name	No	Builder	Type	Built
—	—	R/Hornsby (435398)	4wDM	1959

Access by public transport: Located near to centre of Seaton
On site facilities: Shops Seaton and Colyton, tea bar at Colyton, adventure playground
Length of line: 3 miles, 2ft 9in gauge

Period of public operation: Daily Good Friday-end October, also limited winter service
Special notes: Services operated by open top deck bogie tramcars and enclosed single-deck winter car

Swanage Railway — The Purbeck Line

Overlooked by the historic ruins of Corfe Castle, this railway is slowly extending towards Wareham and a connection to the BR network
Location: Swanage station
Operating society/organisation: Swanage Railway Co Ltd, Station House, Railway Station, Swanage, Dorset
Telephone: Swanage 425800. Purbeck Line 24hr Talking Timetable — Swanage 424276
Main station: Swanage
Other public stations: Herston Halt, Harman's Cross
OS reference: SZ 026789
Car park: Swanage
Access by public transport: Wilts & Dorset buses from Bournemouth, Poole and Wareham stop outside station
On site facilities: Souvenir shop, buffet car on certain trains, hot and cold snacks. Shop open every weekend throughout the year, and on all operating days
Length of line: 3 miles, Swanage-Herston Halt-Harman's Cross
Public opening: Open for viewing daily (except Christmas). Trains run every weekend during January, February and March as well as November and December. Trains run Fridays, Saturdays, Sundays and Mondays between April and May and during October. Daily running June to September (inclusive)
Special events: January, February and March, Pie and Pint Specials (weekends); Teddy Bear Specials 17/18 March; Mother's Day Specials 25 March; Friends of Thomas the Tank Weekend 31 March/1 April; Easter Egg

Locomotives

Name	No	Origin	Class	Type	Built
—	6695	GWR	5600	0-6-2T	1928
—	30053	LSWR	M7	0-4-4T	1905
257 Squadron	34072	SR	BB	4-6-2	1948
Holland America Line	35022	SR	MN	4-6-2	1948
Port Line	35027	SR	MN	4-6-2	1948
—	45160*	LMS/WD	8F	2-8-0	1941
—	80078	BR	4MT	2-6-4T	1954
—	80104	BR	4MT	2-6-4T	1955
—	1708†	MR	1F	0-6-0T	1880
—	D3591	BR	08	0-6-0DE	1958
—	D7594 (25244)	BR	25	Bo-Bo	1964

*Repatriated from Turkey
†Possibly on loan for summer season

Locomotive notes: 30053, 34072 and 80104 are at the Swindon Heritage Centre for restoration, 35027 is on the Bluebell Railway

Industrial locomotives

Name	No	Builder	Type	Built
Cunarder	47160	Hunslet (1690)	0-6-0T	1931
Linda	21	H/Leslie (3931)	0-6-0ST	1938
May	2	Fowler (4210132)	0-4-0DM	1957
Beryl	—	Planet (2054)	4wPM	1937
—	2150	Peckett (2150)	0-6-0T	1954

Stock

3 ex-LSWR coach bodies
4 ex-SR vans
9 ex-SR coaches
18 ex-BR Mk 1 coaches
1 ex-LNWR CCT
1 ex-'Brighton Belle' Pullman 288
1 ex-LMS coach
18 various types of wagons
1 ex-BR Sleeping coach
1 ex-SR 15ton diesel-electric crane
1 Wickham trolley (WD9024)
1 ex-London Transport Plasser & Theurer ballast tamper
1 ex-BR Corridor 2nd, converted to disabled persons coach

Specials 15/16 April; Vintage Transport Weekend 5-7 May; Swanage Railway Steam Gala 19/20 May; Victorian Weekend 16/17 June; Swanage Carnival 28 July-5 August; Steam Gala 15/16 September; Thomas the Tank Weekend 13/14 October; Halloween 27 October; throughout November, Pie and Pint Specials; throughout December, Santa Specials; Mince Pie Specials 29-31 December; New Year Specials 1 January 1991
Facilities for disabled: Access to station, shop and toilets and special coach on train
Feature article reference: RW December 1989, p733 (photo feature)

Owners
6695 (the Great Western Railway Preservation Group)
80078 and 35022 (the Southern Steam Trust)
Cunarder (owned by 1708 Locomotive Preservation Trust Ltd)
34072, 35027 and 80104 (the *Port Line* Project)

Tiverton Museum   M

The Museum, dominated by No 1442, affectionately known as the 'Tivvy Bumper', houses a large collection of railway relics
Location: Tiverton, Devon
OS reference: SS 955124
Operating society/organisation: Tiverton Museum Society, St Andrew Street, Tiverton, Devon EX16 6PH
Telephone: Tiverton (0884) 256295
Car park: Adjoining

Locomotives

Name	No	Origin	Class	Type	Built
—	1442	GWR	1400	0-4-2T	1935

Access by public transport: Rail to Tiverton Parkway, then by bus, or bus from Exeter
On site facilities: Museum, shop and toilets

Public opening: Daily 10.30-16.30; except Sundays and between 1 February-20 December
Special notes: Limited facilities for disabled

West Somerset Railway

Running for 20 miles, this is Britain's longest preserved railway and evokes all the atmosphere of a country railway from a more leisured age. The line is host to several societies and groups, and several stations have their own museum, such as the Somerset and Dorset Trust; at Washford. There are some idyllic country stations in the Quantock Hills and Dunster station served for many years as the model for Hornby Dublo's branch line station
Headquarters: West Somerset Railway, The Railway Station, Minehead, Somerset
Telephone: Minehead (0643) 4996
Main station: Minehead
Other public stations: Dunster, Blue Anchor, Washford, Watchet, Williton, Doniford Beach Halt, Stogumber, Crowcombe, Bishop's Lydeard
OS reference: Minehead SS 975463, Williton ST 085416, Bishops Lydeard ST 164290

Locomotives

Name	No	Origin	Class	Type	Built
—	53808	S&DJR	7F	2-8-0	1925
—	3205	GWR	2251	0-6-0	1946
—	3850	GWR	2884	2-8-0	1942
—	4561	GWR	4500	2-6-2T	1924
—	5542	GWR	4575	2-6-2T	1928
—	6412	GWR	6400	0-6-0PT	1934
Dinmore Manor	7820	GWR	'Manor'	4-6-0	1950
—	D2271	BR	04	0-6-0DM	1952
—	D2994	BR	07	0-6-0DE	1962
—	D7017	BR	35	B-B	1962
—	D9500	BR	14	0-6-0DH	1964
—	D9526	BR	14	0-6-0DH	1964
—	D9551	BR	14	0-6-0DH	1965

Industrial locomotives

Name	No	Builder	Type	Built
Portbury	S3	Avonside (1764)	0-6-0ST	1917
—	—	Bagnall (2473)	0-4-0ST	1932
*Jennifer**	20	H/Clarke (1731)	0-6-0T	1942
Isabel	—	H/Leslie (3437)	0-6-0ST	1919
*Kilmersdon**	—	Peckett (1788)	0-4-0ST	1929

Car parks: Minehead, Williton, Bishops Lydeard. Some parking at all stations except Washford and Doniford Beach

Access by public transport: Nearest BR station, Taunton

Refreshment facilities: Minehead, Bishop's Lydeard (limited opening), Williton (limited opening). Wine and Dine trains. Buffet car on most steam trains

Souvenir shops: Minehead, Bishop's Lydeard

Museum: Somerset & Dorset Railway Museum Trust, Washford. GWR Museum at Blue Anchor

Depots: Bishop's Lydeard, Williton, Washford, Minehead

Length of line: 20 miles

Passenger trains: Steam and diesel trains to Bishops Lydeard

Period of public operation: SAE for details

Special events: Gala Week, 3-10 September

Facilities for disabled: Parking space level with entrance. No steps to shop or booking office, level access to toilets (disabled toilets at Minehead should be commissioned during 1990). Catering facilities can be reached without difficulties. Groups can be catered for. Advanced booking advised to guarantee facilities. No special facilities on train but assistance available

Feature article references: RW July 1988, p411; RW September 1989, p541 (photo feature)

Name	No	Builder	Type	Built
—	24	Ruston (210479)	4wDM	1941
—	—	Ruston (183062)	4wDM	1937
—	57	Sentinel (10214)	0-6-0DM	1964

*May not be on site for all of 1990 season

Stock
18 ex-BR Mk 1 coaches
1 ex-BR Mk 2 coach
2 ex-BR Restaurant cars
7 ex-GWR camping coaches
1 ex-BR Mk 1 Sleeper
1 ex-GWR Sleeping Coach
1 ex-SR 'Ironclad' coach
2 Park Royal 2-car diesel multiple-units (50415, 50414, 56168, 56169)
2 Gloucester 2-car diesel multiple-units (50341, 51118, 56097, 56099)
1 Cravens 2-car diesel multiple-unit (51485, 56121)
1 ex-GWR Hawksworth coach
1 ex-LMS parcels van
1 ex-GWR 5-ton hand crane
More than 40 freight vehicles

Owners
53808, S3, *Isabel, Kilmersdon* and Bagnall 2473 (the Somerset & Dorset Museum Trust)
D7017 and D9526 (the Diesel and Electric Group)
5542 (the 5542 Fund)
3205 (the 2251 Class Fund)
3850 and 7820 (the 3850 Preservation Society)

Below:
National Railway Museum-owned Class 9F No 92220 *Evening Star* climbs Castle Hill, Williton, on 2 July 1989 whilst on loan to the West Somerset Railway. *Melvyn Hopwood*

South-West

Wales

Bala Lake Railway (Rheilffordd Llyn Tegid)

Although narrow gauge, this railway is built over the old standard gauge branch to Bala, which is the line's north-eastern terminus. The railway's headquarters are to be found in the fine old station building at Llanuwchllyn at the other end of the line. Do not be deterred by the fact that the railway runs down the opposite shore of the lake to the main road — it is well worth the detour

Headquarters: Rheilffordd Llyn Tegid (Bala Lake Railway) Llanuwchllyn, Bala, Gwynedd LL23 7DD
Telephone: Llanuwchllyn (067 84) 666
Main station: Llanuwchllyn
Other public stations: Llangower, Bala
OS reference: Llanuwchllyn SH 880300, Bala SH 929350
Car parks: Llanuwchllyn, Llangower and Bala town centre
Access by public transport: Bus Gwynedd service No 94 to both Bala and Llanuwchllyn (from Wrexham or Barmouth)
Road access: Off the A494 Bala-Dolgellau road
Refreshment facilities: Llanuwchllyn. Large picnic site with

Industrial locomotives

Name	No	Builder	Type	Built
Holy War	—	Hunslet (779)	0-4-0ST	1902
Maid Marian	—	Hunslet (822)	0-4-0ST	1903
Meirionnydd	—	Severn Lamb (7322)	Bo-Bo	1973
Alice	—	Hunslet (780)	0-4-0ST	1902
Chilmark	—	R/Hornsby (194771)	4wDM	1939
Indian Runner	—	R/Hornsby (200744)	4wDM	1940
—	—	Lister (34025)	4wDM	1949
—	—	Hudson (38384)	4wDM	1930
—	—	Motorail (5821)	4wDM	1934
—	—	R/Hornsby (209430)	4wDM	1942
—	—	R/Hornsby (189972)	4wDM	1938
—	—	Hibberd (FH2544)	4wDM	1941
—	—	Hunslet (1974)	4wDM	1939
Cernyw	—	R/Hornsby (200748)	4wDM	1940

Locomotive notes: *Alice* is under restoration, *Holy War* and *Maid Marian* will be in regular use, remainder are on static display

toilet facilities by lake at Llangower
Souvenir shop: Llanuwchllyn
Museum: Large collection of antique railway equipment
Depot: Llanuwchllyn
Length of line: 4½ miles, 1ft 11⅝in gauge
Passenger trains: Llanuwchllyn-Bala. Journey takes 25min in each direction

Period of public operation: 7 April-30 September
Facilities for disabled: Facilities available on most trains
Special notes: Small parties (10/12) may just turn up, but a day's notice for large parties would be helpful
Membership details: P. Briddon, 140 Earl Marshal Road, Sheffield S4 8LB

Brecon Mountain Railway

A narrow gauge passenger carrying railway close to Merthyr Tydfil built on part of the trackbed of the former Brecon & Merthyr Railway. Gradually being extended northward, the railway has some interesting narrow gauge steam locomotives imported from East and West Germany and South Africa
Headquarters: Brecon Mountain Railway, Pant Station, Dowlais,

Locomotives

Name	No	Builder	Type	Built
—	—	Baldwin (61269)	4-6-2	1930
Sybil	—	Hunslet (827)	0-4-0ST	1903
San Justo	4	H/Clarke (639)	0-4-2ST	1903
Santa Ana	—	H/Clarke (640)	0-4-2ST	1903
Graf Schwerin-Löwitz	99.3353	Arn Jung (1261)	0-6-2WT	1908
—	—	O&K (12722)	0-4-0WT	1936
Pendyffryn	—	de Winton	0-4-0VBT	1894
Redstone	—	Redstone	0-4-0VBT	1905

Merthyr Tydfil, Mid Glamorgan
CF48 2UP
Telephone: Merthyr Tydfil (0685)
4854
Main station: Pant
Car park: Pant station
OS reference: SO 063120
Access by public transport:
Omnibus to Pant Cemetery — ½
hourly frequency from Merthyr bus
station. BR rail service to Merthyr
from Cardiff Central
Depot: Pant
Length of line: 2 miles, 1ft 11¾in
gauge
Period of public operation: Easter
weekend; May weekend, daily 26 May-
mid-September
Refreshment facilities: Licensed
restaurant at Pant, snackbar at
Pontsticill
Special events: Santa Specials 8/9,
15/16, 22/23 December
Facilities for disabled: Toilets and
ramps

Name	No	Builder	Type	Built
Rhydychen	—	Simplex (11177)	4wDM	1961
Garret	—	M/Rail (7902)	4wDM	1939
—	77	Hanomag (10629)	2-6-2+2-6-2	1928
—	—	Brecon MR (001)	0-6-0DH	1987
—	—	Brecon MR (003)	0-6-0DH	1987

Stock
9 bogie wagons
2 balcony end 39-seat coaches
2 balcony end 40-seat coaches
1 20-seat Caboose
Miscellaneous rail carrying and ballast wagons
South African Railways Box Car
Diesel-hydraulic crane
Wickham petrol trolley

Right:
**Graf Schwerin-Lowitz approaches
Pant with a train from Pontsticill on
27 March 1989.** *Mike Jones*

Caerphilly Railway Society SC

An unusual collection in the historic
surroundings of the old Rhymney
Railway locomotive works, comprising
a rare selection of locomotives and
rolling stock from both main line
railways and South Wales industry.
The restored Brecon & Merthyr
Railway signalbox, with its unique
overlocking Saxby & Farmer lever
frame, is worth seeing
Operating society: Caerphilly
Railway Society Ltd
Location: Harold Wilson Industrial
Estate, Van Road, Caerphilly, Mid
Glamorgan
OS reference: ST 163865
Telephone: (0633) 273182 (evenings
only)
Car parking: Ample car parking
available at the depot
Public transport: Approximately
1 mile from Caerphilly rail and bus
stations

Locomotives

Name	No	Origin	Class	Type	Built
—	41312	LMS	2MT	2-6-2T	1952
—	28	TVR	01	0-6-2T	1897
—	D2178	BR	03	0-6-0DM	1962

Industrial locomotives

Name	No	Builder	Type	Built
Victory	—	Barclay (2201)	0-4-0ST	1945
Forester	—	Barclay (1260)	0-4-0ST	1911
Desmond	—	Avonside (1498)	0-4-0ST	1906
Haulwen	—	V/Foundry (5272)	0-6-0ST	1945
—	—	Hunslet	0-6-0DM	1962
Deighton	—	YEC (2731)	0-4-0DE	1959

Locomotive notes: Locomotives operating from the 1990 season are
expected to be TVR 0-6-2T No 28 and *Victory*. Locomotives currently under
repair are D2178, 41312 and *Deighton*. All others currently static/in store
pending restoration.

On site facilities: Light snacks, refreshments and souvenirs available on steam days
Facilities for the disabled: No steps are involved in gaining access to the depot. Facilities are limited, but help readily given
Length of line: ¾-mile
Public opening: Static display every Sunday 14.00-17.00; 1990 steam days: 25 March; 15/16, 28 April; 7, 27/28 May; 30 June; 29 July; 26/27 August; 29 September; 27 October
Special events: Grand Transport Show 29 September; Santa Specials 15 December (prior booking only)
Membership: Mr N. Radley, 3 Warwick Place, Cardiff, South Glamorgan

Stock
GWR 6-ton hand crane and flat runner wagon
GWR 14-ton ballast wagon 60501
3 wooden 7-plank mineral wagons
2 steel-framed oil tank wagons
BR Mk 1 BSK E34460 (internally converted to buffet facility)
GWR 20-ton Toad goods brake van 35267
SR 4-wheel PMV 1168 (latterly mess and tool van)
GWR/BR Fruit D W92040
LMS 12-ton boxvan 304986
GWR Mink D 28804 (latterly mess and tool van)
Swansea Harbour Trust 4-wheel saloon carriage
TVR coach (body only) No 153

Owners
28 (the National Railway Museum, on loan from the Museum of Wales)
D2178 and Hunslet (on loan from National Smokeless Fuels)

Right:
Taff Vale Railway No 28, a 0-6-2T of 1897, is seen on 30 April 1989. When the locomotive is stored between steamings the cab is boarded in to prevent unauthorised access. *Mike Jones*

Conwy Valley Railway Museum   M

Conveniently situated alongside British Rail's Betws-y-Coed station, the Museum presents some well-displayed distractions to pass the time including model train layouts to delight both adult and child
Location: Adjacent to Betws-y-Coed station
OS reference: SH 796565
Operating society/organisation: Conwy Valley Railway Museum, The Old Goods Yard, Betws-y-Coed, Gwynedd
Telephone: (06902) 568
Car park: On site
Access by public transport: Betws-y-Coed BR station
On site facilities: Refreshments in buffet car. Bookshop and model/gift

Locomotives

Name	No	Builder	Type	Built
Sgt Murphy	—	K/Stuart (3117) (2ft gauge)	0-6-0T	1918

Stock
1 GWR fitter's van
1 LMS 6-wheel van
1 LNER CCT van
1 BR Mk 1 coach
2 SR luggage vans
1 Pullman coach

shop in museum foyer, operating train layouts, miniature railway (1¼-miles, 7¼in gauge) steam-hauled. Picnic area

Public opening: Daily Easter-end of October, 10.30-17.30
Facilities for disabled: Access to museum and toilets

Corris Railway Museum

M

This rather remote Museum merits a detour if only because of the unusual treatment of and detailed research into local history with some fascinating film and photographs that can be seen in the old stone building that houses the Museum

Location: Off A487, opposite Braichgoch Hotel, five miles north of Machynlleth

OS reference: SH 755078

Operating society: The Corris Railway Society, Corris Station Yard, Gwynedd (postal address: Corris, Machynlleth, Powys SY20 9SH)

Car park: Adjacent

Access by public transport: Bus Gwynedd services 34 & 35 (Machynlleth-Aberllefeni and Machynlleth-Dolgellau-Blaenau Ffestiniog respectively) and 'Trawscambria' (stop at Braichgoch Hotel)

Catering facilities: None, but light teas available nearby in village

Locomotives

Name	No	Builder	Type	Built
Alan Meaden	5	M/rail (22258)	4wDM	1965
—	6	R/Hornsby (51849)	4wDM	1966

Locomotive notes: 5 operational and on works trains, 6 currently under repair

Stock

Small number of representative and works wagons, one manriding carriage, with a second currently having a replica body added

On site facilities: Souvenir shop, toilets and children's playground

Length of line: ¾-mile, 2ft 3in gauge construction line, being upgraded to passenger carrying standard

Public opening: 14-16 April; 26-28 May; 23 July-31 August, 10.30-17.00, Monday-Friday and Bank Holiday weekends only. 17-20 April; 29 May-20 July; 3-21 September, 12.00-17.00 Monday-Friday only

Special events: Works train operating on Corris Fun Day — 4 August

Facilities for disabled: Limited

Membership details: A. H. Lawson, 165 Gynsill Lane, Anstey, Leicester LE7 7AN

Fairbourne & Barmouth Railway

Since 1983 this railway has now been regauged from 15in to 12¼in but has been transformed by the introduction of new locomotives and rolling stock, tunnels through the sand dunes, miniaturised stations and signalboxes, new workshops, a créperie overlooking the Barmouth estuary and a butterfly jungle alongside Fairbourne station

Headquarters: North Wales Narrow Gauge Railway Co Ltd, Fairbourne & Barmouth Leisure Park, Beach Road, Fairbourne, Gwynedd, LL38 2EX

Telephone: 0341-250362 or 250083

Main station: Gorsaf Newydd, Fairbourne

Other public stations: Gorsafawddacháidraigd-danheddogleddolôn-penrhynareudraethceredigion, Porth Penrhyn

OS reference: SH 616128

Car parks: Gorsaf Newydd, Gorsafawddach

Access by public transport: Fairbourne BR station. Bus Gwynedd service

Refreshment facilities: Celtic Pavillion at Porth Penrhyn. Porth

Locomotives

Name	No	Builder	Type	Built
Beddgelert	—	Curwen	0-6-4T	1979
Yeo	—	Curwen	2-6-2T	1978
Sherpa	—	Milner	0-4-0STT	1978
Russell	—	FLW	2-6-2T	1985
Lilian Walter	—	FLW	A1-1AD	1985
Gwril	—	FLW	4wBE	1987
Sandy River	24	FLW	2-6-2	1989

FLW — Fairbourne Locomotive Works

Stock

12¼in gauge — 28 coaches (1st, 2nd class)   16 freight

Penrhyn restaurant specialises in Welsh Lamb and Breton Pancakes, with 'Sundowner' evening service for dinner and entertainment (main season) (phone for details)

Souvenir shop: Gorsaf Newydd and Penrhyn Pavillion

Depot: Fairbourne

Length of line: 2¾ miles, 12¼in gauge

Passenger trains: A 2¾-mile journey connecting with ferry at Porth Penrhyn to Barmouth. 20min single journey. Through tickets to Barmouth at reduced price

Period of public operation: Daily Good Friday-1 November (closed Saturdays except at peak season)

Facilities for disabled: Full disabled facilities with Ro-Ro coach

Membership details: Friends of Fairbourne — contact Hon Sec A. de Frayssinet at above address

Special notes: During inclement weather the service may be restricted or cancelled. Extra trains and special parties by arrangement with the manager. Fairbourne Butterfly Jungle at Gorsaf Newydd

Ffestiniog Railway

In many ways, evocative of the early Swiss mountain railways as it climbs high above Porthmadog with some breathtaking views, the railway still operates an interesting variety of locomotives including some unusual Victorian survivors. Passengers have replaced slate as the principal traffic over this former quarry line

Headquarters: Ffestiniog Railway, Harbour Station, Porthmadog, Gwynedd, LL49 9NF
Telephone: Porthmadog (0766) 512340 or 831654
Main stations: Porthmadog Harbour, Blaenau Ffestiniog
Other public stations: Minffordd, Penrhyn, Tan-y-Bwlch, Tanygrisiau
OS reference: SH 571384
Car parks: Porthmadog, Tan-y-Bwlch, Tanygrisiau, Blaenau Ffestiniog
Access by public transport: Minffordd and Blaenau Ffestiniog BR stations. Porthmadog, Minffordd, Tanygrisiau and Blaenau Ffestiniog served by local buses
Refreshment facilities: Licensed restaurant at Porthmadog, buffet at Tan-y-Bwlch (summer only), also on most trains
Souvenir shops: Porthmadog, Tan-y-Bwlch, Blaenau Ffestiniog

Below:
Merddin Emrys, a double Fairlie-type engine, powers its train round the spiral at Dduallt. The four-wheel coaches behind the engine recall the early days before the introduction of bogie coaches.
FR Co

Locomotives

Name	No	Builder	Type	Built
Princess	1	G/England (199/200)	0-4-0STT	1863
Prince	2	G/England	0-4-0STT	1863
Welsh Pony	—	G/England (234)	0-4-0STT	1867
Earl of Merioneth	—	FR	0-4-4-0T	1979
Merddin Emrys	10	FR	0-4-4-0T	1879
Moelwyn	—	Baldwin (49604)	2-4-0DM	1918
Blanche	—	Hunslet (589)	2-4-0STT	1893
Linda	—	Hunslet (590)	2-4-0STT	1893
Britomart*	—	Hunslet (707)	0-4-0ST	1899
Mountaineer	—	Alco (57156)	2-6-2T	1917
Livingston Thompson†	3	FR	0-4-4-0T	1886
—	—	Peckett (2050)	0-6-0ST	1944
—†	K1	B/Peacock (5292)	0-4-0+0-4-0	1909
Upnor Castle	—	Hibberd (3687)	4wDM	1954
Conway Castle	—	Hibberd (3831)	4wDM	1958
Moel Hebog	—	Hunslet (4113)	0-4-0DM	1955
Mary Ann	—	M/Rail (596)	4wDM	1917

7 other 4wDM units
*Privately owned
†On loan to National Railway Museum

Stock
27 bogie coaches
4 4-wheel coaches
2 brake vans, plus numerous service vehicles

Museum: Porthmadog
Depot: Boston Lodge
Length of line: 13½ miles, 1ft 11½in gauge
Passenger trains: Porthmadog-Blaenau Ffestiniog
Period of public operation: Weekends March. Daily April-October, and Christmas
Special events: Special Gala Weekend 5-7 May. Santa Specials — please enquire for details

Facilities for disabled: Porthmadog and Blaenau Ffestiniog easily accessible for wheelchairs. Facilities on trains for disabled in wheelchairs by prior arrangement
Special notes: Reduced return rates available for journeys beginning on diesel services, shown in timetable
Feature article references: RW April 1988, p228 (Ffestiniog Steam 150); RW October 1989, p618 (FR showing the way)

Great Orme Tramway

A cable tramway to the summit of the Great Orme is operated as two sections involving a change half-way. Opened throughout in July 1903, it involves gradients as steep as 1 in 10.3
Location: Great Orme Tramway, Victoria station, Church Walks, Llandudno
OS reference: SH 7781
Operating society/organisation:
Aberconwy Borough Council, Tourism & Amenities Dept, Town Hall, Llandudno
Telephone: Llandudno (0492) 860086
Car park: Approximately 100yd from Lower Terminal. Adjacent to Summit Terminal
Access by public transport: Good
On site facilities: Shop
Period of public operation: Early May-end September (Monday-Friday); end May-end September (Sunday-Friday); August (seven day operation)
Special notes: Cable tramway to summit of Great Orme, approximately 1-mile rising to 650ft (3ft 6in gauge)
Stock: 4 tramcars each seating 48, built 1902/3

Gwili Railway/Rheilffordd Gwili

South Wales' first standard gauge passenger-carrying railway extended services back to Llwyfan Cerrig during 1987
Headquarters: Gwili Railway Co Ltd, Bronwydd Arms station, Bronwydd Arms, Carmarthen, Dyfed
Telephone: Carmarthen (0267) 230666
OS reference:
Bronwydd Arms SN 417239
Llwyfan Cerrig SN 405258,
Conwil SN 386263
Main station: Bronwydd Arms
Other public stations: Llwyfan Cerrig, also Conwil under restoration
Car park: Bronwydd Arms
Access by public transport:
Carmarthen BR station, then Crosville bus service No 400 (not Sundays).
Refreshment facilities: Bronwydd Arms, Llwyfan Cerrig (picnic site). Bar on train
Souvenir shop: Bronwydd Arms
Depot: Llwyfan Cerrig, stock also kept at Bronwydd Arms, Conwil and 'Ironrails', Carmarthen
Length of line: 1¾ miles
Passenger trains: Bronwydd Arms-Llwyfan Cerrig, regular hourly service
Period of public operation: Please contact for details
Public opening: 11.00-17.15 on all operating days
Special events: Santa Specials, 16/17 December. See press for details of other events
Special notes: A guest locomotive is likely for 1990

Right:
On 28 May 1989 *Olwen* heads the 15.15 Bronwydd Arms-Llwyfan Cerrig service at Cwmdwyfran.
Mike Jones

Industrial locomotives

Name	No	Builder	Type	Built
—	1	H/Clarke (1885)	0-6-0ST	1955
Little Lady	1903	Peckett (1903)	0-4-0ST	1936
—	—	R/Hornsby (207103)	4wDM	1941
Trecatty	—	R/Hornsby (421702)	0-6-0DM	1959
Olwen	7058	RSH (7058)	0-4-0ST	1942
—	71516	RSH (7170)	0-6-0ST	1944
Nellie	D2875	YEC (2779)	0-4-0DE	1960
Rosyth No 1	1	A/Barclay (1385)	0-4-0ST	1914*
Swansea Vale No 1	1	Sentinel (9622)	4wVBTG	1958*
Swansea Jack	—	R/Hornsby (393302)	4wDM	1955*
Dylan Thomas	—	N/British (27654)	0-4-0DH	1956*

Stock
1 ex-BR diesel unit trailer car
3 ex-BR Mk 1 coaches
2 ex-BR suburban coaches
1 ex-BR griddle car
1 ex-TVR coach (built 1891)
Coles diesel rail crane
1 ex-GWR Mink van
1 ex-GWR Fruit D
1 ex-GWR Monster
1 ex-GWR Crocodile

1 ex-GWR Loriot D
1 tank wagon
2 GWR Toad brake vans
1 GWR Tube C
1 GWR Tunnel Toad
14 open wagons

Owners
*The Railway Club of Wales

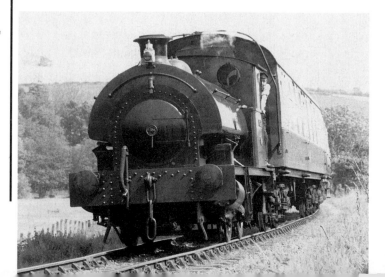

Llanberis Lake Railway (Rheilffordd Lyn Padarn)

A narrow gauge passenger carrying railway starting at the historic Dinorwic Quarry workshops (now part of the National Museum of Wales) and running along the shores of the Llanberis lake using the trackbed of the former slate railway line to Port Dinorwic. Excellent views of Snowdonia and good picnic spots along the line

Headquarters: Llanberis Lake Railway, Gilfach Ddu, Llanberis, Gwynedd LL55 4TY
Telephone: Llanberis (0286) 870549
Main station: Llanberis (Padarn station/Gilfachddu)
Other public stations: Cei Llydan
OS reference: SH 586603
Car park: Llanberis (Padarn station)
Refreshment facilities: Padarn station
Souvenir shop: Padarn Station
Length of line: 2 miles, 1ft 11½in gauge
Passenger trains: Llanberis-Penllyn-Llanberis
Journey time: 40min round trip
Period of public operation: Mondays to Thursdays in April and May and October. Sundays to Fridays, June through September, Saturdays July and August
Facilities for disabled: Level approaches throughout shop, cafe and to train. Special toilet facilities provided. All disabled visitors welcomed

Industrial locomotives

Name	No	Builder	Type	Built
Elidir	1	Hunslet (493)	0-4-0ST	1889
Thomas Bach/Wild Aster	2	Hunslet (849)	0-4-0ST	1904
Dolbadarn	3	Hunslet (1430)	0-4-0ST	1922
Helen Kathryn	5	Henschel (28035)	0-4-0T	1948
—	7	R/Hornsby (441427)	4wDM	1961
Twll Coed	8	R/Hornsby (268878)	4wDM	1956
Dolgarrog	9	M/Rail (22154)	4wDM	1962
—	—	R/Hornsby (425796)	4wDM	1958
—	11	R/Hornsby (198286)	4wDM	1939
Braich	10	R/Hornsby (203031)	4wDM	1942
—	18	M/Rail (7927)	4wDM	1941
Llanelli	19	R/Hornsby (451901)	4wDM	1961
Una*	—	Hunslet (873)	0-4-0ST	1905

*Not part of the railway's motive power stock. Housed at the adjacent slate museum and can sometimes be seen working demonstration freight trains

Stock
13 bogie coaches
20 wagons

Llangollen Railway   SC

The line, which is presently 2 miles long is of standard gauge and is the only preserved standard gauge line in North Wales. Situated in the Dee Valley, it follows the course of the River Dee for much of its route, and affords good views of the surrounding countryside between Llangollen and Berwyn. An hourly service is currently operated although this may be subject to alteration as planned extensions come into use during 1990-91. It is the eventual aim to reach Corwen, some 9 miles from Llangollen where a terminus will be re-established
Location: Llangollen station, A542 from Ruabon, A5 from Shrewsbury, A5 from Betws y Coed
Operating society/organisation: Llangollen Railway Society Ltd, Llangollen station, Llangollen, Clwyd
Telephone: Answerphone (24hr): Llangollen (0978) 860951. Other enquiries: (0978) 860979 (office hours only)

Locomotives

Name	No	Origin	Class	Type	Built
—	2859	GWR	2800	2-8-0	1918
—	5199	GWR	5101	2-6-2T	1934
—	5538	GWR	4575	2-6-2T	1928
Cogan Hall	5952	GWR	'Hall'	4-6-0	1935
—	7754	GWR	5700	0-6-0PT	1930
Ditcheat Manor	7821	GWR	'Manor'	4-6-0	1950
Foxcote Manor	7822	GWR	'Manor'	4-6-0	1950
Odney Manor	7828	GWR	'Manor'	4-6-0	1950
—	03162	BR	03	0-6-0DM	1960
—	D3265 (08195)	BR	08	0-6-0DE	1956
—	25279	BR	25	Bo-Bo	1965
—	25313	BR	25	Bo-Bo	1966
—	D9500*	BR	14	0-6-0DH	1964
—	D9502	BR	14	0-6-0DH	1964

Also ex-BR Class 127 No M51618 and Class 105 No 54456 DMUs

*Undergoing restoration at Williton, West Somerset Railway

Main station: Llangollen
Other stations: Berwyn
OS reference: SJ 214422
Car park: Llangollen (Market Street)
Access by public transport: Nearest station: Ruabon (2hr service), then Crosville bus service No D1 to Llangollen or Nos D93/D94
Refreshment facilities: Llangollen and Berwyn
Souvenir shop: Llangollen
Length of line: 2 miles
Passenger trains: Llangollen-Berwyn, hourly service
Period of public operation: Saturdays and Sundays Easter-July; daily July-mid-September; Saturdays and Sundays mid-September-mid-October. Special event days during winter as advertised. Please see timetable for details of services to Berwyn (hourly)
Special events: Thomas the Tank events June and October; Santa Specials 1/2, 8/9, 15/16, 22/23 December; Mince Pie Specials 26-28 December
Facilities for disabled: Special passenger coach for wheelchairs, also shop and refreshment rooms at Llangollen. Toilet available at Berwyn station. Advance notice required for special coach
Membership details: Mr J. Short, 'Bryn Aber', Llangollen Road, Trevor, Nr Llangollen, Clwyd
Feature article reference: RW October 1989, p605 (photo feature — Great Western Steam at ...)

Industrial locomotives

Name	No	Builder	Type	Built
Darfield No 1	—	Hunslet (3783)	0-6-0ST	1953
Eliseg	—	Fowler (22753)	0-4-0DM	1939
—	—	Fowler (400007)	0-4-0DM	1947
Richboro	—	H/Clarke (1243)	0-6-0T	1917
Burtonwood Brewer	—	Kitson (5459)	0-6-0ST	1932
—	14	H/Clarke (D1012)	0-4-0DM	1956
—	—	North British (27734)	0-4-0DH	1958
—	1	YEC/BTH	0-4-0D	c1950
—	—	YEC	0-6-0DE	—
—	—	R/Hornsby (416213)	0-4-0DE	1957

Stock
17 Mk 1 coaches
2 Mk 1 sleepers
4 GWR coaches
4 wagons
1 Bolster wagon
1 LNWR tool van
2 GWR brake vans
1 GWR Mink D wagon
1 SR 'BY' parcels van
2 tank wagons
1 LNER parcels van
2 BR Fruit vans
1 ex-LNWR brake van
1 Matisa track tamper
1 BR ballast wagon
1 Coles diesel/electric 5-ton crane
1 BR generator van
1 ex-Inspection Machine
1 GWR Siphon G coach
1 LMS box van
1 GWR Mink A van
1 BR CCT
1 Matisa Track Recording Machine
1 BR Bridge/Viaduct Inspection Unit
1 steam crane

Owners
5199, 5952, 7821 and 7828 (the GW Steam Locomotive Group)
7822 (the Foxcote Manor Society)
7754 (the National Museum of Wales)
Richboro (the National Coal Board)
Burtonwood Brewer (the Burtonwood Brewery)
03162 (the Wirral Borough Council)

Right:
Double-headed 'Manors' power the 17.00 Llangollen-Berwyn service over the River Dee on 18 June 1989. The locomotives are Nos 7822 *Foxcote Manor* and 7828 *Odney Manor*, the latter owned by the GW Steam Locomotive Group who have another example of the class, No 7821 *Ditcheat Manor*, under restoration. *Brian Dobbs*

Wales

Narrow Gauge Railway Centre　　　　M

A very extensive collection of narrow gauge railway equipment from the British Isles mainly housed in a purpose-built exhibition hall at the former Oakley Slate Quarries. Close to other tourist attractions in Blaenau Ffestiniog, principally the Llechwedd Slate Caverns and the Ffestiniog Railway
Location: Off the A470 Blaenau Ffestiniog road ½-mile north of the town, turn at the locomotive
OS reference: SH 693470
Operating society/organisation:
Gloddfa Ganol Slate Mine, Blaenau Ffestiniog, Gwynedd, North Wales LL41 3NB
Telephone: (0766 830) 664
Car park: On site
Access by public transport: Blaenau Ffestiniog BR/FR station, bus connection to mine
On site facilities: Licensed restaurant, snack bar and grill. Toilets, children's playground and playroom, slate works, craftshops, mining museum, preserved quarrymen's cottages. Extensive underground workings, Land Rover tours and rail ride
Public opening: Easter-September, Monday-Friday 10.00-17.30; Sundays mid-July-August
Length of line: ½-mile to mine entrance
Facilities for disabled: Toilets, shops, museums, restaurant and section of mine suitable. No advance notice required. Special party rates available

Penrhyn Castle Industrial Railway Museum　　　　M

A collection of historic industrial steam locomotives, both standard and narrow gauge, displayed in Penrhyn Castle, a well known National Trust property in the area regularly open to visitors
Location: Llandegai, near Bangor. One mile east of Bangor on the A5
OS reference: SH 603720
Operating society/organisation: National Trust, Penrhyn Castle, Industrial Railway Museum, Llandegai, near Bangor, Gwynedd
Telephone: Bangor (0248) 353084
Car park: Within castle grounds
Access by public transport: Nearest BR station, Bangor
On site facilities: The castle is open to the public, and contains a gift shop. Light refreshments are available
Public opening: Daily 1 April-4 November
Facilities for disabled: Access to castle and museum
Special notes: For those interested in

Industrial locomotives

Name	No	Builder	Type	Built
Kettering Furnaces No 3	—	B/Hawthorn (859)	0-4-0ST	1885*
Watkin	—	de Winton	0-4-0VBT	1893*
Fire Queen	—	Horlock	0-4-0	1848†
Hawarden	—	H/Clarke (526)	0-4-0ST	1899
Vesta	—	H/Clarke (1223)	0-6-0T	1916
Charles	—	Hunslet (283)	0-4-0ST	1882‡
Hugh Napier	—	Hunslet (855)	0-4-0ST	1904‡
—	1	Neilson (1561)	0-4-0WT	1870
Haydock	—	Stephenson (2309)	0-6-0T	1879
—	—	R/Hornsby (327904)	0-4-0DM	1951

*3ft gauge
†4ft gauge
‡1ft 10¾in gauge

Stock
10 narrow gauge rolling stock exhibits from the Padarn/Penrhyn system. The small relics section includes a comprehensive display of railway signs and model locomotives.

stately homes the castle is well worth a visit. The entrance fee covers both the castle and the railway exhibits housed in the castle courtyard

Pontypool & Blaenavon Railway　　　　SC

The historic Blaenavon site, complete with its railway installations and locomotives can easily be included in a visit to Big Pit Mining Museum
Location: Near Big Pit, Blaenavon, Gwent
OS reference: SO 237093

Locomotives

Name	No	Origin	Class	Type	Built
—	2874	GWR	2800	2-8-0	1918
—	3855	GWR	2884	2-8-0	1942
—	4253	GWR	4200	2-8-0T	1917
—	5668	GWR	5600	0-6-2T	1926
Bickmarsh Hall	5967	GWR	'Hall'	4-6-0	1937

Operating society/organisation:
Pontypool & Blaenavon Railway Co
(1983) Ltd, Council Offices, Lion
Street, Blaenavon, Gwent
Telephone: (0495) 772726 (evenings
only)
Car park: Adjacent to railway
terminus
Access by public transport:
Blaenavon-Brynmawr buses
On site facilities: Light refreshments
and souvenir shop
Public opening: Easter to early
September, Sundays and Bank
Holidays. 12.00-17.00, plus
28-31 August
Special notes: The railway
incorporates the former mineral/
LNWR passenger lines running
through Big Pit. Both north and
southbound extensions are being
considered
Membership details: c/o above
address

Right:
**A line up of potential motive power
awaiting restoration at Blaenavon.
The locomotives, from left to right,
are Nos 5967 *Bickmarsh Hall*, 5668
and 2874.** *Mike Jones*

Industrial locomotives

Name	No	Builder	Type	Built
Brookfield	—	Bagnall (2613)	0-6-0PT	1940
Nora	5	Barclay (1680)	0-4-0ST	1920
Menelaus	—	Peckett (1889)	0-6-0ST	1935
—	8	RSH (7139)	0-6-0ST	1944
—	1	Fowler (22497)	0-6-0DM	1938
—	—	Drewry (2252)	0-6-0DH	1948
—	10083	R/Royce (10083)	0-4-0DH	1961

Stock
1 brake van
5 BR Mk 1 coaches
2 cranes
Several vans, china clay, coke and tank wagons

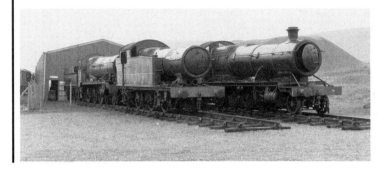

Snowdon Mountain Railway

The only public rack and pinion
railway in the British Isles, this
bustling line climbs up the slopes of
Snowdon, often through the clouds, to
the hotel at the top. The trip should not
be missed
Headquarters: Snowdon Mountain
Railway, Llanberis, Gwynedd
LL55-4TY
Telephone: Llanberis (0286) 870223
Main station: Llanberis
Other public stations: Summit
OS reference: SH 582597
Car park: Llanberis
Access by public transport: Bangor
BR station then by Crosville bus to
Caernarfon and there change to local
bus to Llanberis
Refreshment facilities: Llanberis,
Summit
Souvenir shops: Llanberis, Summit
Depot: Llanberis
Length of line: 4¾ miles, 80cm gauge
Passenger trains: Llanberis-Summit.
Journey time 60 minutes. Departures
from Llanberis at 30 minute intervals
during peak periods
Period of public operation: Daily
15 March-1 November
Special notes: All trains are subject

Locomotives

Name	No	Builder	Type	Built
Enid	2	SLM (924)	0-4-2T	1895
Yr Wyddfa	3	SLM (925)	0-4-2T	1895
Snowdon	4	SLM (988)	0-4-2T	1896
Moel Siabod	5	SLM (989)	0-4-2T	1896
Padarn	6	SLM (2838)	0-4-2T	1922
Ralph	7	SLM (2869)	0-4-2T	1923
Eryri	8	SLM (2870)	0-4-2T	1923
Ninian	9	Hunslet (9249)	0-4-0D	1986
Yeti	10	Hunslet (9250)	0-4-0D	1986

All steam locomotives were built by Swiss Locomotive Works, Winterthur

Stock
8 closed bogie coaches
1 bogie works car
1 4-wheel open wagon

to weather and traffic restrictions. Parties welcome by prior arrangement
Feature article references: RW March 1989, p144

Right:
A view of the platform area at Llanberis is a refreshing change from the usual mountain-side views. Here we see Nos 7 *Ralph* and 5 *Yr Wyddfa* indulging in a spot of shunting, as the locomotives propel their trains uphill. 1 August 1989.
John Stretton

Swansea Maritime & Industrial Museum M

This Museum houses a number of relics from Swansea's industrial maritime past and includes some railway exhibits, some of which are operated on the former dock sidings adjacent to the Museum. Some changes are planned for 1989, please ask for details
Location: On the south side of the town where the shopping centre and the sea in the newly created Maritime Quarter
OS reference: SS 659927
Operating society/organisation: City of Swansea Museum Services. Maritime & Industrial Museum, Museum Square, Maritime Quarter, Swansea SA1 1SN

Industrial locomotives

Name	No	Builder	Type	Built
Sir Charles	—	A/Barclay (1473)	0-4-0F	1919
—	—	Peckett (1426)	0-6-0ST	1916

Telephone: Swansea 50351
Car park: Public car parks close by
Access by public transport: Reached on foot from shopping centre or by car
On site facilities: No refreshments in the Museum but several cafes close by. Museum shop selling souvenirs and produce of the Woollen Mill which operates in the Museum throughout

the year. Education Service available on request to Education Officer
Public opening: 10.30-17.30 seven days a week, closed 25/26/27 December and New Year's Day
Facilities for disabled: Available
Membership details: Museum's Friends Organisation c/o above address

Talyllyn Railway

The very first railway in the country to be rescued and operated by enthusiasts, the line climbs from Tywyn through the wooded Welsh hills past Dolgoch Falls to Nant Gwernol. The trains are hauled by a variety of veteran tank engines all immaculately maintained by the railway's own workshops at Tywyn Pendre
Headquarters: Talyllyn Railway Co, Wharf station, Tywyn, Gwynedd LL36 9EY
Telephone: Tywyn (0654) 710472
Main station: Tywyn Wharf
Other public stations: Tywyn Pendre, Rhydyronen, Brynglas,

Locomotives

Name	No	Builder	Type	Built
Talyllyn	1	F/Jennings (42)	0-4-2ST	1865
Dolgoch	2	F/Jennings (63)	0-4-0WT	1866
Sir Haydn	3	Hughes (323)	0-4-2ST	1878
Edward Thomas	4	K/Stuart (4047)	0-4-2ST	1921
Midlander	5	R/Hornsby (200792)	4wDM	1940
Douglas	6	Barclay (1431)	0-4-0WT	1918
Tom Rolt	7	Barclay (2263)	0-4-2T	1949
Merseysider	8	R/Hornsby (476108)	4wDH	1964
Alf	9	Hunslet (4136)	0-4-0DM	1950

Locomotive notes: In service — 1, 2, 3 and 4; limited use — 6; not yet in service — 7 (scheduled 1990).

Dolgoch Falls, Abergynolwyn, Nant Gwernol
OS reference: SH 586005 (Tywyn Wharf)
Car parks: Tywyn Wharf, Dolgoch, Abergynolwyn
Access by public transport: Tywyn BR station. Bus Gwynedd services to Tywyn
Refreshment facilities: Tywyn Wharf, Abergynolwyn hot and cold snacks available
Souvenir shops: Tywyn Wharf, Abergynolwyn
Museum: Tywyn Wharf
Depot: Tywyn Pendre
Length of line: 7½ miles, 2ft 3in gauge
Passenger trains: Tywyn-Nant Gwernol
Period of public operation: Daily early April to end of October, Christmas and New Year. *Peter Sam,* of Rev Awdry fame operating in 1990
Journey times: Tywyn-Nant Gwernol — single 51min, return 1hr 10/20min
Special events: 5-7 May Model Railway Exhibition in Tywyn; 25-28 May* Vintage Transport Rally in Tywyn; 23-24 June Special event weekend; 2-8 July Vintage trains on the railway; 4-5 August Traction Engine Rally near Tywyn; Unusual

Stock
13 4-wheel coaches/vans
10 bogie coaches
45 wagons

Narrow Gauge Museum, Tywyn

Name	No	Builder	Type	Built
Dot	—	B/Peacock (2817)	0-4-0ST	1887
Pet*	—	LNWR	0-4-0ST	1865
Rough Pup	—	Hunslet (541)	0-4-0ST	1891
—	2	K/Stuart (721)	0-4-0WT	1902
Jubilee 1897	—	M/Wardle (1382)	0-4-0ST	1897
George Henry	—	de Winton	0-4-0T	1877
—	13	Spence	0-4-0T	1895
Nutty	—	Sentinel (7701)	0-4-0VB	1929

*On loan from National Railway Museum

Stock
Various wagons and miscellaneous equipment

'Race the Train' event 18 August; Santa Special 22 December; October Special trains to commemorate last train operated prior to formation of TRPS (dates to be announced). *Provisional date
Facilities for disabled: No problem for casual visitors, advanced notice preferred for groups. Access to shop and cafeteria possible at Tywyn and Abergynolwyn. Disabled toilet facilities near Abergynolwyn. Access possible to lower floor of museum. Limited capacity for wheelchairs on trains. New vehicle for wheel chairs now in operation
Special notes: Special parties and private charter trains by arrangement. Children under 5 years of age free. Narrow gauge 'Wanderer' four- and eight-day tickets accepted
Membership details: Mr A. Johnston, 9 Reynolds Way, Croydon, Surrey CR0 5JW

Vale of Rheidol Railway

This narrow gauge railway offers a 23-mile round trip from Aberystwyth to Devils Bridge providing spectacular views which cannot be enjoyed by road. At Devils Bridge there are short walks to the Mynach Falls and Devils Punch Bowl. Many artists have been inspired by the magnificence of Devils Bridge and the Rheidol Valley
Operating company: Brecon Mountain Railway, Pant station, Dowlais, Merthyr Tydfil, Mid Glamorgan CF48 2UP
Telephone: Merthyr Tydfil (0685) 4854
Main station: Aberystwyth (adjacent to BR station)
Other public stations: Devil's Bridge, Rhiwfron, Rheidol Falls, Aberffrwd, Nantyronen, Capel Bangor, Glanrafon, Llanbadarn
OS reference: SN 587812
Car parks: Aberystwyth, Devil's Bridge
Access by public transport: Aberystwyth BR station: and bus services to Aberystwyth

Locomotives

Name	No	Origin	Ex-BR Class	Type	Built
Owain Glyndwr	7	GWR	98	2-6-2T	1923
Llywelyn*	8	GWR	98	2-6-2T	1923
Prince of Wales	9	GWR	98	2-6-2T	1924
—	10	Brecon MR (002)	98/1	0-6-0DH	1987

*Currently runs unnamed in Cambrian Railways livery

Stock
16 bogie coaches including one Vista coach
1 4-wheel baggage van
12 wagons for maintenance use
1 inspection trolley

Refreshment facilities: Aberystwyth (not railway-owned), Devil's Bridge
Souvenir shop: Aberystwyth, Devil's Bridge
Depot: Aberystwyth (not open to the public)
Length of line: 11¾ miles, 1ft 11½in gauge

Passenger trains: Aberystwyth-Devil's Bridge
Period of public operation: Daily 13 April-30 September
Feature article reference: RW February 1988, p76 (sale of)

North Wales Steam

Above:
New for 1989 was a series of main line steam workings on the North Wales main line. LMS Class 7P No 6201 *Princess Elizabeth* is seen here passing through Abergele on 3 September 1989 bound for Holyhead. A triangle has been installed at Valley for the purpose of turning the locomotive to face in the right direction for the return working. *Don Smith*

Below:
During August rebuilt 'West Country' class Pacific No 34027 *Taw Valley* was working on the route and we see No 34027 standing at Llandudno after arriving from Crewe. *P. Q. Treloar*

The 1964 company operates services over a short section at the south-western end of the old Welsh Highland line which linked the North Wales line with the Cambrian Coast. Negotiations are in hand to extend the line northward through the more spectacular scenery that attracted passengers from far and wide in the early part of the century. In the meantime, you have the compensation of low fares

Location: Porthmadog, Gwynedd, adjacent to BR station

OS reference: SH 571393

Operating society/organisation: Welsh Highland Light Railway (1964) Ltd, Gelert's Farm Works, Madoc Street West, Porthmadog, Gwynedd LL49 9DY

Telephone: Porthmadog (0766) 513402 (weekends and operating days) or 051-327 3576 (evenings) or 051-608 2696 (day)

Car park: At terminus

Catering facilities: Station buffet — 'Russells' supplying hot meals, cold buffet, sandwiches and light refreshments

Access by public transport: Rail service to Porthmadog BR station. Festiniog Railway Harbour station. Bws Gwynedd service 1 and 3 to Porthmadog

On site facilities: Souvenir shop, information boards, taped commentary on coaches, sheds and workshops open to visitors. Afternoon tea served on 15.00, 15.45 and 16.30 trains on Wednesdays during June and September

Length of line: ¾-mile, 1ft 11½in gauge

Passenger trains: Porthmadog-Pen-y-Mount. Return journey time 30 minutes approximately, steam hauled bank holidays, weekends during high season and every day (except Mondays and Fridays) in August

Locomotives

Name	No	Builder	Type	Built
Moel Tryfan	—	Bagnall (2875)	0-4-2T	1948
Snowdon Ranger	—	Bagnall (3050)	0-4-2T	1953
Russell	—	Hunslet (901)	2-6-2T	1906
Pedemoura	—	O&K (10808)	0-6-0WT	1924
Karen	—	Peckett (2024)	0-4-2T	1942
Glaslyn	1	R/Hornsby (297030)	4wDM	1952
Kinnerley	2	R/Hornsby (354068)	4wDM	1953
—	—	R/Hornsby (191658)	4wDM	1938
—	—	R/Hornsby (237914)	4wDM	1946
Cnicht	36	M/Rail (8703)	4wDM	1941
LBLR	9	M/Rail (9547)	4wDM	1950
Katherine	—	M/Rail (60S363)	4wDM	1968
Pilkingtons No 4	—	M/Rail (60S333)	4wDM	1959
Pilkingtons No 6	—	M/Rail (11165)	4wDM	1968
Felin Foel	—	Hunslet (6285)	4wDM	1968

Locomotive notes: 1990 steam service will be worked by *Russell*, the only surviving locomotive from the original Welsh Highland Railway, *Karen* will be the stand-by engine. Diesel service will be worked by *Glaslyn* with *Kinnerley* on stand-by.

Stock

A collection of rolling stock including bogie coaches and numerous service construction vehicles including Vale of Rheidol brake van (1902)

Period of public operation: 13-22, 28/29 April; 5-13, 15-20, 22-31 May; 1-3, 5-30 (not Mondays) June; daily in July and August; 1-9, 11-27 (not Mondays or Fridays) 29/30 September; 20-28 Ocotber

Special events: Porthmadog Transport Gala 26-28 May; Model Railway Exhibition 11/12 August

Facilities for disabled: Disabled passengers can be accommodated without prior notice — except in parties

Membership details: Membership Secretary, c/o above address

Right:
Russel is the sole surviving example of the original Welsh Highland's fleet of steam locomotives, and following an eventful life, now sees action almost back on home territory. The Hunslet-built 2-6-2T is seen here leaving Porthmadog in **August 1989.** *D. W. Allan*

Welshpool & Llanfair Light Railway

There is a decidedly foreign atmosphere to the trains over this line. The steam locomotive collection embraces examples from three continents, and the coaches are turn-of-the-century balcony saloons from Austria or 1960s bogies from Africa. The line follows a steeply graded route (maximum 1 in 24) through very attractive rolling countryside, and is rather a gem in an area too often missed by the traveller heading for further shores

Headquarters: Welshpool & Llanfair Light Railway Preservation Co Ltd, Llanfair Caereinion station, Powys

Telephone: Llanfair Caereinion (0938) 810441

Main station: Llanfair Caereinion

Other public stations: Castle Caereinion, Sylfaen, Welshpool (Raven Square)

OS reference: SJ 107069

Car park: Llanfair Caereinion, Welshpool (both free)

Access by public transport: BR station at Welshpool, one mile from Raven Square. Crosville buses from Shrewsbury, Oswestry and Newtown

Refreshment facilities: Light refreshments at Llanfair Caereinion

Souvenir shops: Llanfair Caereinion

Depot: Llanfair Caereinion

Length of line: 8 miles, 2ft 6in gauge

Passenger trains: Welshpool-Llanfair Caereinion

Period of public operation: Weekends and Bank Holidays Easter to early October. Daily mid-July-mid-September

Special events: Santa trains on three weekends before Christmas; Teddy Bears Outing 12/13 May; Epicurean Express Dining Train 30 June; Thomas the Tank Engine Weekend 7/8 July; Garden Railways Exhibition 1/2 September; Postman Pat Weekend 29/30 September

Facilities for disabled: Wheelchair access to trains by prior arrangement. Easy access to shop, but no special toilet arrangements

Membership details: John Parkinson, 124 London Road, Long Sutton, Spalding, Lincolnshire PE12 9EE

Right:
Diminutive *Dougal* stands alongside the new workshop extension on 1 July 1989.
Alan C. Butcher

Locomotives

Name	No	Builder	Type	Built
The Earl	1	B/Peacock (3496)	0-6-0T	1902
The Countess	2	B/Peacock (3497)	0-6-0T	1902
Monarch	6	Bagnall (3024)	0-4-4-0T	1953
Chattenden	7	Drewry (2263)	0-6-0DM	1949
Dougal	8	Barclay (2207)	0-4-0T	1946
Sir Drefaldwyn	10	Franco-Belge (2855)	0-8-0T	1944
Ferret	11	Hunslet (2251)	0-4-0DM	1940
Joan	12	K/Stuart (4404)	0-6-2T	1927
SLR 85	14	Hunslet (3815)	2-6-2T	1954
—	15	Tubize (2369)	2-6-2T	1948

Locomotive notes: Locomotives expected in service 1990 — *Countess, Joan, Sir Drefaldwyn, Dougal. The Earl* will be on display at the Didcot Railway Centre. The remainder can be seen at Llanfair station, 15 is displayed with access to the footplate.

Stock
1 Wickham trolley
6 W&LLR wagons
8 ex-Admiralty wagons
2 ex-Bowater wagons
5 ex-Zillertalbahn coaches
4 ex-Sierra Leone coaches

Great Western Visitors

Above and below:

During 1989 the Great Western Society based at Didcot lent a couple of its locomotives to other railways. The view above shows 'heavy freight' locomotive No 3822 whilst on loan to the Nene Valley Railway emerging from Wansford Tunnel with an afternoon service on 26 March 1989. The second view illustrates Prairie tank No 6106 hauling the 14.00 Loughborough-Rothley service on the Great Central Railway; by coincidence this view was taken on the same date.

J. H. Cooper-Smith/W. A. Sharman

West Midlands

Birmingham Museum of Science & Industry | M

Location: Newhall Street, Birmingham B3 1RZ
OS reference: SP 064874
Organisation: Birmingham City Council
Telephone: 021-236 1022
Car park: Public multi-storey nearby in Newhall Street
Access by public transport: Birmingham New Street or Snow Hill stations, then short walk following signs
Facilities: Shop, refreshments
Opening times: Monday-Saturday 09.30-17.00; Sunday 14.00-17.00
Special notes: Facilities for the disabled (toilets and lifts). Special parking facility

Locomotives

Name	No	Origin	Class	Type	Built
City of Birmingham	46235	LMS	8P	4-6-2	1939

Industrial locomotives

Name	No	Builder	Type	Built
Secundus	—	B/Seekings	0-6-0WT	1874*
Leonard	1	Bagnall (2087)	0-4-0ST	1919†
Lorna Doone	56	K/Stuart (4250)	0-4-0ST	1922†

*2ft 8in gauge
†2ft gauge

Birmingham Railway Museum | SC

The old motive power depot is slowly being transformed into an imaginative museum of local railway history. The climax of any visit must be the view from the elevated walkway in the engine shed over the locomotives below, particularly if one has been lit up in preparation for a tour over the main line and is gently hissing steam
Location: 670 Warwick Road (A41), Tyseley, Birmingham B11 2HL
OS reference: SP 105841
Operating society/organisation: Birmingham Railway Museum Trust
Telephone: 021-707-4696
Car park: Site
Access by public transport: West Midlands Travel bus routes Nos 37, 44 from city centre. BR service to Tyseley station (no Sunday service)
On site facilities: The Museum is on the site of a former GWR/BR steam shed and has been equipped with much specialised railway engineering machinery. Souvenir shop, restaurant,

Locomotives

Name	No	Origin	Class	Type	Built
Albert Hall	4983	GWR	'Hall'	4-6-0	1931
Earl of Mount Edgcumbe	5043	GWR	'Castle'	4-6-0	1936
Defiant	5080	GWR	'Castle'	4-6-0	1939
King Edward 1	6024	GWR	'King'	4-6-0	1930
Thornbury Castle†	7027	GWR	'Castle'	4-6-0	1949
Clun Castle	7029	GWR	'Castle'	4-6-0	1950
—	7752	GWR	5700	0-6-0PT	1930
—	7760	GWR	5700	0-6-0PT	1930
Cornwall	3020	LNWR	—	2-2-2	1847
—	9395	LNWR	G2	0-8-0	1921
—	9600	GWR	5700	0-6-0PT	1945
Kolhapur*	5593	LMS	'Jubilee'	4-6-0	1934
Scots Guardsman	6115	LMS	'Royal Scot'	4-6-0	1927
—	13029	BR	08	0-6-0DE	1953
—	27059	BR	27	Bo-Bo	1962
—	40118	BR	40	1Co-Co1	1961

*On loan to the Great Central Railway
†On loan to the Dart Valley Railway

passenger demonstration line and station, viewing gallery, schools education service

Refreshment facilities: Full range of hot and cold meals available in 'Chuffs' restaurant plus wine & dine facilities on 'Shakespeare Express' trains to Stratford-on-Avon

Length of line: ⅓-mile

Public opening: Static display daily 10.00-17.00 except Christmas and New Year. Steam days every Sunday and Bank Holiday, Easter-October

Special events: Santa and Halloween (see press for details)

Special notes: Tyseley is a centre for 'Steam on BR' railtours over the BR lines to Stratford upon Avon and Didcot (via Oxford). Development plans envisage the construction of a roundhouse, small exhibits museum, and other ancillary features over the next 10 years financed by Local Authority grants. In 1983 an Education Service for schools began operating, providing a service of visits to schools in the Midlands and party visits from schools to the museum. Membership is available to the public providing free entry to site events, magazines, members' evenings, etc.

Membership facilities: From the museum office

Feature article references: RW February 1988, p94 ('Bloomer' project — also RW April 1988, p226; RW June 1988, p360; RW August 1988, p482; RW August 1989, p501; RW November 1989, p667)

Note: All attractions and facilities are advertised subject to availability

Industrial locomotives

Name	No	Builder	Type	Built
Rocket	—	Peckett (1722)	0-4-0ST	1926
—	1	Peckett (2004)	0-4-0ST	1942
—	—	Baguley (800)	0-4-0PE	1920
Henry	—	H/Leslie (2491)	0-4-0ST	1901
Count Louis†	—	B/Lowke (32)	4-4-2	1924

†15in gauge — on static display

Owners

9395 (on loan from National Railway Museum)
27059 (Sandwell District Council)
6024 (the 6024 Preservation Society Ltd)

Stock

1 Pullman bar car
1 Gresley buffet car
1 LNWR semi-Royal Saloon
1 GWR VIP Saloon
1 30-ton steam crane and sundry goods vehicles
1 5-ton hand crane
1 GWR Inspection Saloon
1 Tourist 3rd open coach
2 TPO vehicles (1 LNWR, 1908; 1 LMS 1950)
1 GWR brake 3rd corridor coach
1 BR Mk 1 BFK coach
1 LMS 50ft parcels van
1 LNWR 6-wheel guard's van
1 GWR 'Toad' guard's van
1 SR PMV
1 GWR 6-wheel Mess Tool van
Plus varied goods vehicles
2 Leamington & Warwick Horse Trams

Below:
A line up of top link GWR motive power is seen at Birmingham Railway Museum. 'Castle' class locomotives Nos 5080 *Defiant* **and 7029** *Clun Castle* **flank 'King' class No 6024** *King Edward I.* **The 'King' was transferred from the Buckinghamshire Railway Centre for running-in prior to use over British Rail metals.** *Robin Stewart-Smith*

West Midlands

Above:

Sir Cecil A. Cochrane perches on the new locomotive turntable at Marley Hill shed on the Tanfield Railway on 14 October 1989. As can be seen the turntable is little longer than the locomotive it is turning; does it qualify for the smallest standard gauge locomotive turntable to have existed? *W. A. Sharman*

Below:

Contrast in saddletanks at Embsay. The left-hand locomotive is a Hunslet-built 0-6-0ST of 1944. Named *Wheldale*, and purchased from the NCB, it is equipped with a system to burn coal more economically — hence the unusual chimney. By contrast No 22 is a Barclay product from 1952 which was also purchased from the NCB. This view was taken on 6 September 1989 when both locomotives were out of service and their cabs boarded-up as a security measure. *G. D. King*

The Centre, opened in 1968, is principally a standard gauge museum and home of two main line express locomotives *King George V* and *Princess Elizabeth*. Both are normally maintained in full working order and, as such, can be absent on main line operations elsewhere. The centre also houses a collection of other locomotives, including industrial, as well as various items of rolling stock. From time to time the centre holds steam events and also serves as a depot for the servicing of steam locomotives engaged on main line operations in the region.

Location: H. P. Bulmer Ltd (Cider Makers), Whitecross Road, Hereford. The site is ¼-mile from city centre on A438 Hereford-Brecon road

OS reference: SO 505402

Operating society: The 6000 Locomotive Association in conjunction with the Princess Elizabeth Locomotive Society and the Worcester Locomotive Society, on behalf of H. P. Bulmer Ltd

Telephone: Whitchurch (Avon) (0272) 834430 for enquiries

Car park: Free parking on site

Access by public transport: Midland Red bus services and local private bus services. Hereford (BR) station (1 mile)

On site facilities: Souvenir/book stall. Light refreshment facilities generally available

Length of line: About ¾-mile

Public opening: Weekends and bank holidays Easter/April-September inclusive. Static display (14.00-17.00). With regular steam-operated brake van trips, on specified Sundays and bank holidays (11.00-17.00). Telephone for details. Closed on normal weekdays (Mon-Fri)

Special events: Steam open days Easter Sunday and Monday and last Sunday in September. Santa Specials in December (enquire for details)

Special notes: Centre for steam events and servicing depot for main line steam operations in the area

Facilities for disabled: Wheelchair access to most of the site, train rides need assistance (available), no special toilet facilities

Feature article references: RW March 1988, p166 (locomotive 6201)

Membership details: 6000 Locomotive Association, 8 Chancel View, Abbots Mead, Hereford HR2 7XD

Locomotives

Name	No	Origin	Class	Type	Built
King George V	6000	GWR	'King'	4-6-0	1927*
—	5786	GWR	5700	0-6-0PT	1930
Princess Elizabeth	6201	LMS	7P	4-6-2	1933*
Cider Queen	2 (D2758)	Hunslet (6999)	05	0-6-0DH	1955

*Telephone to check presence on site

Industrial locomotives

Name	No	Builder	Type	Built
Pectin	—	Peckett (1579)	0-4-0ST	1921
Carnarvon	47	Kitson (5474)	0-6-0ST	1934
—	1254	H/Clarke	0-6-0	1962

Locomotive notes: During 1990, *King George V* will almost certainly be absent undergoing a major overhaul elsewhere. Similarly, No 6201 will be away on main line operations during part of the year as it did in 1989. No 5786 and *Pectin* will carry out the official steaming requirements at the Centre.

Stock

Gresley Buffet coach
Several ex-BR Mk 1 coaches
Pullman car from ex-SR 6-PUL electric unit
Small number of freight vehicles including GWR tank wagon and BR Conflat

Owners

6201 (the Princess Elizabeth Locomotive Society)
6000 (on loan from the National Railway Museum)
5786 and 47 (the Worcester Locomotive Society)
Pectin and 1254 (the 6000 Locomotive Association)
2 (D2758) (H. P. Bulmer Ltd)

Below:
GWR Pannier tank No 5786 giving brake van rides at the Bulmer Railway Centre on 20 August 1989 following an overhaul. *Melvyn Hopwood*

Cadeby Light Railway

The collection of a genial clergyman whose personality dominated all about him during his lifetime, this narrow gauge railway running in the grounds of the old rectory has been saved by Teddy Boston's enterprising widow and a small band of dedicated supporters in the face of considerable odds. Echoes of the *Titfield Thunderbolt* and Ancient and Modern. Their endeavours deserve your support

Location: One mile south of Market Bosworth on A447

OS reference: SK 426024

Operating society/organisation: Mrs J. A. Boston, The Old Rectory, Cadeby, Nuneaton, Warwicks CU13 0AS

Telephone: Market Bosworth (0455) 290462

Car park: In local side roads

Access by public transport: Leicester City, 178 from Hinckley, Leicester Corp/Gibson Bros (Comfort Coaches) from Leicester to Market Bosworth (1¼-miles away)

On site facilities: 2ft gauge railway, also traction engines and a model railway

Locomotives

Name	No	Builder	Type	Built
Pixie	—	Bagnall (2090)	0-4-0ST	1919
—	2	O&K (7529)	0-4-0WT	1914
—	—	Baguley (1695)	0-4-0PM	1928
New Star	—	Lister (4088)	4wPM	1931
—	20	M/Rail (8748)	4wDM	1942
—	42	M/Rail (7710)	4wDM	1939
—	87004	M/Rail (2197)	4wDM	1922
—	87009	M/Rail (4572)	4wDM	1929
—	—	M/Rail (5853)	4wDM	1934
—	—	H/Clarke (D558)	4wDM	1930
—	87008	R/Hornsby (179870)	4wDM	1936
—	87051	R/Hornsby (404967)	4wDM	1957

Standard gauge

—	—	Peckett (2012)	0-4-0ST	1942

Stock
Penrhyn Quarrymans coach
2 flat trucks
7 open trucks
2 platelayers trolleys

Refreshment facilities: Catering by arrangement
Public opening: 2nd Saturday of every month, plus 1st Saturday in November and Boxing Day or by arrangement
Special events: Bonfire Night Steaming 5 November; Santa Special 11 December

---

Cambrian Railways Society

SC

Location: Oswestry station yard, Oswald Road, Oswestry, Shropshire

OS reference: SJ 294297

Operating society/organisation: Cambrian Railways Society Ltd, C. W. Mottram, 'Delamere', Old Chirk Road, Gobowen, Oswestry, Shropshire SY11 3LH

Telephone: (0691) 661648

Car park: In Society's depot

Length of line: 400yd, opening 1990

Public opening: Wednesday 10.00-17.00 (market day) and Sunday 11.00-17.00 throughout the year

Industrial locomotives

Name	No	Builder	Type	Built
—	1872	B/Peacock (1827)	0-4-0ST	1879
—	1	H/Clarke (D843)	0-4-0DM	1954
Adam	1	Peckett (1430)	0-4-0ST	1916
—	3	Hunslet (D3526)	0-6-0DM	1954
—	6	Peckett (2131)	0-4-0ST	1951
—	8	Barclay (885)	0-6-0ST	1900
—	322	Planet (3541)	4wDM	1952
Norma	3770	Hunslet (3770)	0-6-0ST	1952
—	—	Sentinel (9374)	4w	1947
—	—	Hibberd (3057)	4wDM	1946

Stock
1 GWR auto-trailer
1 LMS brakevan
2 tank wagons
1 open wagon

Anniversary Feature

Above:

On 14 May 1951 the first train to be operated by a preservation society left Wharf station on the Talyllyn Railway. This is the scene prior to the breaking of the ribbon. The locomotive, No 2 *Dolgoch*, was the only serviceable locomotive available. Throughout its life the railway only possessed two loooomotives, to which the society has added a number of additional machines.   *J. Adams*

Left:

The other original locomotive was No 1 *Talyllyn* which is seen here at Dolgoch Falls station.   *I. Davies*

Below left and below:

The first standard gauge railway to be preserved was the Middleton Railway and its first passenger trains consisted of a diesel locomotive and ex-London Tram. Here we see No 7401 on the first passenger working in 1960, and in 1988 (below) Sentinel 0-4-0VBT No 54 nears the summit of the line with the last passenger train of the day.   *Ian Smith/Mike Taylor*

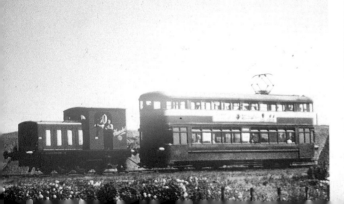

Above:

The Bluebell Railway was the second standard gauge line to be reopened. This was the scene at Sheffield Park station on 1 April 1962 on the occasion of a through train being run from London Bridge and hauled by a privately preserved LNER Class J52 0-6-0ST. No 1247 can be seen on the right as 'P' class 0-6-0T No 323 *Bluebell* operates a service train consisting of Metropolitan Railway stock. One of the events taking place during 1990 will be a re-enactment of the excursion, albeit using a different route and stock. *Brian Haresnape*

Right:

Standard Class 4MT No 80064 pounds up the bank towards Horsted Keynes with a service train well over 25 years later. *Don Smith*

Founded in 1959 as the Railway Preservation Society (West Midlands District) the Group celebrated 30 years of existence in 1989. Activities now centre on 1-mile of track in Chasewater Pleasure Park
Location: Chasewater Pleasure Park, Brownhills, West Midlands
OS reference: SK 034070
Operating society/organisation: Chasewater Light Railway & Museum Co
Telephone: (0543) 452623
Car park: Pleasure park
Access by public transport: WMPTE 155 from Birmingham, 345 and 394 from Walsall. Midland Red and Chase Coaches 154 and 156 from Birmingham and Cannock
On site facilities: Refreshments (buffet coach), museum and souvenir shop. Extensive small relics collection. Lakeside walk
Catering facilities: Hot and cold buffet
Length of line: 1-mile
Public opening: Site open 2pm-dusk Saturdays and Sundays throughout

Below:
Chasewater Light Railway's Barclay 0-4-0ST *Invicta* and Neilson 0-4-0ST *Alfred Paget* are seen here.
Mike Wood

Industrial locomotives

Name	No	Builder	Type	Built
—	—	Peckett (917)	0-4-0ST	1902
Invicta	8	Barclay (2220)	0-4-0ST	1946
—	3	Barclay (1223)	0-4-0ST	1911
Lion	—	Peckett (1351)	0-4-0ST	1914
Alfred Paget	11	Neilson (2937)	0-4-0ST	1882
—	S100	H/Clarke (1822)	0-6-0T	1949
—	15	H/Clarke (431)	0-6-0ST	1895
Asbestos	4	H/Leslie (2780)	0-4-0ST	1909
—	21	Kent Cont (1612)	4wDM	1929
—	7	R/Hornsby (548641)	0-4-0DE	1961
—	—	Smiths	4wD crane	1951
—	59632	Sentinel (9632)	4wVBT	1957
—	1	M/Rail (1947)	4wPM	1919
—	61/50011	Fowler (4220015)	0-4-0DM	1962

Stock
Passenger services provided with ex-BR DMU trailer cars.
A selection of freight vehicles is also housed at the site, also several pre-Grouping coaches.

the year. Timetable on application
Special events: Easter 15/16 April; Railwayana Fair 22 April; May Day Fundays 6/7 May; Spring Bank Holiday 27/28 May; Transport Scene Vintage Vehicle Rally 17 June; Schools Day 2 July; British Motor Cycle Rally 15 July; Military Day 12 August; August Bank Holiday 26/27 August; Enthusiasts Day and Railwayana Fair 9 September; Transport Rally 7 October; Bonfire Night Party 4 November; Santa Specials (booking required) 16 December; Mince Pie specials 30 December
Facilities for disabled: Access to station only, car park adjacent
Membership details: Brownhills West Station, Hednesford Road, Brownhills West, Walsall WS8 7LT

Chatterley Whitfield Mining Museum M

Location: Tunstall, Stoke-on-Trent, Staffs ST6 8UN
Operating society/organisation: Chatterley Whitfield Mining Museum Trust
Telephone: (0782) 813337
Car parks: Main car park has capacity for up to 50 coaches; other overflow car parks are also available
Access by public transport: Nearest British Rail station, Longport. By bus, PMT Services operate regular (10min intervals Monday to Saturday) routes between Hanley
Refreshment facilities: Pit Canteen, 100-seat capacity, open 10.00 to 16.30, seven days a week
Other on-site facilities: Shire horse trips, underground tours, British Coal's National Collection, film shows, restored winding engines, toilets, museum shop, education services, vintage car workshops
Length of line: ½-mile; currently non-passenger carrying; operated as a colliery railway siding
Public opening: Site open 10.00 to 17.00, seven days per week, 51 weeks

Industrial locomotives

Name	No	Builder	Type	Built
—	2	Stoke	0-6-2T	1923
—	6	Robert Heath	0-4-0ST	1886
The Welshman	—	M/Wardle (1207)	0-6-0ST	1890
Joseph	—	Hunslet (3163)	0-6-0ST	1944
—	9	YEC (2521)	0-6-0ST	1952
Hem Heath	3D	Bagnall (3119)	0-6-0DM	1956
—	—	NBL (27876)	0-4-0DM	1959
—	LO52	YEC (2745)	0-6-0DE	1960
—	13D	T/Hill (181V)	6wDH	1967

Stock
3 2ft 6in gauge underground manrider trains
2 2ft 4in gauge underground manrider trains
1 2ft gauge underground manrider train
1 Taylor & Hubbard steam crane
1 25-ton brake van
Various coal wagons

per year
Period of public operation: Locomotive in steam on most opening days
Special events: Various throughout the year including annual Steam Carnival

Facilities for disabled: Disabled toilet, surface collection building, sections of underground accessible, driving for the disabled utilising retired pit pony

Cheedleton Railway Centre SC

A Victorian country station set in the attractive Staffordshire moorlands, situated adjacent to the River Churnet. Pleasant walks can be taken alongside the Caldon Canal, and the Flint Mill Museum is only ⅔-mile away
Location: Cheddleton station, near Leek, Staffordshire
OS reference: SJ 983519
Operating society/organisation: North Staffordshire Railway Company (1978) Ltd
Telephone: Churnetside (0538) 360522, Sundays and Bank Holidays only (10.00-17.00). (0782) 503458 (evenings only)
Car park: Riverside car park and picnic area opposite the station
Access by public transport: BR Stoke-on-trent (10 miles). A regular bus service operated by Proctors, PMT and Stevensons from Hanley, Longton and Leek to Cheddleton village
On site facilities: The station contains a refreshment room, souvenir shop and small relics museum. On

Locomotives

Name	No	Origin	Class	Type	Built
—	4422	LMS	4F	0-6-0	1927
—	80136	BR	4MT	2-6-4T	1956
—	D3420	BR	08	0-6-0DE	1957

Industrial locomotives

Name	No	Builder	Type	Built
Josiah Wedgwood	52	Hunslet (3777)	0-6-0ST	1952

Locomotive notes: 4422 is now nearing completion and it is hoped to steam it in 1990. Negotiations are continuing to bring a main line diesel to Cheedleton in the near future. 52 and D3420 will also be in operation in 1990.

Owners
4422 (the 4422 Locomotive Fund)
D3420 (the NSR Diesel Group)

Stock
2 ex-BR Mk 1 CK coaches
2 ex-BR brake suburban coaches
1 ex-NSR coach body
1 ex-LMS 6-wheel full brake
2 ex-LMS box vans

NYMR Contrasts

Left:
Beck Hole on the North Yorkshire Moors Railway is the location for this photograph as BR-built, but NER-designed, 'J72' No 69023 blasts its way up the hill. No 69023 is hauling a brake van up to Goathland prior to working a demonstration freight train on 25 March 1989.   *T. J. Gregg*

Below:
Clayton Class 17 No D8568 is seen at Grosmont on 24 April 1989, whilst one of its coaches is having a wash and brush up. This design of centre cab Bo-Bo diesel was unsuccessful but this example managed to survive in industrial ownership prior to preservation.
Don Smith

open days visitors are allowed to visit the yard, signalbox and new locomotive display hall. Modern toilets are also on site

Length of line: 400yd

Public opening: Easter–September inclusive — Sundays and bank holiday Mondays, 11.00-17.30 June, July and August, Monday-Saturday 14.00-17.00. Sundays October-March 12.00-17.00

Special events: Model Railway Day 10 June; Classic Car Day 30 September. Santa and Steam 16/23 December. Other steam open days and steaming of 4422 — see press

Facilities for disabled: Access to most of the site is possible by wheelchair. Train rides by arrangement

Membership details: Richard Waterhouse c/o above address

Special notes: Coach parties catered for by prior arrangement. Guided tours available for parties on request. The Railway Centre is adjacent to a BR freight line which is now mothballed pending a decision on its future. The NSR Co would like to re-open the line to passenger trains as the 'Churnet Valley Railway'

Right:
Josiah Wedgwood **was built by Hunslet in 1952 to their 'Austerity' design. The design originated during World War 2 and the type continued to be built postwar for industrial use, and the last standard gauge steam locomotive to be constructed was to this design.** ***Josiah Wedgwood*** **is seen in action on the centre's demonstration line, 1 May 1989.**   *Tom Heavyside*

Stock
2 ex-BR box vans
2 ex-LMS 5-plank wagons
1 ex-LMS hopper wagon
1 Esso tank wagon
1 7-ton diesel rail-mounted crane

Crewe Heritage Centre   SC

Location: Crewe Heritage Centre, Vernon Way, Crewe

OS reference: SJ 709552

Operating society/organisation: Crewe Heritage Centre Trust/Railside Ltd

Telephone: (0270) 212130

Car park: Town Centre, Forge Street, Oak Street

Access by public transport: BR Crewe

Refreshment facilities: Cafe in APT

On-site facilities: Souvenir shop, collector's corner

Public opening: Limited opening during 1990 due to building work, please see press for details

Locomotives

Name	No	Origin	Class	Type	Built
—	D5233	BR	25	Bo-Bo	1963
—	D1842	BR	47	Co-Co	1965

Industrial locomotives

Name	No	Builder	Type	Built
Jane Derbyshire	2	Barclay (1969)	0-4-0ST	1929
—	—	K/Stuart (4388)	0-4-0ST	1926
Robert	—	H/Clarke (1752)	0-6-0T	1943
Joseph	—	Hunslet (3163)	0-6-0T	1944

Rolling stock
APT vehicle Nos 48103, 48106, 48602, 48603, 48606, 49002, 49002 in use as cafe.
1 BR Mk 1 BSK
2 BR brake vans

Facilities for disabled: Toilets
Membership details: Heritage
Centre Supporters Association, c/o
above address
Notes: Steam locomotives passed for
use over BR tracks are often stabled
between duties on the North Wales
Coast Line

Right:
**Crewe Heritage Centre is the home
for the first Class 47 to be
preserved, and its seen here on
30 September 1989 whilst on loan
to the East Lancashire Railway for
its Diesel Weekend. The location is
Bury Bolton Street station.**
Doug Birmingham

Dean Forest Railway SC

Steam train rides previously operating
alongside the Lydney to Parkend line
have been extended southwards to
Lydney town
Location: Norchard Steam Centre on
the B4234, ¾-mile off A48 at Lydney,
Glos
OS reference: SO 629044
Operating society/organisation:
Dean Forest Railway Society in
conjunction with owning company,
Forest of Dean Railway Ltd
Telephone: Dean (0594) 843423
Car park: Adequate for cars and
coaches — no charge
Access by public transport: None
On site facilities: A shop and
refreshments are available at
Norchard along with a museum,
photographic display, riverside walk,
forest trail and picnic area
Catering facilities: Hot and cold
snacks, ploughman's lunches etc on
steam days. Parties catered for by
appointment
Length of line: ¾-mile
Public opening: Daily for static
display — shop, museum,
refreshments open every Saturday
and Sunday 11.00-17.00 and weekdays
Easter to October. Steam days Easter,
May Day, Spring and August Bank
Holiday Saturdays, Sundays and
Mondays. Sundays June to September.
Wednesdays June to August
Special events: Thomas the Tank
Engine's Friends 23/24 June,
29/30 September; Preservation Rally
21 October; Santa Specials 1/2, 8/9,
15/16, 23/24 December
Special events: Preservation rally
15 October; Santa Specials 3, 9/10 and
16/17 December

Locomotives

Name	No	Origin	Class	Type	Built
—	4121	GWR	5101	2-6-2T	1937
Pitchford Hall	4953	GWR	'Hall'	4-6-0	1928
—	5521	GWR	4575	2-6-2T	1928
—	5541	GWR	4575	2-6-2T	1928
—	9681	GWR	5700	0-6-0PT	1949
—	03.062	BR	03	0-6-0DM	1958
—	03.119	BR	03	0-6-0DM	1958
—	08.377	BR	08	0-6-0DE	1957

Industrial locomotives

Name	No	Builder	Type	Built
—	—	Barclay (2221)	0-4-0ST	1946
Jessie	—	Hunslet (1873)	0-6-0ST	1937
Uskmouth No 1	—	Peckett (2147)	0-4-0ST	1952
Wilbert	—	Hunslet (3806)	0-6-0ST	1953
Warrior	—	Hunslet (3823)	0-6-0ST	1954
—	—	Hunslet (2145)	0-4-0DM	1940
—	—	Fowler (4210101)	0-4-0DM	1955
—	—	Fowler (4210127)	0-4-0DM	1957
—	—	Hibberd (3947)	4wPM	1960
Cabot	39	R/Royce (10218)	0-6-0DH	1965
Lord Marshall of Goring	392	A/Barclay (392)	0-4-0DM	1954

Stock
8 ex-GWR coaches
16 ex-BR coaches
3 Wickham trolleys
1 steam crane Thos Smith (Rodley) TS 5027 (1 ton)
1 45 ton steam crane (Cowans Sheldon) ADRC 95222
50+ wagons

Facilities for disabled: Access to
museum and toilets
Special notes: During 1989 it is
intended to extend train rides from
Norchard to Lydney (Lakeside)
Membership details: Mr
P. Brammell, 4 Pool Gardens, Higham,
Gloucester

Foxfield Steam Railway

The railway, built in 1893 to connect a colliery to the national system, closed in 1965, has been re-opened. Views of the 13th century Caverswall Castle can be obtained

Headquarters: Foxfield Light Railway, Blythe Bridge, Stoke on Trent

Telephone: (0782) 396210 (weekends), 314532 (weekdays)

Main station: Blythe Bridge (Caverswall Road)

OS reference: SJ 957421

Car park: Blythe Bridge

Access by public transport: BR Blythe Bridge (400yd). PMT bus service to Blythe Bridge

Refreshment facilities: Blythe Bridge

Souvenir shop: Blythe Bridge

Passenger trains: Steam-hauled trains operate from Blythe Bridge (Caverswall Road) to Dilhorne Park and return

Length of line: 2¾ miles

Period of public operation: Steam trains operate Sundays and Bank Holidays only, April-September inclusive between Blythe Bridge and

Industrial locomotives

Name	No	Builder	Type	Built
Whiston	—	Hunslet (3694)	0-6-0ST	1950
Wimblebury	—	Hunslet (3839)	0-6-0ST	1956
Roker	—	RSH (7006)	0-4-0CT	1940
Cranford	—	Avonside (1919)	0-6-0ST	1924
Lewisham	—	Bagnall (2221)	0-6-0ST	1927
Hawarden	—	Bagnall (2623)	0-4-0ST	1940
Wolstanton No 3	—	Bagnall (3150)	0-6-0DM	1960
Bagnall	—	Bagnall (3207)	0-4-0DH	1961
Little Barford	—	Barclay (2069)	0-4-0ST	1939
—	—	E/Electric (788)	4wBE	1930
Spondon No 2	—	E/Electric (1130)	4wBE	1939
Henry Cort	—	Peckett (933)	0-4-0ST	1903
Ironbridge No 1	—	Peckett (1803)	0-4-0ST	1933
—	11	Peckett (2081)	0-4-0ST	1947
C.P.C.	—	Barclay (1964)	0-4-0ST	1929
Moss Bay	—	K/Stuart (4167)	0-4-0ST	1920
Rom River	—	K/Stuart (4421)	6wDM	1929
—	1	Barclay (1984)	0-4-0F	1930
Helen	—	Simplex (2262)	4wDM	1924
Coronation	—	N/British (27097)	0-4-0DH	1953
—	—	R/Hornsby (395305)	0-4-0DM	1956
Gas-oil	—	R/Hornsby (408496)	0-4-0DM	1957
Hercules	—	Ruston (242915)	4wDM	1946
—	—	Thomas Hill (103C)	0-4-0DH	1957

Below:
The Foxfield Railway's gala was held on 30 July 1989, and Bagnall 0-6-0ST *Lewisham* is seen at Caverswall Road. Coupled to *Lewisham* is *The King*, a Borrows 0-4-0WT on loan from the Battlefield Line for the event.
Melvyn Hopwood

Dilhorne Park. Special trains at other times by prior arrangement with the secretary, Tel: (0782) 314532
Special events: Santa Specials, weekends in December (advanced booking essential)
Facilities for disabled: Access to majority of facilities is on the level. For special requirements prior notice is desirable
Special notes: Wine and Dine Specials will operate on a number of Saturday evenings during the operating season for all specials
Feature article references: RW November 1988, p674

Stock
3 coaches
1 Dynamometer car
4 scenery vans (some converted for other uses)
19 wagons
1 steam crane

Ironbridge Gorge Museum   M

The railway items form only a small part of the displays on two of the museum's main sites, Blists Hill and Coalbrookdale. The Blists Hill site offers an opportunity to see a number of industrial and other activities being operated in meticulously reconstructed period buildings. A working foundry and ironworks are just two of the exciting exhibits. The Ironbridge Gorge was designated a World Heritage Site in 1987
Location: Ironbridge, Shropshire
OS reference: SJ 694033
Operating society/organisation: Ironbridge Gorge Museum Trust, Ironbridge, Telford, Shropshire TF8 7AW
Telephone: Ironbridge (095 245) 3522
Car park: At the sites
Access by public transport: Various private bus companies, including

Industrial locomotives

Name	No	Builder	Type	Built
—	—	Sentinel/Coalbrookdale (6185)	0-4-0VBT	1925
—	—	Sentinel/M/Wardle (6155)	0-4-0VBT	1925
—	5	Coalbrookdale	0-4-0ST	1865

All locomotives are at the Museum of Iron, Coalbrookdale

Midland Red, Williamson's Shearings, Elcocks, Boultons.
On Sundays in the summer British Rail run a special Ironbridge Express from Birmingham via Wolverhampton to the Museum of Iron (for further details contact the Museum on the above telephone number).
A frequent 'Park & Ride' bus service operates on weekdays during school holidays, and on weekends from Easter to September. Vintage vehicles are used at weekends

Catering facilities: Licensed Victorian pub, sweet shop and tea rooms at the Blists Hill site, serving drinks and mainly cold snacks. Tea, coffee and light refreshments at the Museum of Iron
Public opening: Main sites including Museum of Iron and on Blists Hill, daily (except Christmas Eve and Christmas Day) 10.00-17.00, 10.00-18.00 during British Summer Time
Special notes: Tickets for all the sites or just for single sites available

Moseley Railway Museum   SC

The collection concentrates on diesel and petrol power with some battery units. There are also hand, rope and chain operated vehicles on site. Emphasis is placed on operational locomotives and stock which, by prior appointment, can be observed and photographed performing the tasks for which they were originally designed. There are a number of unique running exhibits including the Kent petrol and Greenbat electric locomotives, and single cylinder Simplex and Ruston diesel units. Passenger train rides are

Industrial locomotives

Name	No	Builder	Type	Built
—	—	G/Batley (2345)	4wBE	1951
—	—	G/Batley (2960)	4wBE	1959
—	—	G/Batley (420172)	4wBE	1969
—	—	H/Hunslet (6299)	4wDM	1964
—	—	Hunslet (4758)	4wDM	1954
—	—	Kent	4wDM	c1926
Ald Hague	—	Hiberd (3465)	4wDM	1954
—	—	Lister (8022)	4wDM	1936
—	—	Lister (38296)	4wDM	1952
—	—	Lister (52031)	4wDM	1960
—	—	M/Rail (4565)	4wDM	1928

always available on official open days

Location: Grounds of The Manor School, Northdowns Road, Cheadle, Cheshire SK8 5HA

OS reference: SJ 864871

Operating society: The Moseley Industrial Narrow Gauge Tramway Museum Society (MTM), address as above

Telephone: School hours 061-485 4372, any other time 061-485 4448, Colin Saxton

Car park: Extensive, free, adjacent to the museum buildings

Station: One boarding area adjacent to the museum. Other request stops

Length of line and gauge: Approximately ½-mile, 2ft gauge. Static lines in short lengths at other gauges

Access by public transport: Nearest BR station Cheadle Hulme (10min walk). Bus from Manchester 157, bus from Stockport S13, ask for Cheadle Adult Education Centre/Manor School

On site facilities: Free access and parking, a small selection of cold drinks and chocolate, access to all site

Period of public operation: Throughout the year. Second Sunday of every month plus any other time by appointment

Name	No	Builder	Type	Built
—	—	M/Rail (7512)	4wDM	1938
—	—	M/Rail (7552)	4wDM	1948
—	—	M/Rail (8663)	4wDM	1941
—	—	M/Rail (8669)	4wDM	1941
—	—	M/Rail (8878)	4wDM	1944
The Lady D	—	M/Rail (8934)	4wDM	1944
Nick the Greek	—	M/Rail (8937)	4wDM	1944
—	—	M/Rail (9104)	4wDM	1942
—	—	M/Rail (11142)	4wDM	1960
Knothole Worker	—	M/Rail (22045)	4wDM	1959
Moseley	—	R/Hornsby (177639)	4wDM	1936
—	—	R/Hornsby (198278)	4wDM	1940
—	—	R/Hornsby (223667)	4wDM	1943
—	—	R/Hornsby (279647)	4wDM	1944
Neath Abbey	—	R/Hornsby (476106)	4wDM	1964
—	—	R/Hornsby	4wDM	—

Stock
Nearly 80 items of rolling stock, gauges from 10¼in to 2ft
3 Wickham Target Trolleys

Train services: Return journey (round trip) approximately 20min

Facilities for the disabled: The museum operates policy as Stockport Education Authority. Every effort is made to accommodate disabled persons who may find a visit easier during school hours when the main school premises are open

Special notes: Part of the site, including museum buildings and displays are now open

Membership details: Colin Saxton, Member of Staff in charge. School address or 60 Pingate Lane, Cheadle Hulme, Cheshire SK8 7LT or John Rowlands, Secretary/Treasurer School address

Severn Valley Railway

The railway hosts more main line engines than any other preserved line in the country, enjoying the backup of a large volunteer and professional workforce and extensive engineering workshops and equipment. Railway travel like it used to be

Headquarters: The Railway Station, Bewdley, Worcestershire

Telephone: Bewdley (0299) 403816; 24hr timetable — Bewdley (0299) 401001

Main stations: Bridgnorth, Bewdley, Kidderminster Town

Other public stations: Arley, Highley, Hampton Loade, Northwood Halt

OS reference: Bridgnorth SO 715926, Bewdley SO 793753

Car parks: At all stations

Access by public transport: Midland Red bus service X92 to Kidderminster and Bewdley and 890 to Bridgnorth. BR Sprinter service to Kidderminster (BR) with immediate connections to SVR station. Through tickets available from a wide range of BR stations

Refreshment facilities: Bridgnorth, Hampton Loade, Bewdley, Arley, Highley, Kidderminster Town and on

Locomotives

Name	No	Origin	Class	Type	Built
The Great Marquess	3442	LNER	K4	2-6-0	1938
Gordon	AD600	LMR	WD	2-10-0	1943
—	43106	LMS	4MT	2-6-0	1951
—	46443	LMS	2MT	2-6-0	1950
—	46521	LMS	2MT	2-6-0	1953
—	5000	LMS	5MT	4-6-0	1934
RAF Biggin Hill	45110	LMS	5MT	4-6-0	1935
Leander	5690	LMS	'Jubilee'	4-6-0	1936
Galatea	5699	LMS	'Jubilee'	4-6-0	1936
—	47383	LMS	3F	0-6-0T	1926
—	8233	LMS	8F	2-8-0	1940
—	2968	LMS	5P4F	2-6-0	1933
—	813	GWR	—	0-6-0ST	1901
—	2857	GWR	2800	2-8-0	1918
—	5164	GWR	5101	2-6-2T	1930
—	4150	GWR	5101	2-6-2T	1947
—	5764	GWR	5700	0-6-0PT	1929
—	7714	GWR	5700	0-6-0PT	1930
Raveningham Hall	6960	GWR	'Hall'	4-6-0	1944
—	4566	GWR	4500	2-6-2T	1924
Bradley Manor	7802	GWR	'Manor'	4-6-0	1939
Hinton Manor	7819	GWR	'Manor'	4-6-0	1939
Erlestoke Manor	7812	GWR	'Manor'	4-6-0	1939
Hagley Hall	4930	GWR	'Hall'	4-6-0	1929
—	1501	GWR	1500	0-6-0PT	1949
—	9303	GWR	4300	2-6-0	1932
Taw Valley	34027	SR	WC	4-6-2	1946

most trains. Fully licensed bars at Bridgnorth and Kidderminster Town
Souvenir shops: Bridgnorth, Bewdley, Kidderminster Town and Model Railway at Bewdley
Depots: Bridgnorth (locomotives), Bewdley (stock)
Length of line: 16¼ miles
Passenger trains: Steam-hauled trains running frequently from Kidderminster Town to Bewdley and Bridgnorth. Diesel-hauled service on limited occasions
Period of public operation: Weekends March-October and Santa Steam specials in late November and December. Daily service mid-May to end September and all public Bank Holidays. Open for limited viewing at other times
Special events: Steam Enthusiasts' weekends in April and September; Diesel Gala weekends in May and October; Santa Specials end November and December; Mince Pie Specials in December/early January 1990
Facilities for disabled: Facilities available, special vehicle available to carry wheelchairs
Special notes: A number of special enthusiasts' weekends and special events are held when extra trains are operated. In addition supplementary trains with diesel haulage may be run on special occasions. 'Severn Valley Limited' Restaurant Car service operates on Sundays and dining car service on selected Saturday evenings. Advanced booking recommended
Membership details: Mrs Gwen Bailey c/o above address
Share details: Mr M. J. Draper, c/o above address
Feature article references: RW July 1988, p418; RW June 1989, p364 (Bewdley — pre-preservation)

Name	No	Origin	Class	Type	Built
—	80079	BR	4MT	2-6-4T	1954
—	78019	BR	2MT	2-6-0	1954
—	75069	BR	4MT	4-6-0	1955
Western Ranger	D1013	BR	52	C-C	1962
Western Courier	D1062	BR	52	C-C	1963
—	D3022	BR	08	0-6-0DE	1952
—	D3586	BR	08	0-6-0DE	1953
—	D7633	BR	25	Bo-Bo	1965

Industrial locomotives

Name	No	Builder	Type	Built
—	4	Peckett (1738)	0-4-0ST	1928
Warwickshire	—	M/Wardle (2047)	0-6-0ST	1926
The Lady Armaghdale	—	Hunslet (686)	0-6-0T	1898
—	—	Ruston (319290)	0-4-0DM	1953
Alan	—	R/Hornsby (414304)	0-4-0DM	1957
Archibald	—	R/Hornsby (418789)	0-4-0DM	1957
William	—	R/Hornsby (408297)	0-4-0DM	1957

Stock
27 ex-GWR coaches
13 ex-LMS coaches
24 ex-BR Mk 1 coaches
8 ex-LNER coaches
Numerous examples of ex-GWR, LMS and other freight vehicles and two 30-ton steam cranes

Owners
3442 (family of the late Earl of Lindsay)
AD600 (The Royal Corps of Transport Museum Trustees)
43106 (the Ivatt 4 Fund)
46443 (SVR 46443 Fund)
5000 (on loan from the National Railway Museum)
47383 (the Manchester Rail Travel Society)
8233 (the Stanier 8F Locomotive Society)
2968 (the Stanier Mogul Fund)
813 (the GWR 813 Fund)
2857 (the 2857 Fund)
5164 (The 51XX Fund)
4150 (the 4150 Locomotive Fund)
5764, 7714 (the Pannier Tank Fund)
4566 (the 4566 Fund)
7802, 7812 (the Erlestoke Manor Fund)
7819 (the Hinton Manor Fund)
1501 (the 15XX Trust)
9303 (the Great Western (SVR) Association)
80079 (the Passenger Tank Fund)
75069 (the 75069 Fund)
6960, 34027, 46521, 78019, D1013 (private)
D1062 (the Western Locomotive Association)
D3022 (the Class 08 Society)
D7633 (the SVR P/W Fund)

Telford Horsehay Steam Trust   SC

Location: Horsehay, Telford, Shropshire
OS reference: SJ 675073
Operating society/organisation: Telford Horsehay Steam Trust, The Old Loco Shed, Horsehay, Telford, TF4 2LT
Public opening: Please contact for details

Stock
1 ex-BR Mk 1 coach
1 ex-GWR auto-trailer
1 ex-GWR Toad brake van
1 ex-GWR 3-ton hand crane.   1 Wickham trolley.   Various wagons

Locomotives

Name	No	Origin	Class	Type	Built
—	5619	GWR	5600	0-6-2T	1925

Industrial locomotives

Name	No	Builder	Type	Built
Peter	—	Barclay (782)	0-6-0ST	1896
Tom	—	N/British (27414)	0-4-0DH	1954
Ironbridge No 3	—	Peckett (1990)	0-4-0ST	1940
—	—	Sentinel (9535)	4wVBT	1952
—	D2959	R/Hornsby (382824)	4wDM	1955

The Battlefield Steam Railway

A quiet country railway operated by members of the Shackerstone Railway Society Ltd, who are undertaking the extension of the line to Shenton and the battlefield of Bosworth
Headquarters: Market Bosworth Light Railway, Shackerstone station, near Market Bosworth, Leicestershire
Telephone: (0827) 715790 (weekdays only); (0827) 880754 (weekends only)
Main station: Shackerstone
Other public station: Market Bosworth
OS reference: SK 379066
Car park: Shackerstone
Access by public transport: Leicester City Bus, Lex Gibson Bros service 123 (tel: 24326). Leicester (Horsefair St) to Market Bosworth (square) weekdays and Sundays
Refreshment facilities: Shackerstone cafe on station. Licensed bar on train
Souvenir shop: Shackerstone
Museum: Shackerstone
Depot: Shackerstone
Length of line: 2¾ miles
Passenger trains: Shackerstone-Market Bosworth
Period of public operation: Passenger steam service will operate: Sundays only 1 April-28 October. Station and museum only are open weekends throughout the year
Special events: Grandparents' Day 29 April; Teddy Bears' Picnic 13 May; Fathers' Day 17 June; Friends of Thomas the Tank Engine Day 5 August; Car Boot 19 August; Postman Pat Day 9 September; Bonfire Special 4 November; Santa Specials 1/2, 8/9, 15/16, 22/23 December
Special notes: An extension of the line from Market Bosworth to Shenton and the battlefield of Bosworth is being undertaken and it is hoped to open in 1990

Locomotives

Name	No	Origin	Class	Type	Built
–	D2245	BR	04	0-6-0DM	1956

Industrial locomotives

Name	No	Builder	Type	Built
Linda	–	Bagnall (2648)	0-4-0ST	1941
The King	–	Borrows (48)	0-4-0WT	1906
–	11	Hunslet (1493)	0-4-0ST	1925
Dunlop No 7	–	Peckett (2130)	0-4-0ST	1951
–	3	RSH (7537)	0-6-0T	1949
–	4	RSH (7684)	0-6-0T	1951
Lamport No 3	–	Bagnall (2670)	0-6-0ST	1942
Florence	2	Bagnall (3059)	0-6-0ST	1953
–	–*	R/Hornsby (235513)	4wDM	1945
–	–	R/Hornsby (263001)	4wDM	1949
The 1211 Squadron	–	R/Hornsby (347747)	0-6-0DM	1957
–	–	R/Hornsby (393304)	4wDM	1956
–	–	R/Hornsby (423657)	4wDM	1958
–	–	S/Crossley (7697)	0-6-0DM	1953

*Converted to steam power 1983

Stock
3 ex-BR Mk 1 coaches
2 ex-BR converted DMU coaches
3 parcels vans
2 rail mounted steam cranes
1 rail mounted diesel crane
Small number of wagons
ex-BR Griddle car
SR brake van

Below:
Industrial power storms along the Battlefield Line in the shape of *The King* and *Linda*. 1 May 1989 was a busy day and the 17.15 is seen approaching Market Bosworth.
Melvyn Hopwood

Home for several locomotives used for main line running, with considerable engineering facilities, the depot also houses several smaller locomotives, other stock and railwayana
Location: Dinting Railway Centre Ltd, Dinting, Glossop, Derbyshire
OS reference: SK 021946
Operating society/organisation: Bahamas Locomotive Society
Telephone: Glossop (045 74) 5596
Car park: Free parking on site
Access by public transport: BR services to Dinting station and buses Nos 215, 236, 237 and 394
Refreshment facilities: Hot and cold buffet
On site facilities: Souvenir shop. Picnic area. Miniature steam railway (Bank Holiday and most steaming Sundays)
Length of line: ¼ mile
Public opening: Daily except Christmas and Boxing Day. In operation Sundays March-October and Bank Holiday Mondays, also Wednesdays July and August
Special events: Please see press for details of events
Membership details: Mr J. Winters, 427 Stockport Road, Denton, Manchester M34 1FQ
Special notes: Dinting is a centre for steam-hauled main line railtours
Feature article references: RW September 1988, p532

Locomotives

Name	No	Origin	Class	Type	Built
Bahamas*	45596	LMS	'Jubilee'	4-6-0	1935
—	102	GCR	04	2-8-0	1911
—	1054	LNWR	—	0-6-2T	1888

*Currently based at Steamtown, Carnforth, for main line running

Industrial locomotives

Name	No	Builder	Type	Built
Southwick	—	RSH (7069)	0-4-0CT	1942
Warrington	150	RSH (7136)	0-6-0ST	1944
Nunlow	—	H/Clarke (1704)	0-6-0T	1938
—	1883	Avonside (1883)	0-6-0ST	1923
Tiny	—	Barclay (2258)	0-4-0ST	1949
—	—	B/Peacock (2734)	0-4-0VB tram	1886
—	RS8	Avonside/RR (1913)	0-4-0DH	1923
Jacob	—	McEwan Pratt (680)	Petrol loco	1916
James	—	R/Hornsby (431763)	0-4-0DE	—

Stock
Sundry freight vehicles

Owners
1054 (the National Trust)
B/Peacock (2734) and 102 (on loan from the National Railway Museum)

Note:
Due to difficulties surrounding the lease of the site, the Society may be required to move in the near future. *Railway World* will carry full details should the need to relocate arise.

Below:
Whilst the future of the Bahamas Locomotive Society's Dinting headquarters is uncertain at the time of writing, the future of *Bahamas* itself is brighter. Here No 45596 is seen at Blea Moor heading towards Carlisle. *Robin Stewart-Smith*

Great Central Railway

The original Great Central Railway's extension to London in 1899 was the last main line to be built in this country, most of which was closed in the 1960s. Steam-hauled services are now operating again through attractive rolling Leicestershire countryside crossing the picturesque Swithland reservoir. The collection of locomotives, includes the only surviving GCR express locomotive — *Butler Henderson*

Headquarters: Great Central Railway, (1976) PLC (Main Line Steam Trust Ltd), Loughborough Central Station, Great Central Road, Loughborough, Leicestershire LE11 1RW

Telephone: Loughborough (0509) 230726

Main station: Loughborough Central

Other public stations: Quorn & Woodhouse, Rothley

OS reference: SK 543194

Car park: Quorn, Rothley

Access by public transport: Loughborough BR station (¾-mile). Trent, South Notts, L'boro Coach & Bus Co and Midland Fox bus services to Loughborough bus station (¾-mile)

Refreshment facilities: Licensed buffet car and light refreshments on most trains. Sunday lunches on 13.00 train 'The Carillon'. Dinner train 'The Charnwood Forester' runs on certain Saturday nights, please contact railway for dates and reservations (advance booking only). Refreshment buffets at Loughborough and Rothley

Souvenir shop: Loughborough

Museum: Loughborough

Depot: Loughborough

Length of line: 5½ miles (3-mile extension in progress)

Passenger trains: Loughborough-Rothley

Period of public operation: Weekends throughout the year and Bank Holiday Mondays and Tuesdays. Midweek-Tuesdays

Right:
LNER Class N2 No 69523 is seen here leaving Quorn whilst masquerading as No 69531. During the line's gala weekend the locomotive ran with a variety of numbers. In this view it is hauling the 15.50 Rothley-Loughborough service. The locomotive is now scheduled to undergo a major overhaul. *John B. Gosling*

Locomotives

Name	No	Origin	Class	Type	Built
Butler Henderson	506	GCR	'Director'	4-4-0	1919
—	68088	NER	Y7	0-4-0T	1923
—	5224	GWR	5205	2-8-0T	1924
Witherslack Hall	6990	GWR	'Hall'	4-6-0	1948
Kolhapur	5593	LMS	'Jubilee'	4-6-0	1934
—	48305	LMS	8F	2-8-0	1943
—	1264	LNER	B1	4-6-0	1947
Mayflower	1306	LNER	B1	4-6-0	1948
—	69523	LNER	N2	0-6-2T	1921
Boscastle	34039	SR	WC	4-6-2	1946
Canadian Pacific	35005	SR	MN	4-6-2	1941
Brocklebank Line	35025	SR	MN	4-6-2	1948
—	92212	BR	9F	2-10-0	1959
—	D3101	BR	08	0-6-0DE	1955
—	D4067	BR	10	0-6-0DE	1961
Atlantic Conveyor	40106	BR	40	1Co-Co1	1960
Royal Highland Fusilier	55019	BR	55	Co-Co	1961

3-car DMU, Class 120 M59276, Class 127 M51616 and M51622

Industrial locomotives

Name	No	Builder	Type	Built
—	7597	RSH (7597)	0-6-0T	1949
—	68009	Hunslet (3825)	0-6-0ST	1953
Qwag	1	Ruston (371971)	4wDM	1954
Arthur Wright	D4279	Fowler (4210079)	0-4-0DE	1952
Alen Grice	11	Sentinel (134C)	4wDH	1963
—	28	A/Barclay (400)	0-4-0DM	1956

3 July-4 September; Wednesdays
23 May-5 September; Thursdays
5 July-6 September
Special events: Easter Fair; Thomas
the Tank weekend, Bonfire Special
and Santa trains planned
Facilities for disabled: Special
carriage for wheelchair/disabled
persons (advance notice required).
Wheelchair access good at Quorn and
Rothley, can be arranged at
Loughborough with advance
notification. Boarding ramps at all
stations
Membership details: *Share
enquiries:* Company Secretary, Great

Owners
506 (on loan from the National Railway Museum)
68088 (the Y7 Locomotive Society)
69523 (the Gresley Society)
6990 (the Witherslack Hall Locomotive Society)
61264 (the Thompson B1 Locomotive Society)
92212 (the 92212 Holdings Ltd)
7597 (Railway Vehicle Preservation Society)
55019 (the Deltic Preservation Society)
5593 (on loan from the Birmingham Railway Museum)

Central Railway (1976) PLC
Membership: Membership Secretary,
Main Line Steam Trust PLC. Both c/o

above address
Feature article reference: RW
August 1989, p493 (Locomotive 35025)

Leicestershire Museum M

Narrow gauge site railway (1ft 11½in
gauge) formerly part of sewage
pumping station that now forms
museum site. Railway renovated in the
last two years using MSC CP scheme.
Original route totally relaid and reset
in concrete. Additional track laid on
sleepers. Original Simplex locomotive
kept on site (non-operational at
present) and Planet type locomotive
used to demonstrate railway with
typical tipper wagons on Special
Event Days. Both locomotives petrol
driven. Line originally used for
transferring solid material from
screens to tip (about 100yd). Now
demonstration line in museum only
Location: Museum of Technology,
Abbey Pumping Station, Corporation
Road, off Abbey Lane, Leicester
LE4 5PW
Operating group: Leicestershire
County Council Museum Department
and Site Railway Volunteer Group
Telephone: (0533) 661330
Car park: Available and free
Nearest BR station: Leicester
(London Road). Access to museum by
Leicester CityBus route 29 or 29A
direct from station (alight at
Beaumont Leys Lane)

Industrial locomotives

Name	No	Builder	Type	Built
Mars II	—*	RSH (7493)	0-4-0ST	1948
—	2*	Barclay (1815)	0-4-0F	1924
—	3*†	Brush (314)	0-4-0ST	1906
—	—	M/Rail (52600)	4wPM	1931
—	—	Planet (1776)	4wPM	1931

*Standard gauge, accessible by appointment only at present
†Originally Powlesland & Mason Railway 6, taken over by GWR in 1924

Stock
Several narrow gauge wagons

Length of line/gauge: About 150yd
and 1ft 11½in gauge. No public riding
on line
Operation: On Special Event Days:
1989 Season's dates are Sunday
23 April, 14.00 to 17.30; Saturday and
Sunday 17 and 18 June, 11.00 to 17.30;
Sundays 17 September and December,
both 14.00 to 17.30. At all other times
museum is open 10.00 to 17.30 Monday
to Saturday and 14.00 to 17.30 Sunday
On site facilities: Museum/shop/
toilets/car park. Refreshments only on
Special Event Days
Facilities for disabled: Access to
grounds and lower floor of museum.

Steps to Engine House and Beam
Engines. Regret steps also to
refreshments
Volunteer contact: Mr F. Crammond,
26 Brambling Way, Oadby, Leicester
Museum contact: Mr R. Bracegirdle,
Industrial Museum, Snibston Mine,
Ashby Road, Coalville, Leicestershire
LE6 2LN. Telephone: 0530 510851
Other attractions: Museum holds
various other railway items both
standard and narrow gauge. Small
exhibit on Leicester & Swannington
Railway in museum. Some items only
viewable by appointment or on Special
Event Days

Midland Railway Centre 🚂

This centre is being established as not
only an operating railway, but also as
a 57-acre museum site and a 35-acre
country park which will make the
centre unique. A wide variety of
exhibits are being collected

Locomotives

Name	No	Origin	Class	Type	Built
Princess Margaret Rose	46203	LMS	8P	4-6-2	1936
—	44027	LMS	4F	0-6-0	1924
—	44932*	LMS	5MT	4-6-0	1945

Location: Midland Railway Centre, Butterley station, near Ripley, Derbyshire
OS reference: SK 403520
Operating society/organisation: Midland Railway Trust Ltd
Telephone: Ripley (0773) 747674/570140
Car park: Butterley station on A61 1-mile north of Ripley
On site facilities: Souvenir shop, display vehicles and exhibition coach. First stages of museum complex
Refreshment facilities: Small restaurant for hot/cold meals, bar on most trains and extensive Wine & Dine service, the 'Midlander' (details from above address)
Length of line: 3½ miles
Public opening: Every Sunday and Bank Holiday Weekend throughout the year. Every Saturday April-October and December. Daily 13-22 April, 20 May-3 June; Tuesday-Sunday 7 July-9 September
Journey time: Approximately 1hr
Special events: North Midland 150 5-7 May; Diesel Spectacular 19/20 May; Friends of Thomas the Tank 26 May-3 June; Steam Spectacular 25/27 August; Santa Specials 24/25 November, 1/2, 8/9, 15/16, 22-24 December
Facilities for disabled: Toilets, special coach, access to shop and cafeteria, special weekend
Feature article references: RW March 1988, p148
Membership details: J. E. Hett, at above address

Name	No	Origin	Class	Type	Built
—	47564	LMS	3F	0-6-0T	1928
—	47327	LMS	3F	0-6-0T	1926
—	47357	LMS	3F	0-6-0T	1926
—	47445	LMS	3F	0-6-0T	1927
—	158A	MR	—	2-4-0	1866
—	41708	MR	1F	0-6-0T	1880
—	48151	LMS	8F	2-8-0	1942
—	53809	S&DJR	7F	2-8-0	1925
—	73129	BR	5MT	4-6-0	1956
—	80080	BR	4MT	2-6-4T	1954
—	80098	BR	4MT	2-6-4T	1955
—	D2138	BR	03	0-6-0DM	1960
—	12077	BR	11	0-6-0DE	1950
—	24061	BR	24	Bo-Bo	1960
—	D7671	BR	25	Bo-Bo	1967
—	40012	BR	40	1Co-Co1	1959
Great Gable	D4	BR	44	1Co-Co1	1959
Tuylar	55015	BR	55	Co-Co	1961

*Shares time between here and Steamtown, Carnforth

Locomotive notes: In service 44932, 46203, 47327, 47357, 41708, 53809, 80080, 48151, 12077, 55015 and D7671. Under restoration 73129, 44027, D4, 40012, D2138. Awaiting repairs or stored 80098, 47445. Boiler and frames only 47564. Static display 158A.

Industrial locomotives

Name	No	Builder	Type	Built
Gladys	—	Markham (109)	0-4-0ST	1894
Stanton	24	Barclay (1875)	0-4-0CT	1925
Victory	—	Peckett (1547)	0-4-0ST	1917
—	4	N/Wilson (454)	0-4-0ST	1894
—	—	Sentinel (9370)	4wVBT	1947
Andy	—	Fowler (16038)	0-4-0DM	1923
—	RS9	M/Rail (2024)	0-4-0DM	1921
—	RS12	M/Rail (460)	0-4-0DM	1912
—	—	M/Rail (1930)	0-4-0PM	1919
Boots	2	Barclay (2008)	0-4-0F	1935
—	D2959	R/Hornsby (384139)	0-4-0DE	1955
Handyman*	—	H/Clarke (573)	0-4-0ST	1900
Albert Fields	—	H/Clarke (D1114)	0-6-0DM	1958
—†	—	Deutz (10249)	4wDM	1932
Campbell Brick Works†	—	M/Rail (60S364)	4wDM	1968
—†	—	M/Rail (5906)	4wDM	1932
—†	—	M/Rail (11246)	4wDM	1963
Hucknall Colliery‡	1	Ruston (480080)	4wDM	1963
Hucknall Colliery‡	3	Ruston	4wDM	1963
Oddson‡	—	Marshall	4wVBT	1970

*3ft gauge
†2ft gauge
‡2ft 6in gauge

Locomotive notes: In service Sentinel 9370, D2959, Deutz 10249, 1, Oddson M/Rails 5906/60S364. Under restoration, Handyman, Andy RS12. Awaiting repairs or stored Stanton, RS9, Ruston 480080. Static display Gladys, 4, Boots No 2, Albert Fields, 3.
Victory and M/Rail (1930) on loan to Derby Industrial Museum

Stock
Numerous carriages, wagons and cranes including MR Royal saloon, MR brake van, LD&ECR six-wheel coach, L&YR saloon — all on display in new museum. MR six-wheel coach and BR horsebox should be restored and on display for 1990

East Midlands

Below:
Swanwick on the Midland Railway Centre's line now boasts a section of narrow gauge line. *Oddson,* **a 4wVBT built in 1970, is seen here providing a 'frame' for BR Standard Class 4MT 2-6-4T No 80080 on 10 September 1989.**
Robin Stewart-Smith

Owners
158A, 44027 (on loan from the National Railway Museum)
41708 (the 1708 Locomotive Preservation Trust)
53809 (the 13809 Preservation Group)
47357, 47327, 47445, 47564, 73129 (Derby City Council)
80080, 80098 (the 80080 Holdings Ltd)
55015 (the Deltic Preservation Society)
D4 (the Peak Locomotive Preservation Co Ltd)
D7671 (Derby Industrial Museum)

National Tramway Museum

A journey back in time — an experience of living transport history with vintage horse-drawn, steam and electric trams running through a recreated townscape of authentic buildings, stone setts, iron railings and historic street furniture. The heart of the Museum is its collection of over 40 vintage trams and you can enjoy the thrill of travelling on the scenic mile-long track
Location: Crich, near Matlock, Derbyshire DE4 5DP
OS reference: SK 345549
Operating society/organisation: Tramway Museum Society
Telephone: 0773 852565
Car park: Site, coach parking also available

Locomotives

Name	No	Builder	Type	Built
—	—	B/Peacock (2464)	0-4-0VB tram loco	1885
—	—	E/Electric (717)	4wE	1927
Rupert	—	R/Hornsby (223741)	4wDM	1944
GMJ	—	R/Hornsby (326058)	4wDM	1952
—	—	R/Hornsby (373363)	4wDM	1954

Also some 40 trams (including examples from Czechoslovakia, Portugal, USA and South Africa), about a third of which have been restored to working order

Access by public transport: Maun International bus services. Nearest stations: Cromford (BR) or Alfreton & Mansfield Parkway (BR) then by bus; or Whatstandwell (BR) and steep uphill walk

On site facilities: Souvenir shop, bookshop and picnic areas. 1-mile electric tramway. Tramway period street, depots, displays, exhibitions and video theatre
Refreshment facilities: Hot and cold

snacks and meals
Public opening: Saturdays, Sundays and bank holidays, 31 March to end October, plus Mondays to Thursdays 7 May to end September. Also open daily 9-20 April, and Fridays, 1 June and 20 July through to end August. Additional openings: daily during autumn half-term week. Open: 10.00am to 5.30pm (6.30pm Saturdays/Sundays/Bank Holidays) **Facilities for disabled:** Access available for most of site **Special Notes:** Crich houses the largest collection of preserved trams in Europe and has a 1-mile working tramway on which restored electric trams are regularly operated. Special events are arranged throughout the season. Part of tram line occupies route of narrow gauge mineral railway built by George Stephenson **Membership details:** From above address

Northampton Steam Railway

Headquarters: Pitsford & Brampton Station
Location: About 5 miles north of Northampton, Pitsford road off A50 or A508
Operating society/organisation: Northampton Steam Railway Preservation Society
Telephone: (0604) 22709
Car parks: Yes, extension under construction
Access by public transport: None
On site facilities: Bar and restaurant open daily from 11.00 in the old station master's house, called the 'pines'. Sales stand
Length of line: ½-mile at present
Public opening: Possible opening date, Easter 1990. For details of opening times, events and journey times, please see railway press
Membership details: Mr F. Collins, Membership Secretary, 2 Watson Road, Long Buckby, Northants NN6 7PS

Locomotives

Name	No	Origin	Class	Type	Built
—	3862	GWR	2884	2-8-0	1942
Castel Dinas Bran	25035	BR	25	Bo-Bo	1963
—	27056	BR	27	Bo-Bo	1962

Industrial locomotives

Name	No	Builder	Type	Built
Colwyn	45	Kitson (5470)	0-6-0ST	1933
Yvonne	2945	Cockerill (2945)	0-4-0VBT	1920
—	2104	Peckett (2104)	0-4-0ST	1948
Bunty	—	Fowler (4210018)	0-4-0DM	1950
—	1	R/Hornsby (275886)	4wDM	1949
Sir Gyles Isham	764	R/Hornsby (319286)	0-4-0DM	1953

Stock
1 ex-SR double-decker motor coach
1 Pullman car
1 BR Mk 1 FK
2 BR Suburban coaches (1 CL, 1 BS)
1 BR Mk 2 SO
1 BR Mk 1 BSK
2 GWR coaches
1 GWR Siphon
2 LMS coaches
1 BR full brake
1 BR GUV
A number of various wagon types

Owners
3862 (the LNWR Preservation Society)
Colwyn (the *Colwyn* Preservation Society)

Northamptonshire Ironstone Railway Trust   SC

Location: Hunsbury Hill Industrial Museum. Hunsbury Hill Country Park, Hunsbury Hill Road, Camp Hill, Northampton
OS reference: SP 735584
Operating organisation: Northamptonshire Ironstone Railway Trust Ltd, c/o Mr G. Williams, 68 Sentinel Road, West Hunsbury, Northampton. Tel: (0604) 764862
Telephone: Northampton (0604) 767216

Industrial locomotives

Name	No	Builder	Type	Built
Vigilant	—	Hunslet (287)	0-4-0ST	1882
Brill	14	M/Wardle (1795)	0-4-0ST	1912
—	87	Peckett (2029)	0-6-0ST	1942*
Belvedere	—	Sentinel (9365)	0-4-0TG	1946
Musketeer	—	Sentinel (9369)	0-4-0TG	1946
Hylton	—	Planet (3967)	0-4-0DM	1961
Spitfire	39	R/Hornsby (242868)	4wDM	1946
—	16	Hunslet (2087)	0-4-0DM	1940
—	—	R/Hornsby (386875)	0-4-0DM	1955
—	—	M/Rail (9711)	0-4-0DM	1946†

Access by public transport: Terminus of Northampton Transport bus routes, 24, 26 to Camp Hill from Northampton Greyfriars bus station. Operated by United Counties Bus Co on Sundays
On site facilities: Light refreshments, shop, toilets in car park. Brake van rides given on standard gauge railway. Children's playground and picnic areas within the park boundary
Length of line: 2¼ miles
Public opening: Easter Sunday to end of September and Bank Holidays
Times of opening: Museum: 11.00-17.00. Railway: First train 14.00, last train 17.10

Name	No	Builder	Type	Built
—	—	M/Rail	0-4-0DM	1954†
—	—	Lister (14006)	0-4-0PM	1950†

*Metre gauge
†2ft gauge

Facilities for the disabled: Site relatively flat. Members willing to assist.
Special notes: Museum to the Ironstone Industry of Northamptonshire, the museum houses photographs, documents and other items connected with the Ironstone Industry of Northamptonshire. The railway has been relaid on part of the trackbed of the former 3ft 8½in gauge line of now defunct Hunsbury Ironstone Co
Membership details: Mrs J. Clayton, PO Stores, High Street, Hallaton, Leicestershire

Peak Rail PLC   SC

Locations: Buxton Midland Station Site, Buxton, Derbyshire BR station, Matlock, Derbyshire
OS reference: Buxton SK 296603, Matlock SK 060738
Operating society/organisation: Peak Rail PLC, Buxton Midland Station, Buxton, Derbyshire
Car parks: On sites
Access by public transport: BR DMU service between Manchester Piccadilly and Buxton daily. Monday to Saturday between Derby and Matlock
Length of line: 350yd
On site facilities: Main site at Buxton. Shops at Matlock and Buxton. Steam rides at Buxton Sundays and bank holidays, Easter-October. Saturdays July and August
Public opening: Buxton shop and site open at weekends and midweek. Matlock shop open at weekends and most weekdays during summer
Facilities for disabled: Advance notice not necessary but contact telephone is (0298) 79898
Special events: Santa Specials 1/2, 8/9, 15/16 December
Special notes: Peak Rail (Operations) Ltd, has outline planning permission to relay the 20-mile line from Buxton to Matlock. Track laying is now underway between Matlock and Darley Dale, with working parties present most weekends of the year
Feature article references: RW March 1988, p156

Locomotives

Name	No	Origin	Class	Type	Built
—	47406	LMS	3F	0-6-0T	1926
—	48624	LMS	8F	2-8-0	1943
—	92214	BR	9F	2-10-0	1959
—	92219	BR	9F	2-10-0	1959
Penyghent	D8*	BR	44	1Co-Co1	1959
3rd Carabinier	D99*	BR	45	1Co-Co1	1961
Sherwood Forester	D100*	BR	45	1Co-Co1	1961
—	D3429	BR	08	0-6-0DE	1958
—	D5705*	BR	28	Co-Bo	1958
—	D7615	BR	25	Bo-Bo	1963

*At Matlock

Industrial locomotives

Name	No	Builder	Type	Built
Shropshire†	193	Hunslet (3793)	0-6-0ST	1953
Vulcan	—	V/Foundry (3272)	0-4-0ST	1918
Lytham No 1	—	Peckett (2111)	0-4-0ST	1949
Harry	—	Barclay (1823)	0-4-0ST	1924
Brookes No 1	—	Hunslet (2387)	0-6-0ST	1941
The Duke	2746	Bagnall (2746)	0-6-0ST	1944
William*	—	Sentinel (9599)	0-4-0T	1956
—	E1	H/Clarke (D1199)	0-6-0DM	1960
—	—	Hunslet (1684)	0-4-0T	1931
Arthur	1601	M/Wardle (1601)	0-6-0ST	1903
—	1684	Hunslet (1684)	0-4-0T	1931
Meteor	7604	RSH (7604)	0-6-0T	1956
Lucy	—	Cockerill	0-4-0VBT	1890
Janine*	—	YEC	0-6-0DE	1963
—*	—	Simplex	0-4-0D	—
Robert	2068	Avonside (2068)	0-6-0ST	1933
Cynthia*	—	R/Hornsby	0-4-0DM	—

*At Darley Dale
†On loan to the East Lancashire Railway

Owners
D8 (the North Notts Loco Group)
Vulcan (the Vulcan Loco Trust)
47406 (the Rowsley Locomotives Trust)

Right:
Peak Rail are in the process of relaying the 20 miles from Buxton to Matlock, the first section being between Matlock and Darley Dale. This is the view towards Matlock on 21 May 1989. *S. Groves*

Rutland Railway Museum

SC

This museum is dedicated to portraying the railway in industry, particularly iron ore mining, and has a wide range of industrial locomotives and rolling stock. Indeed, its collection of freight rolling stock is probably the most comprehensive in the country and regular demonstrations are a feature of the 'steam days'.

Location: Cottesmore Iron Ore Mines Siding, Ashwell Road, Cottesmore, near Oakham, Leicestershire — museum situated mid-way between villages of Cottesmore and Ashwell, approximately 4 miles north of Oakham (locally signposted)

OS reference: SK 886137

Operating society/organisation: Rutland Railway Museum, Cottesmore Iron Ore Mines Siding, Ashwell Road, Cottesmore, Nr Oakham, Leicestershire LE15 7BX

Telephone: Information, Stamford (0780) 63092/62384; Site, Oakham (0572) 813203

Car park: Free car park on site

Access by public transport: Nearest BR station, Oakham. Blands bus service, Leicester-Oakham-Cottesmore. Bartons buses, Nottingham-Melton Mowbray-Oakham-Ashwell, Corby/Peterborough-Oakham-Ashwell (services 117 and 125).

On site facilities: Free train rides, demonstration freight trains,

Locomotives

Name	No	Origin	Class	Type	Built
NCB No 7	(D9518)	BR	14	0-6-0DH	1964
NCB No 3	D9521	BR	14	0-6-0DH	1964
BSC45	(D9520)	BR	14	0-6-0DH	1964
—	D9555	BR	14	0-6-0DH	1965

Industrial locomotives

Name	No	Builder	Type	Built
Albion	—	Barclay (776)	0-4-0ST	1896
Uppingham	—	Peckett (1257)	0-4-0ST	1912
Rhos	39	H/Clarke (1308)	0-6-0ST	1918
BSC No 2	—	Barclay (1931)	0-4-0ST	1927
Dora	—	Avonside (1973)	0-4-0ST	1927
Elizabeth	—	Peckett (1759)	0-4-0ST	1928
Singapore	Yard No 440	H/Leslie (3865)	0-4-0ST	1936
Swordfish	—	Barclay (2138)	0-6-0ST	1941
Drake	—	Barclay (2086)	0-4-0ST	1940
Sir Thomas Royden	—	Barclay (2088)	0-4-0ST	1940
Carlton No 3	—	Barclay (352)	0-4-0DM	1941
S and L No 24	—	Hunslet (2411)	0-6-0ST	1941
Salmon	8410/39	Barclay (2139)	0-6-0ST	1942
Coal Products No 6	—	Hunslet (2868)	0-6-0ST	1943
		(Rebuilt Hunslet 3883 1963)		
—	No 1	Hunslet (6688)	0-4-0DH	1969
—	8	Peckett (2110)	0-4-0ST	1950
—	3	N/British (27656)	0-4-0DH	1957
—	—	R/Hornsby (306092)	4wDM	1950
—	—	R/Hornsby (305302)	4wDM	1951
Phoenix	—	Hibberd (3887)	4wDM	1958
Janus	No 28	YEC (2791)	0-6-0DE	1962
Colsterworth	1382	YEC (2872)	0-6-0DE	1962
—	65	Hunslet (3889)	0-6-0ST	1964
—	20-90-01	Barclay (499)	0-4-0DH	1965
—	20-90-02	R/Hornsby (504565)	0-4-0DH	1965

refreshments, toilets, museum, shop, picnic sites, demonstration line with lineside walk and viewing areas, static displays of over 30 steam and diesel locomotives; over 70 wagons, vans and coaches (believed to be the largest collection of preserved freight stock in the UK)

Length of line: ¾-mile

Passenger trains: Regular shuttle service operates on open days using brake vans (approximately every 15min)

Public Opening: Open weekends or by arrangement. Regular steam days: 14*/15/16 April (Easter); 5*/6/7 May (May Day Bank Holiday); 26*/27/28 May (Spring Bank Holiday); 30 June*, 1 July; 4*/5, 11*/12, 18*/19, 25/26/27 August (Summer Bank Holiday); 29*/30 September; 8/9, 15/16, 22/23 December. (*Diesel service). Open 11.00-17.00

Below:
Following its acquisition from the NCB colliery at Ashington, No D9555 is seen at the Rutland Railway Museum.
Robin Stewart-Smith

Name	No	Builder	Type	Built
Betty	8411/04	R/Royce (10201)	0-4-0DM	1965
—	—	E/Electric (D1231)	0-6-0DH	1967
—	No 1	Hunslet (6688)	0-4-0DH	1968

Locomotive notes: In service *Singapore, Dora, Salmon,* BSC45, NCB 3, D9555, *Colsterworth, Betty, Janus,* E/Electric D1231 and 1.

Stock
4 coaches
5 brake vans
12 covered goods vans
57 wagons (includes rakes of wagons as used in local ironstone and industrial railways)
2 rail cranes

Special events: Children's Weekend 5/6/7 May; Teddy Bear Weekend 26/27/28 May; Ironstone Weekend 11/12 August; Rutland Steam Gala 25/26/27 August (extra attractions); Grand Prize Draw 29/30 September; Santa Steam Weekends 8/9, 15/16, 22/23 December

Facilities for disabled: Site relatively flat. Members willing to assist.

Special notes: The museum houses an extensive collection of industrial locomotives and rolling stock typifying past activity in local ironstone quarries, nationwide mines and factories. A demonstration line approximately ¾-mile long has been relaid on the former MR Cottesmore mineral branch (originally built to tap local ironstone quarries), on which restored locomotives and stock are run. Among the latter is the only surviving Wisbech & Upwell Tramway Coach and the last locomotive built for BR service at Swindon Works

Membership details: Membership Secretary, c/o above address

Eastern Counties

Bressingham Steam Museum   SC

Five miles of various gauges of railway running through extensive gardens and a collection of well maintained and impressive main line locomotives. All the fun of the fair, with something for everyone including the mother who never wants to see another steam engine
Location: Two miles west of Diss on the A1066
OS reference: TM 080806
Operating society/organisation: Bressingham Steam Preservation Co Ltd, Bressingham Hall, Diss, Norfolk IP22 2AB
Telephone: Bressingham (037 988) 386 and 382
Car park: Steam Centre (free)
Access by public transport: Diss BR station (3 miles)
On site facilities: 9½/15/24in and standard gauge lines, totalling nearly 5 miles. Museum, steam roundabout, souvenir shop and restaurant, extensive gardens
Public opening: Museum open daily 14 April-14 October. Steam days and gardens open every Sunday, Thursday and bank holiday from 15 April-30 September, Wednesdays from 25 July to 5 September
Special events: Norfolk & Norwich Rover P4 Owners' Club Rally 27 May. 4th Annual Fire Rally 5 August
Facilities for disabled: Toilets, wheelchairs available. Able to take wheelchairs on Nursery Line Railway
Special notes: Reduced rates for coach parties. Prices on application
Feature article reference: RW June 1989, p338

Locomotives

Name	No	Origin	Class	Type	Built
Martello	662	LBSCR	A1X	0-6-0T	1875
Thundersley	80	LTSR	3P	4-4-2T	1909
Granville	102	LSWR	B4	0-4-0T	1893
—	490	GER	E4	2-4-0	1894
—	2500	LMS	4P	2-6-4T	1934
Royal Scot	6100	LMS	7P	4-6-0	1927
Duchess of Sutherland	6233	LMS	8P	4-6-2	1938
Oliver Cromwell	70013	BR	7MT	4-6-2	1951
Peer Gynt	5865	NSB	52	2-10-0	1944
Tom Paine	141R73	SNCF	141R	2-8-2	1948
King Haakon VII	377	NSB	21c	2-6-0	1919

Industrial locomotives

Name	No	Builder	Type	Built
Beckton	1	Neilson (4444)	0-4-0ST	1892
Beckton	25	Neilson (5087)	0-4-0ST	1896
William Francis	6841	B/Peacock (6841)	0-4-0+0-4-0T	1937
Millfield	—	RSH (7070)	0-4-0CT	1942
Bluebottle	—	Barclay (1472)	0-4-0F	1916

Narrow gauge locomotives

Name	No	Builder	Type	Built
Gwynedd	—	Hunslet (316)	0-4-0ST	1883
George Sholto	—	Hunslet (994)	0-4-0ST	1909
Bronllwyd	—	H/Clarke (1643)	0-6-0WT	1930
Eigiau	—	O&K (5668)	0-4-0WT	1912
—	—	M/Rail (22120)	4wDM	1964
—	—	M/Rail (22253)	4wDM	1965

15in gauge locomotives

Name	No	Builder	Type	Built
Rosenkavalier	—	Krupp (1662)	4-6-2	1937
Mannertreu	—	Krupp (1663)	4-6-2	1937
Flying Scotsman	4472	W. Stewart (4472)	4-6-2	1976

9½in gauge locomotives

Name	No	Builder	Type	Built
Princess	—	Motor Gear & Engine Co	4-6-2	1947

Owners
80, 490, 2500, 70013 (on loan from the National Railway Museum)

Bure Valley Railway

Headquarters: BVR Ltd, Boundary Road, Great Yarmouth, Norfolk NR31 0JY
Telephone: (0493) 655358/657338
Fax: (0493) 655131
Main public station: Aylsham (Norwich Road)
Other public stations: Coltishall, Brampton and possibly Buxton

Car parks: 150 spaces at Aylsham, 60 spaces at Wroxham
Journey time: Approximately 40min each way with 20min turnround (provisional)
Opening times: Easter-end October daily. November-Easter weekends (opening July 1990) (all provisional)
Facilities for disabled: Toilets at both ends but as yet no special rolling stock
Locomotives and carriages: On hire from RH&D — *Winston Churchill* and *Samson*. Diesel hydraulic built by BVR. 20 coaches seating 20 people each

Colne Valley Railway   SC

An immaculate country station surrounded by green fields, the railway offers much to entertain as well as to educate. A well-deserved reputation for good food
Location: Castle Hedingham station, Yeldham Road, Castle Hedingham, Halstead, Essex CO9 3DZ
OS reference: TL 774362
Operating society/organisation: Colne Valley Railway Preservation Society
Telephone: Hedingham (0787) 61174
Car park: At the site (access from A604 road) between Castle Hedingham and Gt Yeldham
Access by public transport: Eastern National bus services No 88 Colchester-Halstead, 89 Halstead-Hedingham and Hedingham & District Nos 4 Braintree-Hedingham, 5 Sudbury-Hedingham. Nearest BR station — Braintree
On site facilities: Depot, museum, souvenir shop and restaurant, 4-acre riverside wooded picnic area, toilets, video carriage
Catering facilities: Restaurant carriage open daily 10.00-17.00 and 19.00-22.00 except 22 December-1 March and Mondays out of peak season. Pullman on train service on steam days for Brunch, Cream Teas, private hire and evening wine and dine also Sunday lunches and Saturday evening wine and dine Pullman service. *All must be prebooked.* Buffet carriage open steam days also
Length of line: ¾-mile
Public opening: Daily for static displays except Christmas, New Year and January. Locomotives in steam most Sundays of the month between Easter and October inclusive, also

Locomotives

Name	No	Origin	Class	Type	Built
—	D2041	BR	03	0-6-0DM	1959
—	03063	BR	03	0-6-0DM	1959
—	D2184	BR	03	0-6-0DM	1962
—	E79978	BR	—	AC Cars Railbus	1958

Industrial locomotives

Name	No	Builder	Type	Built
—	—	Barclay (349)	0-4-0DM	1941
Victory	—	Barclay (2199)	0-4-0ST	1945
—	190	Hunslet (3790)	0-6-0ST	1952
—	72	Vulcan (5309)	0-6-0ST	1945
Jupiter	—	RSH (7671)	0-6-0ST	1950
—	40	RSH (7765)	0-6-0T	1954
Barrington	—	Avonside (1875)	0-4-0ST	1921
—	1	H/Leslie (3715)	0-4-0ST	1928
—	YD43	R/Hornsby (221639)	0-4-0DM	1943
—	—	Hibbard (3147)	0-4-0DM	1947

Stock
10 ex-BR Mk 1 coaches
1 ex-Norwegian State Railway Class B 65 18803 (built 1926) Balcony Open Second (teak)
2 ex-Pullman cars, *Aquila* and *Hermione*
1 ex-BR Mk 1 (BG) exhibition carriage
1 ex-LNER BTO 43571 bar saloon
1 ex-GWR Engineers Observation Saloon
Steam crane DRG 80103
Sundry items of freight stock

every Bank Holiday and preeceding Sunday except Christmas and New Year. Schools' steam operation most weekdays in June and Santa Specials in December
Special events: Playgroup Specials, Rising Five Specials, Victorian Specials, Santa Specials, please telephone for details
Facilities for disabled: To look and ride only
Special notes: The railway has been completely rebuilt on part of the original Colne Valley line track-bed. The railway offers much of educational value specialising in school party visits by appointment at any time of the year. Catering approved by Egon Ronay 'Just-a-bite' guide 1989, also new conference Pullman train
Membership details: J. Dunn, 24 Slades Close, Glemsford, Sudbury, Suffolk CO10 7PT

East Anglian Railway Museum SC

Location: Chappel & Wakes Colne station, near Colchester CO6 2DS
OS reference: TL 898289
Operating society/organisation: Stour Valley Railway Preservation Society, Chappel & Wakes Colne station, Essex CO6 2DS
Telephone: Colchester (0206) 242524
Car park: On site
Access by public transport: Chappel & Wakes Colne BR station. Also Eastern National/Hedingham Omnibus service No 88 Colchester-Halstead. Sundays Eastern National No 188 Colchester-Halstead
On site facilities: Light refreshments, bookshop, museum, souvenir shop and toilets
Public opening: Daily 09.00-17.30
Special events: Santa Specials in December (please see press for details)
Special notes: Special steam days are held first Sunday of month March-October inclusive, plus Bank Holidays, Wednesdays in August. Three restored signalboxes, large goods shed and restoration shed. Victorian country junction station. School days and Stanta steamings. Disabled visitors welcome — prior advice appreciated. Rail Riders sticker station. Now heritage centre open
Membership details: Membership Secretary, 24 Olivia Drive, Leigh-on-Sea, Essex SS9 3EG

Locomotives

Name	No	Origin	Class	Type	Built
—	69621	GER	N7	0-6-2T	1924
—	80151	BR	4MT	2-6-4T	1956
—	D2279	BR	04	0-6-0DM	1960

Industrial locomotives

Name	No	Builder	Type	Built
Jubilee	—	Bagnall (2542)	0-4-0ST	1936
—	1074	Barclay (1047)	0-4-0ST	1905
Belvoir	—	Barclay (2350)	0-6-0ST	1954
Gunby	68067	Hunslet (2413)	0-6-0ST	1941
—	2	M/Vick	0-4-0E	1912
—	1438	Peckett (1438)	0-4-0ST	1916
—	2039	Peckett (2039)	0-4-0ST	1943
Penn Green	54	RSH (7031)	0-6-0ST	1941
—	AMW144	Barclay (333)	0-4-0DM	1938
—	23	Fowler (4220039)	0-4-0DH	1965
—	2029	Simplex (2029)	0-4-0PM	1920

Locomotive notes: 69621 returned to service in August 1989.

Stock
1 ex-LNER coach
4 ex-BR Mk 1 coaches
1 ex-BR sleeping coach
1 ex-LNER Buffet car
1 GER 6-wheel full brake
1 GER 6-wheel family saloon
1 GER 4-wheel coach
2 MSL 6-wheel coaches
3 GER coach bodies
2 Grafton 4-ton steam cranes

1 SR PMV
1 ex-BR CCT
1 ex-BR 13-ton open wagon
1 ex-LMS 12-ton open wagon
1 ex-GE bogie coach
2 Wickham Trolleys
1 GWR Toad Brakevan
1 ex-BR brake van
1 ex-LNER Pigeon van

East Anglia Transport Museum SC

The East Suffolk Light Railway is the title given to the 2ft gauge railway, which winds its way some 300yd or so along the northern perimeter of the museum site, between the stations of Chapel Road and Woodside. The railway commenced operation in 1973 and aims to re-create a typical passenger-carrying light railway of years gone by. Many aspects of railway interest can be found along its length. The track came from Leziate sand-quarry and Canvey island, as

Industrial locomotives

Name	No	Builder	Type	Built
—	1	M/Rail (5902)	4wDM	1932
—	2	M/Rail (5912)	4wDM	1934
—	4	R/Hornsby (177604)	4wDM	1936

Locomotive notes: During the 1990 season, R/Hornsby locomotive 4 (177604) will be the sole source of motive-power. The two Motor-rail locomotives are under course of restoration, as finance and time allows. The return journey takes 10 to 15min.

well as from the Southwold Railway. There is also a signalbox from the Lowestoft-Great Yarmouth line, and signals from various local locations; all of which help to set the overall scene
Location: Carlton Colville, three miles south-west of Lowestoft in Suffolk
OS reference: TM 505903
Operating society/organisation: East Anglia Transport Museum Society Ltd, Chapel Road, Carlton Colville, Lowestoft, Suffolk NR33 8BL
Telephone: (0502) 518459
Car park: On site
Access by public transport: Services

Stock
Locally designed and built covered coach
Small selection of wagons
Van body ex-Southwold Railway

111, 119, 631, 671 from Lowestoft. BR Oulton Broad South (1 mile)
On site facilities: Refreshments, souvenir and bookshop, toilets, working transport museum, including trams, narrow-gauge railway, trolleybuses, steam-rollers and other commercial and public transport vehicles
Period of public opening: Easter Sunday and Monday, and Sundays from beginning of May to end of September, also other Bank Holidays in this period; open from 11.00. Saturdays from the beginning of June to the end of September, and every weekday during August; open from 14.00
Special notes: Limited facilities for the disabled
Membership details: From the above address

Leighton Buzzard Railway

In places, this line bears the air of a Continental roadside tramway, running as it does behind the backs of houses before it passes into the open countryside; there is no denying the quaintness of its engines or the friendliness of the little trains and their staff
Headquarters: Leighton Buzzard Railway, Page's Park station, Billington Road, Leighton Buzzard LU7 8TN
OS reference: Page's Park SP 928242
Telephone: (0525) 373888, 24hr answerphone with service and event details
Main station: Pages Park (A4146, Leighton Buzzard)
Other public stations: Halts at Vandyke Road and Stonehenge Works
Car park: Pages Park
Access by public transport: Leighton Buzzard BR station then by bus to town centre
Refreshment facilities: Pages Park
Souvenir shop: Pages Park
Depots: Pages Park and Stonehenge Works
Length of line: 3 miles, 2ft gauge
Journey time: Single 25min, return 65min
Passenger trains: Pages Park-Stonehenge Works
Period of public operation: Sundays 1 April-7 October; Good Friday; Easter Saturday; Bank Holiday Mondays 16 April, 7/28 May, 27 August; Saturdays 21 July-25 August; Wednesdays 25 July-29 August
Special events: Summer Steam Gala 17 June; September Steam Up 8/9 September
Facilities for disabled: Access to shop, buffet, platform. Toilet facilities are specially available June-

Locomotives

Name	No	Builder	Type	Built
Chaloner	1	de Winton	0-4-0VBT	1877
Pixie	2	K/Stuart (4260)	0-4-0ST	1922
Rishra	3	Baguley (2007)	0-4-0T	1921
The Doll	4	Barclay (1641)	0-6-0T	1919
Elf	5	O&K (12740)	0-6-0WT	1936
Caravan	6	Simplex (7129)	4wDM	1938
Falcon	7	O&K (8986)	4wDM	1939
Gollum	8	Ruston (217999)	4wDM	1942
Haydn Taylor	10	Simplex (7956)	4wDM	1945
P. C. Allen	11	O&K (5834)	0-4-0WT	1912
Carbon	12	Simplex (6012)	4wPM	1930
Arkle	13	M/Rail (7108)	4wDM	1937
—	14	Hunslet (3646)	4wDM	1946
Tom Bombadil	15	Hibberd (2514)	4wDM	1941
Thorin Oakenshield	16	Lister (11221)	4wDM	1939
Damredub	17	Simplex (7036)	4wDM	1936
Fëanor	18	M/Rail (11003)	4wDM	1956
—	19	M/Rail (11298)	4wDM	1965
—	20	M/Rail (60s317)	4wDM	1966
Festoon	21	Simplex (4570)	4wPM	1929
—	22	under construction	—	—
—	23	Ruston (164346)	4wDM	1932
Ad-a-Cab	25	Simplex (7214)	4wDM	1938
Yimkin	26	Ruston (203026)	4wDM	1942
Poppy	27	Ruston (408430)	4wDM	1957
RAF Stanbridge	28	Ruston (200516)	4wDM	1949
Creepy	29	Hunslet (6008)	4wDM	1963
—	30	M/Rail (8695)	4wDM	1941
—	33	Hibberd (3582)	4wDM	1954
T. W. Lewis	39	Ruston (375316)	4wDM	1954
—	43	Simplex (10409)	4wDM	1954
Kestrel	44	Simplex (7933)	4wDM	1941
Madge	—	O&K (7600)	4wDM	1935
—	—	Ruston (172892)	4wDM	1934
—	—	Hunslet (2536)	4wDM	1941
—	—	Lister (4228)	4wDM	1931
—	—	Hunslet (6619)	0-4-0DM	1966

Dismantled for spares: M/Rail 4805, 5613, 5612, 5603; Ruston 218016
Converted to brake vans: M/Rail 5608, 5875

Locomotive notes: 20 of these locomotives operated during 1989 and steam locomotives 1 and 5 are potentially operational during 1990, though possibly only during Gala Days.

Eastern Counties

September. Wheelchairs can be conveyed on trains. Those persons who can be transferred from chair to train are conveyed by first available train
Membership details: Membership secretary c/o above address

Stock
8 coaches and a number of miscellaneous vehicles

Nene Valley Railway

This unique railway's collection includes locomotives and coaches from 10 countries and two continents. It is a regular location for TV and film makers — from films like *Octopussy* with Roger Moore as 007 to TV — *Hanney, Christobel* — to commercials for cars, beer and soft drinks. The railway and the pleasant Cambridgeshire countryside have doubled for as diverse locations as Russia and Spain. *Thomas* also makes regular appearances to delight the children
Headquarters: Nene Valley Railway, Wansford station, Stibbington, Peterborough, Cambs PE8 6LR
Telephone: Stamford (0780) 782854; talking timetable (0780) 782921
Main station: Wansford
Other public stations: Orton Mere, Ferry Meadows, Peterborough NVR ½-mile from city centre
OS reference: TL 903979
Car park: Wansford, Orton Mere, Ferry Meadows, Peterborough NVR
Access by public transport: Buses from Peterborough to Orton Mere and Ferry Meadows
Refreshment facilities: Wansford, (restaurant bar coach on platform 4). Orton Mere. Light snacks available. Bar coach on most trains
Souvenir shops: Wansford, Orton Mere, Ferry Meadows
Museum: Wansford
Depot: Wansford
Length of line: 7½ miles
Passenger trains: Yarwell Mill-Wansford-Orton Mere-Peterborough NVR
Period of public operation: Weekends April-end-October; Sundays March and November, bank holidays; Mid-week July and August. School specials 12-14 and 19-21 June and Bank Holidays, mid-week June, July and August
Special events: Thomas the Tank Weekends May, August and end October; Santa Specials in December (phone for details)
Facilities for disabled: Ramp access to all stations and shops. Toilets

Locomotives

Name	No	Origin	Class	Type	Built
—	80.014	DB	80	0-6-0T	1927
—	656	DSB	F	0-6-0T	1949
DFDS Danish Seaways	740	DSB	S	2-6-4T	1927
—	1697 (101)	SJ	B	4-6-0	1943
—	1178	SJ	S	2-6-2T	1914
—	3.628	SNCF	230D	4-6-0	1911
92 Squadron	34081	SR	BB	4-6-2	1948
—	5231	BR	5MT	4-6-0	1936
Britannia*	70000	BR	7MT	4-6-2	1951
City of Peterborough	73050	BR	5MT	4-6-0	1954
—	D9516	BR	14	0-6-0DM	1964
—	D9520	BR	14	0-6-0DM	1964
—	D9523	BR	14	0-6-0DM	1964
—	064-305-6	DB	64	2-6-2T	1936

*Currently based at Steamtown, Carnforth, for restoration to BR standards for main line operations

Industrial locomotives

Name	No	Builder	Type	Built
—	804	Alco (77778)	Bo-Bo	1949
—	—	Avonside (1945)	0-6-0ST	1926
—	90432	Barclay (2248)	0-4-0ST	1948
—	—	Cockerlll (1626)	0-4-0VBT	1890
Ryan	—	H/Clarke (1539)	0-6-0ST	1924
Thomas	—	H/Clarke (1800)	0-6-0T	1947
Jacks Green	—	Hunslet (1953)	0-6-0ST	1939
—	68081	Hunslet (2855)	0-6-0ST	1943

Stock
11 BR Mk 1 coaches
2 ex-SR EMU vehicles
Wagons Lits sleeping car, Italian-built
Wagons Lits sleeping car, Belgian-built
6 coaches from Denmark
1 coach from France
1 coach from Norway
Leyland Vehicles Experimental coach
3 steam rail cranes
SR Travelling Post Office

Owners
34081 (the Battle of Britain Locomotive Preservation Society)
73050 (Peterborough City Council)
3.628 (Science Museum)
70000 (the Britannia Locomotive Society)
804 (Museum of World Railways)

adjacent to Wansford station souvenir shop. Disabled persons and helpers are eligible for concessionary fares. Passengers can be assisted on and off trains
Membership details: Mrs D. Foster, 409 Oundle Road, Peterborough

Right:
Wansford station on the Nene Valley Railway on 25 March 1989 with GWR '2884' No 3822 awaiting the right of way. No 3822 was on loan from the Didcot Railway Centre. *Melvyn Hopwood*

North Norfolk Railway

Part of the former Midland & Great Northern Joint Railway, other elements of the LNER have crept in in the guise of the Great Eastern 'J15', the 'B12' now being restored and a variety of Gresley coaches. The newly opened extension to Holt has opened up extensive views of the Norfolk coast and the steep gradients belie the county's reputation for flatness
Headquarters: North Norfolk Railway, Sheringham station, Sheringham, Norfolk, NR26 8RA
Telephone: Sheringham (0263) 822045. Talking timetable: (0263) 825449
Main station: Sheringham
Other public stations: Weybourne, Kelling Heath Park, Holt
OS reference: Sheringham TG 156430, Weybourne TG 118419
Car parks: Sheringham (old goods yard), Weybourne, Holt
Access by public transport: Sheringham BR station (200 yards)
Refreshment facilities: Sheringham, Weybourne
Souvenir shops: Sheringham, Weybourne
Museum: Sheringham
Depot: Weybourne
Length of line: 5¼ miles

Locomotives

Name	No	Origin	Class	Type	Built
—	564	GER	J15	0-6-0	1912
—	61572	LNER	B12	4-6-0	1928
—	12131	BR	11	0-6-0DE	1952
—	27066	BR	27	Bo-Bo	1962

Industrial locomotives

Name	No	Builder	Type	Built
Pony	—	H/Leslie (2918)	0-4-0ST	1912
Ring Haw	—	Hunslet (1982)	0-6-0ST	1940
—	3809	Hunslet (3809)	0-6-0ST	1954
Harlaxton	—	Barclay (2107)	0-6-0T	1941
Birchenwood	4	Bagnall (2680)	0-6-0ST	1944
John D Hammer	5	Peckett (1970)	0-6-0ST	1939
—	12	RSH (7845)	0-6-0T	1955
—	10	E/Electric (C8431)	0-4-0DH	1963
—	4	Fowler (4210080)	4wDM	1953
Wissington	—	H/Clarke (1700)	0-6-0ST	1938
—	—	Bagnall (2370)	0-6-0F	1929
Edmundsons	—	Barclay (2168)	0-4-0ST	1940

Stock
2 Wagon und Maschinenbau ex-BR diesel railbuses
10 ex-BR coaches
2 ex-SR 'Brighton Belle' Pullman cars
7 ex-LNER coaches
Small number of wagons

Owners
564 and 61572 (the Midland & Great Northern Railway Society)

Passenger trains: Steeply graded, Sheringham-Weybourne-Holt
Period of public operation: Please contact for details
Special events: Santa Specials in December
Facilities for disabled: Specially adapted Pullman Car available, advanced booking essential
Feature article references: RW July 1989, p433 (last days of the M&GNJR)

Right:
Built by Peckett in 1939 this 0-6-0ST now sees action on the North Norfolk Railway. Named *John D. Hammer* it is seen at Weybourne on 6 August 1989 on its way to Holt. *Melvyn Hopwood*

Wells & Walsingham Light Railway

One man's railway, the life and love of retired naval commander, Roy Francis, this delightful line which is totally uncommercialised runs along the old Wells branch to Walsingham where the old station has been transformed into a Russian Orthodox Church by the addition of an onion-shaped dome to its roof. A must if you find yourself nearby

Location: On A149, Stiffkey Road, Wells next the Sea, Norfolk
Operating organisation: Wells & Walsingham Light Railway
Car park: Yes
Access by public transport: Eastern Counties buses
On site facilities: Souvenir and tea shop
Length of line: 4 miles, 10¼in gauge

Public opening: Daily Easter to the end September
Special notes: Journey may be commenced at either end, believed to be world's longest 10¼in gauge line. Built on the old Wells & Fakenham Railway trackbed. Old Swainsthorpe signalbox on site at Wells. Motive power is provided by a Garratt locomotive

Wolferton Station Museum   M

Location: In the village of Wolferton which is on the Sandringham Estate in Norfolk
OS reference: TF 661286
Operating society/organisation: Operated by Roger E. Hedly-Walker, 'Downside', Wolferton, King's Lynn, Norfolk PE31 6HA
Telephone: Dersingham (0485) 40674

Car and coach park: Available in former goods yard
Access by public transport: None (nearest bus stop from King's Lynn is one mile away)
On site facilities: Museum and souvenir shop
Period of public opening: 1 April-30 September, Monday-Friday, 11.00-

13.00 and 14.00-17.30. Saturday closed. Sunday 14.00-17.30
Special notes: On display are the former Royal Retiring Rooms and display of rail relics and general Victoriana and Edwardiana. On one level, so suitable for wheelchairs

North West

Blackpool & Fleetwood Tramway

Operating organisation: Blackpool Transport Services Ltd, Rigby Road, Blackpool, Lancashire FY1 5DD
Telephone: (0253) 23931
Length of line: 11½ miles, standard gauge
Period of public operation: Daily throughout the year
Number of trams: 86 double- and single-deck trams

The Blackpool & Fleetwood Tramway is the sole surviving street tramway system in the United Kingdom and attracts visitors from all over the country. During the autumn the streets are illuminated and several specially decorated trams are used

East Lancashire Railway

A very popular yet newly opened railway by the East Lancs Railway Society in close co-operation with local authorities, the line won the 1987 ARPS award. Visit the line to find out the cause of the line's popularity and success
Location: Bolton Street Station, Bury, Lancashire BL9 0EY
OS reference: SD 803109
Operating society/organisation: East Lancashire Railway Preservation Society
Telephone: 061 764 7790
Access by public transport: BR to Bury Interchange (not Sundays). GM Buses, Rossendale Transport and Ribble Motor Services to Bury
On site facilities: Refreshments normally available when trains are running. Buffet car service on most trains. Souvenir shop, transport museum
Length of line: Approximately 4 miles
Public opening: Steam and diesel-hauled services operate on Saturdays, Sundays and Bank Holidays throughout the year. Santa Specials (advanced booking only) in December
Special events: Diesel Enthusiast's Weekend 16/17 June and 6/7 October; Teddy Bear Picnic 27 August; Santa Specials (please see press for details)

Locomotives

Name	No	Origin	Class	Type	Built
—	7298	LMS	3F	0-6-0T	1924
—	45337	LMS	5MT	4-6-0	1937
—	46428	LMS	2MT	2-6-0	1948
—	73156	BR	5MT	4-6-0	1956
—	76079	BR	4MT	2-6-0	1957
—	80097	BR	4MT	2-6-4T	1954
Morning Star	92207	BR	9F	2-10-0	1959
—	D335*	BR	40	1Co-Co1	1961
—	40145*	BR	40	1Co-Co1	1961
Onslaught	D832	BR	42	B-B	1961
Western Prince	D1041	BR	52	C-C	1962
—	D2587	BR	05	0-6-0DM	1959
—	D2767	BR	—	0-4-0DH	1960
—	D2774	BR	—	0-4-0DH	1960
—	D2956	BR	01	0-4-0DM	1956
—	D5054	BR	24	Bo-Bo	1960
—	D7076	BR	35	B-B	1963
—	25901	BR	25	Bo-Bo	1966
—	D7659	BR	25	Bo-Bo	1966
—	D9531	BR	14	0-6-0DH	1965

*May not be on site for all of 1990

Industrial locomotives

Name	No	Builder	Type	Built
Gothenburg	32	H/Clarke (680)	0-6-0T	1903
Phoenix	70	H/Clarke (1464)	0-6-0T	1921
Sir Robert Peel	8	Hunslet (3789)	0-6-0ST	1953
—	193	Hunslet (3793)	0-6-0ST	1953
—	1	Barclay (1927)	0-4-0ST	1927

Special Notes: The Society re-opened a section of the former Bury-Rawtenstall line as far as Ramsbottom, in July 1987 and carried over 26,000 passengers in its first three months of operation. The remaining 4½ miles is due to re-open in 1990

MEA No 1	1	RSH (7683)	0-6-0T	1951
—	DH16	Sentinel (10175)	4wDH	1964
Mr Mercury	1	Hibberd (3438)	4wDM	1950
Winfield	—	M/Rail (9009)	4wDM	1948

Stock
19 BR Mk 1 coaches
Battery-electric multiple-unit Nos SC79998/9
1 L&YR coach
2 Bogie Guards coaches
3 Newspaper vans
Cravens 50-ton steam crane RS1013/50 (1930), NER 5-ton hand crane DB915390 (1880) and Smiths 5-ton diesel crane (1939) plus a small number of other goods vehicles

Owners
D345 (the Class 40 Preservation Society)
193 (on loan from Peak Rail)
Battery-electric MU (on loan from the West Yorkshire Transport Museum)

Greater Manchester Museum of Science & Industry   M

Location: Liverpool Road Station, Castlefield, Manchester (off Deansgate near Granada)
OS reference: SJ 831987
Operating society/organisation: Greater Manchester Museum of Science & Industry, Liverpool Road Station, Liverpool Road, Castlefield, Manchester M3 4JP
Telephone: 061 832 2244
Car parks: On site, plus parking in the area (museum car park 50p)
Access by public transport: Manchester Victoria, Piccadilly and Oxford Road BR stations. GM bus 33
On site facilities: Oldest passenger railway station, weekend train rides, former railway warehouses containing exhibitions about science, industry, aviation, space, water supply and sewage disposal and electricity. New exhibitions include The Manchester Story and Xperiment! Also a licensed buffet and shop
Public opening: Daily except 23, 24 and 25 December, including Saturdays and Sundays, 10.00-17.00. Entrance in Lower Byrom Street. Admission charged
Special events: Castlefield Carnival held during the August Bank Holiday weekend
Special notes: Some wheelchair access, toilets for the disabled, lecture and conference facilities

Locomotives

Name	No	Origin	Class	Type	Built
Magpie	44806	LMS	5MT	4-6-0	1944
Pender	3*	IoMR	—	2-4-0T	1873
Novelty	Powered replica of 1929 locomotive using some original parts				
—	3157†	PR	—	4-4-0	1911
—	2352‡	SAR	GL	4-8-2+2-8-4	1929
Ariadne	1505 (27001)	BR	EM2 (77)	Co-Co	1954
Hector	26048	BR	EM1 (76)	Bo-Bo cab only	—

Industrial locomotives

Name	No	Builder	Type	Built
Agecroft No 3	—	RSH (7681)	0-4-0ST	1951
—	—	Barclay (1964)	0-4-0ST	1929
—	—	E/Electric (1378)	4wBE	1944
—	—	H/Leslie (3682)	Bo-Bo	1927
—	—	Fowler	0-6-0	—

*Ex-Isle of Man Railways, 3ft gauge, sectioned (B/Peacock 1255)
†Ex-Pakistan Railways, 5ft 6in gauge (V/Foundry 3064)
‡Ex-South African Railways, 3ft 6in gauge (B/Peacock 6693)

Rolling stock
BR Restaurant Car (RU(A), BRCW Co Ltd, 1959
31217 BR passenger bogie brake van, LMS (Wolverton), 1944
B955209 20-ton goods brake van, BR (Ashford), 1962
B782903 4-wheeled covered goods van, BR (Wolverton), 1961
B783709 4-wheeled covered goods van, BR (Wolverton), 1962
3-plank loose coupled goods wagon, MSLR (Dukinfield)?, c1890

Owners
Novelty on loan from the Science Museum, London
RU (A) Birmingham Railways Coach & Wagon Co Ltd

Lakeside & Haverthwaite Railway

Originally this Furness Railway branch line carried passengers and freight from Ulverston to Lakeside but now the only part remaining is the 3½-mile section from Haverthwaite to the terminus at Lakeside where connections are made with the 'Windermere Cruises' which ply the 10-mile length of Lake Windermere

Headquarters: Haverthwaite station, near Ulverston, Cumbria LA12 8AL

Telephone: Newby Bridge (05395) 31594

Main station: Haverthwaite

Other public stations: Intermediate station at Newby Bridge. Terminus at Lakeside

OS reference: SD 349843

Car parks: Haverthwaite, Lakeside

Access by public transport: Windermere Cruises ships on Lake Windermere call at Lakeside. Ribble bus to Haverthwaite

Refreshment facilities: Haverthwaite

Souvenir shop: Haverthwaite

Depot: All rolling stock at Haverthwaite

Length of line: 3½ miles

Passenger trains: Steam-hauled Haverthwaite-Lakeside

Period of public operation: Easter then daily from early-May to end of September. Sundays only in October.

Special events: Santa Specials 15/16 December (advance booking essential)

Special notes: Combined railway/lake steamer tickets available, from the station at Haverthwaite and 'Windermere Cruises' piers at Bowness and Ambleside. 'Windermere Cruises' is operated by Windermere Iron Steamboat Co Ltd

Locomotives

Name	No	Origin	Class	Type	Built
—	2073	LMS	4MT	2-6-4T	1950
—	42085	LMS	4MT	2-6-4T	1951
—	8(D2117)	BR	03	0-6-0DM	1959
—	17(AD601)	LMS	—	0-6-0DE	1945
—	03.072	BR	03	0-6-0DM	1959
—	5643*	GWR	5600	0-6-2T	1925

*Under restoration at Steamtown, Carnforth

Industrial locomotives

Name	No	Builder	Type	Built
Caliban	1	Peckett (1925)	0-4-0ST	1937
Rachel	9	M/Rail (2098)	4wDM	1924
Repulse	11	Hunslet (3698)	0-6-0ST	1950
Princess	14	Bagnall (2682)	0-6-0ST	1942
Askam Hall	15	Avonside	0-4-0ST	1935
Alexandra	12	Barclay (929)	0-4-0ST	1902
David	13	Barclay (2333)	0-4-0ST	1953
Cumbria	10	Hunslet (3794)	0-6-0ST	1953
—	7	Fowler (22919)	0-4-0DM	1940
Fluff	16	Hunslet/Fowler	0-4-0DM	1937
—	20	Jones crane	0-4-0DM	1952
—	21	Barclay (1550)	0-6-0F	1917
—	22	Fowler (4220045)	0-4-0DM	1967

Stock

10 ex-BR Mk 1 coaches
1 ex-LNER BG
1 ex-BR Mk 1 miniature buffet coach
Small selection of freight vehicles

Liverpool Museum   M

A fine selection of vehicles in a traditional 'stuffed and mounted' display. The railway vehicles are due to move to nearby premises in January 1990. But at the time of going to press their availability for public viewing is uncertain. Visitors are advised to enquire by telephone before arranging a visit

Locomotives

Name	No	Origin	Class	Type	Built
Lion*	57	L&MR	—	0-4-2	1838

*Lion is the oldest working locomotive in the world

Industrial locomotives

Name	No	Builder	Type	Built
—	1	Avonside (1465)	0-6-0ST	1904

Location: William Brown Street, Liverpool
Operating society/organisation: National Museums and Galleries on Merseyside, William Brown Street, Liverpool L3 8EN
Telephone: 051-207 0001
Car parks: Public car parks nearby
Access by public transport: Adjacent Lime Street stations (BR and Merseyrail).

Stock
LOR electric coach of 1893
L&MR replica coaches built Derby 1929

Numerous bus routes
On site facilities: Cafe, shop
Public opening: Please contact for details
Special notes: Transport gallery
within large general museum.
Facilities for disabled visitors
Feature article references: RW April 1988, p218 (*Lion* — also RW May 1988, p277)

Ravenglass & Eskdale Railway

Originally built to serve iron ore mines in Eskdale, this delightful line makes an ideal 'tourist' line running as it does through wooded valleys and along rugged hillsides
Headquarters: Ravenglass & Eskdale Railway, Ravenglass station, Cumbria
Telephone: 0229 717171
Main station: Ravenglass
Other public stations: Muncaster Mill, Irton Road, The Green, Eskdale (Dalegarth)
OS reference: SD 086964
Car parks: All stations
Access by public transport: BR services to Ravenglass
Refreshment facilities: Ravenglass, Dalegarth. Bar meals at 'Ratty Arms'
Souvenir shops: Ravenglass, Dalegarth
Museum: Ravenglass
Length of line: 7 miles, 15in gauge
Passenger trains: Steam or diesel-hauled narrow gauge trains Ravenglass-Dalegarth
Period of public operation: Daily from late March-late October. Limited winter service November-March
Special events: Family Day 26 May

Locomotives

Name	No	Builder	Type	Built
River Irt	—	Heywood	0-8-2	1894
River Esk	—	Davey Paxman (21104)	2-8-2	1923
River Mite	—	Clarkson (4669)	2-8-2	1966
Northern Rock	—	R&ER	2-6-2	1976
Bonny Dundee	—	K/Stuart (720)*	0-4-2WT	1901
Shelagh of Eskdale	—	R&ER/Severn-Lamb	4-6-4DH	1969
Quarryman	—	Muir-Hill (2)	0-4-0P/Paraffin	1928
Perkins	—	Muir Hill (NG39A)	0-4-4DM	1929
Silver Jubilee	—	R&ER	DMU	1977
Lady Wakefield	—	R&ER	Bo-Bo	1980
Synolda	—	Bassett-Lowke	4-4-2	1912
—	—	Greenbat (2782)	0-4-0B	1957
Cyril	—	Lister	0-4-0DM	1987

*Rebuilt to 15in gauge 1981

Facilities for disabled: Special coaches for wheel-chair passengers. Advance notice preferred. Wheelchair access to toilets and museum at Ravenglass; toilets, shop and cafe at Eskdale (Dalegarth)
Special notes: At Ravenglass the R&ER has two camping coaches and the company also operates the 'Ratty Arms' public house formed by conversion of the former BR station buildings. During the high summer, mid-July through August, five steam locomotives are normally in use Monday-Thursday
Membership details: A. N. Grayston, 'Brunel', 10 Harriot Hill, Cockermouth, Cumbria CA13 0BL

South Tynedale Railway

A narrow gauge line passing through the attractive scenery of the South Tyne valley, in the North Pennine area of outstanding natural beauty
Location: Approximately ¼-mile north of Alston town centre, on A686 Hexham road
OS reference: NY 717467
Operating society: South Tynedale Railway Preservation Society, The Railway Station, Alston, Cumbria CA9 3JB

Locomotives

Name	No	Builder	Type	Built
Phoenix	1	Hibberd (2325)	4wDM	1941
Ayle	2	Hudson-Hunslet (2607)	4wDM	1942
Sao Domingos	3	O/K (11784)	0-6-0WT	1928
Naworth	4	H/Clarke (DM819)	0-6-0DM	1952
—	5	Simplex (11297)	4wDM	1964
Thomas Edmondson	6	Henschel (16047)	0-4-0T	1918
The Peril	8	Hunslet (6347)	4wDM	1975
Naklo	10	Chrzanow (3459)	0-6-0WTT	1957
Tiny Tim	—	Hunslet (6619)	0-4-0DM	1966

Telephone: Alston (0434) 381696
Car park: Alston station
Access by public transport: Wright Bros buses, Haltwhistle-Alston and Newcastle-Alston-Keswick.
Enquiries: Tel: Alston (0434) 381200. Also summer Sunday buses from Stanhope in connection with 'Heritage Line' trains. Details: (091 386) 4411 ext 2498. Bus links from Langwathby in connection with 'Dalesrail' trains on certain dates — see 'Dalesrail' publicity for details
On site facilities: Book and souvenir shop, tourist information centre, refreshments, picnic area, toilets (including disabled persons)
Catering facilities: Tea room at Alston, serving selection of snacks and home baking
Length of line: 1½ miles, 2ft gauge
Public opening: Passenger train service from Alston to Gilderdale: April — Easter weekend then Sundays; May — Saturday, Sundays, May Day Holiday, Spring Bank Holiday Week; June and September — Tuesdays, Wednesdays, Thursdays, Saturdays, Sundays; July and August — daily; October — Sundays. Departures from 11.15 until 16.00 or 17.00. Steam haulage scheduled at weekends from Spring Bank Holiday until end of September, also Easter and May Day weekends
Journey time: c40min
Special events: Children's Day — 30 May; Teddy Bear Day — 24 June; Steam Enthusiasts' Weekend — 28/29 July; Edwardian Day — 9 September; Diesel Day — 14 October; Santa Specials — 8/9, 15/16 December; Mince Pie Specials 29/30 December
Special notes: The line has been constructed on the trackbed of the former BR Haltwhistle-Alston branch. Extension of the line from Gilderdale towards Slaggyford, a further 3 miles, has commenced
Membership details: Membership Secretary c/o above address
Feature article reference: RW February 1989, p92

Locomotive notes: In addition to several of the above, the visiting Hunslet steam locomotive *Chaka's Kraal No 6* is expected to be in service during the 1990 season

Stock
6 bogie coaches
1 brake van
1 bogie box van
1 bogie open wagon
5 4-wheel open wagons
1 4-wheel box van
1 4-wheel flat wagon
1 fuel tank wagon
2 bogie well wagons
6 bogie hopper wagons

Owners
2, 3, 4, 8 and 9 (the Durham Narrow Gauge Group)
Tiny Tim (the Ayle Colliery Co)

Right:
Contrasts on 2ft gauge. Visiting locomotives to the South Tynedale Railway for its Enthusiasts' Weekend were *Chaka's Kraal No 6* and *Peter Pan*. They are seen at Alston. *N. E. Stead*

Exhibits include ex-Liverpool Riverside signalbox and the restored turntable facilities using the turntable from York (Queen St). A working ex-Midland Railway water column from London St Pancras is a dominant feature of the site. Steamport has been a servicing point for the annual Southport-Manchester steam specials since 1985

Location: Five minutes from BR station, via London Street. Behind car park

OS reference: SD 341170

Operating society/organisation: Steamport Southport Ltd, Derby Road, Southport PR9 0TY

Telephone: Southport (0704) 30693

Car park: Derby Road

Access by public transport: BR station, Merseyrail from Liverpool

On site facilities: Souvenir shop. Cafe open Sundays and Bank Holidays at weekends. Steam hauled rides in LMS brake vans June-end September, plus special events. Buffet car in operation on special events. Santa Steam trains in December

Length of line: 600yd

Public opening: Weekends May-September 11.00-17.00, October-April 14.00-17.00; Weekdays June-mid September 13.00-17.00 (July-August 11.00-17.00)

Facilities for disabled: Access to all parts of museum. No toilets. No advanced notice required

Locomotives

Name	No	Origin	Class	Type	Built
Cecil Raikes	5	Mersey Railway	—	0-6-4T	1886
—	5193	GWR	5101	2-6-2T	1934
—	D2148	BR	03	0-6-0DM	1960
—	D2953	BR	05	0-6-0DM	1959
—	24081	BR	24	Bo-Bo	1958

Industrial locomotives

Name	No	Builder	Type	Built
—	5	Peckett (2153)	0-6-0ST	1954
North Western Gas Board	—	Peckett (1999)	0-4-0ST	1941
Waleswood	—	H/Clarke (750)	0-4-0ST	1906
Fitzwilliam	—	Hunslet (1954)	0-6-0ST	1939
—	—	Hunslet (3155)	0-6-0ST	1943
Glasshoughton	4	Hunslet (3855)	0-6-0ST	1954
Persil	—	Fowler (4160001)	0-4-0DM	1952
*Lucy**	—	Avonside (1568)	0-6-0ST	1909
*Efficient**	—	Barclay (1598)	0-4-0ST	1918
Agecroft No 2	—	RSH (7485)	0-4-0ST	1948
St Monans	—	Sentinel (9373)	4wVBT	1947
Hornet	—	Peckett (1935)	0-4-0ST	1937
Whitehead	—	Peckett (1163)	0-4-0ST	1908
—	—	Greenwood & Batley (2000)	0-4-0BE	1958
Sefton	—	T/Hill (123V)	4wDM	1963
Stanlow No 4	4	T/Hill (160V)	0-4-0DM	1966
—	—	N/British (27653)	0-4-0DH	1956
—	D2870	YEC (2677)	0-4-0DM	1960

Stock

Small selection of rolling stock including Class 502 EMU, M28361M and M29896M on loan from NRM, and buffet car Sc1839 and BSK 35128
1 Smith-Rodley diesel crane

Owner

Cecil Raikes (Liverpool Museum)
*Stock (Liverpool Locomotive Preservation Group)

Right:
Following a number of years' industrial use by the NCB, former BR Class 03 shunter No D2148 is now restored to original condition at Steamport, Southport. It was photographed in August 1989.
W. C. Knox

Formerly BR Carnforth motive power depot. Carnforth is a centre for 'Steam on BR' steam-hauled railtours over BR main lines.

Location: Steamtown Railway Centre, Warton Road, Carnforth, Lancashire LA5 9HX

OS reference: SD 496708

Operating society/organisation: Steamtown Railway Museum Ltd

Telephone: Carnforth (0524) 734220

Car park: Free car park on site

Access by public transport: BR services to Carnforth station. Bus services to Carnforth by Ribble and Lancaster City Transport

Catering facilities: Cafe for meals and snacks, several picnic areas

On site facilities: Model railway, signalbox, collectors' corner, shop, cafe, 15in gauge railway

Length of line: Standard gauge ¾-mile, 15in gauge 1-mile

Public opening: Weekends all year round, daily Easter-October. Summer 10.00-16.00, winter 11.00-16.00. Locomotives in steam on Bank Holidays, Sundays from Easter-October, and daily during July-August

Below:
On Good Friday, 24 March 1989, LMS 'Black 5' No 5407 was caught as it coasted through Denton, south of Guide Bridge. The train was bound for Chester and Crewe having run from Carnforth, Blackburn and Manchester Victoria. *David Eatwell*

Locomotives

Name	No	Origin	Class	Type	Built
Britannia*	70000	BR	7MT	4-6-2	1951
Flying Scotsman†	4472	LNER	A3	4-6-2	1923
Lord Nelson	850	SR	LN	4-6-0	1926
—	5643	GWR	5600	0-6-2T	1925
Sovereign	44871	LMS	5MT	4-6-0	1945
—	44932‡	LMS	5MT	4-6-0	1945
—	5407	LMS	5MT	4-6-0	1937
—	6441	LMS	2MT	2-6-0	1950
—	1300	L&Y	27	0-6-0	1896
—	D2381	BR	03	0-6-0DM	1960
—	03120	BR	03	0-6-0DM	1959
—	D5500	BR	31	A1A-A1A	1957
—	D335§	BR	40	1Co-Co1	1961
—	40145§	BR	40	1Co-Co1	1961
La France	231K22	SNCF	231K	4-6-2	1914
—	01.2104-6	DB	01	4-6-2	1940

*On site for restoration to BR standards for main line operation
†Sometimes based in London area for main line running
‡Shares time between here and Midland Railway Centre
§Expected to arrive during 1990

Industrial locomotives

Name	No	Builder	Type	Built
Sirapite	6158	A/Porter (6158)	0-4-0TG	1906
Elizabeth	—	Avonside (1865)	0-4-0ST	1922
Pitsford	—	Avonside (1917)	0-6-0ST	1923
John Howe	5	Barclay (1147)	0-4-0ST	1908
Coronation	3	Barclay (2134)	0-4-0ST	1942
Cooke & Nuttal	1	Barclay (2230)	0-4-0ST	1947
British Gypsum	4	Barclay (2343)	0-4-0ST	1953
Glenfield	1	Barclay (880)	0-4-0CT	1902
May	—	Peckett (1370)	0-4-0ST	1915
Trimpell	—	Bagnall (3019)	0-6-0F	1953
Cranford No 2	—	Bagnall (2668)	0-6-0ST	1942
Great Central	39	RSH(6947)	0-6-0T	1938
Barrow Steel No 7	FR 18	S/Stewart (1435)	0-6-0ST	1863

Facilities for disabled: Limited, toilets available, standard gauge trains can accommodate wheelchairs
Special notes: Scheduled steam hauled excursions during summer season, operate from Carnforth with through connections from main centres
Feature article reference: RW July 1988, p405

Name	No	Builder	Type	Built
Barrow Steel No 17	FR 25	S/Stewart (1585)	0-4-0ST	1865
Lindsay	—	Wigan Coal & Iron Co	0-6-0ST	1887
Flying Flea	D3	R/Hornsby (294266)	0-4-0DM	1951
Joyce	—	Sentinel (7109)	4wVBTG	1950
Gasbag	—	Sentinel (8024)	4wVBTG	1923
Esso	—	General Electric (30483)	Bo-Bo	1949
Lord Leverhulme	—	Barclay (388)	0-4-0DM	1953
Lord Trenchard	—	Barclay (401)	0-4-0DM	1956
Tom Rolt	7049	Hunslet (2697)	0-6-0DM	1944

Stock
4 pre-Grouping vehicles
1 GWR saloon
5 LNER coaches
2 LMS coaches
6 BR coaches
Small selection of freight vehicles
3 steam cranes
1 diesel crane

Owners
1300 (the Fairclough Corporation)
850 and D5500 (on loan from the National Railway Museum)
5643 (the Lakeside & Haverthwaite Railway)

West Lancashire Light Railway   SC

Location: Alty's Brickworks. Station Road, Hesketh Bank, near Preston, Lancashire
OS reference: SD 448229
Operating society/organisation: The West Lancashire Light Railway Association, Secretary, 790 Ormskirk Road, Pemberton, Wigan WN5 8AX
Telephone: (0942) 218078 (Secretary)
Car parks: On site
Access by public transport: BR to Preston or Southport. Bus route 100 and 102. Between Preston and Southport
On site facilities: Gift shop, light refreshments, 2ft gauge line
Public opening: Easter weekend (not Saturday); May Day Bank Holiday Sunday and Monday; Spring Bank Holiday, then every Sunday until end of October. Opening times 13.00-17.30
Special events: Enthusiast's Day 15 July; Santa Specials 9, 16 December
Special notes: Disabled welcome. Wheelchairs carried in brake van

Industrial locomotives

Name	No	Builder	Type	Built
Clwyd	1	R/Hornsby (264251)	4wDM	1951
Tawd	2	R/Hornsby (222074)	4wDM	1943
Irish Mail	3	Hunslet (823)	0-4-0ST	1903
—	4	Hibberd (1777)	4wPM	1931
—	5	R/Hornsby (200478)	4wDM	1940
—	7	M/Rail (8992)	4wDM	1946
—	8	H/Hunslet (4480)	4wDM	1953
—	9	K/Stuart (2405)	0-6-0T	1915
—	10	Hibberd (2555)	4wDM	1946
—	16	R/Hornsby (202036)	4wDM	1941
Trent	18	R/Hornsby (283057)	4wDM	1949
—	19	Lister (10805)	4wPM	1939
—	20	Baguley (3002)	4wPM	1937
—	21	H/Hunslet (1963)	4wDM	1939
—	25	R/Hornsby (297054)	4wDM	1950
—	26	M/Rail (11223)	4wDM	1963
Mill Reef	27	M/Rail (7371)	4wDM	1939
Red Rum	29	M/Rail (7105)	4wDM	1936
—	30	M/Rail (11258)	4wDM	1964
Montalban	34	O&K (6641)	0-4-0WT	1913
Utrillas	35	O&K (2378)	0-4-0WT	1907
—	36	R/Hornsby (339105)	4wDM	1953
—	38	Hudswell (D750)	0-4-0DM	1949
Jonathan*	—	Hunslet (678)	0-4-0ST	1898

*On loan from The Lytham Creek Motive Power Museum
Note: 30 M/Rail (11258) is presently on loan to Steamport Southport

Stock
Southport Pier railway coach
Saloon coach built by WLLR
Toastrack coach built 1986 by WLLR
Brake van built 1987 by WLLR
Large collection various wagons

North East

Beamish   SC

The railway station, signalbox and goods shed have been completely recreated along with the other exhibits to show a way of life long past. There are some very old locomotives in the collection
Location: The North of England Open Air Museum, Beamish, County Durham DH9 0RG
OS reference: NZ 217547
Telephone: Stanley (0207) 231811
Car park: At museum
Access by public transport: Bus service from Worswick Street, Newcastle upon Tyne; Bus service Nos 775 and 778 from Sunderland via Chester-le-Street; Bus service 720 from Milburngate, Durham City
On site facilities: 200-acre open air museum vividly recreates life in the North of England around the turn of the century. The town with dentist's home and surgery, solicitor's office, the Sun Inn public house, Co-operative shops and printer's workshop. The railway station with country station, goods yard, signalbox and rolling stock and locomotives often in steam. The Colliery Village with furnished pit cottages, 'drift' mine and colliery buildings. Home Farm with farm house, livestock and exhibitions. Tea Room, souvenir shop and picnic areas
Public opening: April-October (inclusive) daily 10.00-18.00.

Locomotives

Name	No	Origin	Class	Type	Built
—	876	NER	C1	0-6-0	1889
Locomotion	1*	—	—	0-4-0	1975

*Replica

Industrial locomotives

Name	No	Builder	Type	Built
Twizell	3	Stephenson (2730)	0-6-0T	1891
—	14	H/Leslie (3056)	0-4-0ST	1914
South Durham Malleable	No 5	Stockton Ironworks	0-4-0ST	c1880
Coffee Pot	—	Head Wrightson	0-4-0VB	1871
—	18	Lewin (683)	0-4-0WT	1863
—	E1	Black, Hawthorn (897)	2-4-0CT	1883
Hetton Loco	—	G. Stephenson (1)	0-4-0	1822
—	—	R/Hornsby (476140)	0-4-0DM	1963

Owner
Hetton Loco (on loan from National Railway Museum)

Note
Not all exhibits on display

November-March (inclusive) daily except Mondays 10.00-17.00. Last admission is always 4pm. Please check for Christmas opening times. Locomotives do not steam, and some areas are closed in winter months
Special events: Beamish Commercial Vehicle Event 2 September
Length of line: Approx ½-mile single line connecting rebuilt NER station to colliery sidings. No through passenger trains
Facilities for disabled: Not ideal for wheelchairs. Rolling stock not converted. Advanced notice for parties to Bookings Officer preferred
Special notes: European Museum of the Year 1987

Bowes Railway   SC

The railway includes the only preserved rope-hauled standard gauge inclines, whose operation requires considerable skill and sleight of hand. You should not miss the opportunity of inspecting the inclines and cable house and haulage engine when you can

Industrial locomotives

Name	No	Builder	Type	Built
WST	—	Barclay (2361)	0-4-0ST	1954
—	22	Barclay (2274)	0-4-0ST	1949
—	—	Barclay	0-6-0DH	1977
—	6163	Hunslet	0-4-0DM	1964
Norwood	77	RSH (7412)	0-6-0ST	1948

Location: Bowes Railway, Springwell Village, near Gateshead, Tyne & Wear (on B1288)
OS reference: NZ 285589
Operating society/organisation: Bowes Railway Co Ltd
Telephone: Tyneside (091) 4161847 (Answerphone)
Car park: Springwell
Access by public transport: Northern Buses services Nos 184 Washington/Birtley, 187/188 Gateshead Metro/Sunderland, 189 Washington (Brady Sq)-Gateshead 638 Ryton/Sunderland
On site facilities: Exhibition of Railway's history, wagon exhibition, workshop displays. On operating days — shop, refreshments and guided tours. Steam hauled brake van rides. Rope haulage demonstration trains
Public opening: Bank Holidays, also first and third Sundays in each month, Easter-September (tel: (091) 2622651 for confirmation)
Length of line: 1¼ miles total length; 1¼ miles of rope haulage; ¾-mile used for passenger trains
Special notes: Preserved section of the Pontop & Jarrow Railway; designed G. Stephenson; opened 1826; the only standard gauge rope-hauled incline railway in the world; Railway's own historic workshops preserved, with examples of all of the Railway's wagon types
Facilities for disabled: Toilet only
Membership details: Management

Name	No	Builder	Type	Built
—	101	Planet (3922)	4wDM	1959
—	—	Smith (18773)	4wCT	1948

Owners
22 (On loan from Thomas Ness Ltd)
WST (On loan from British Gypsum Ltd)
Norwood (On loan from National Smokeless Fuels)
Barclay 0-6-0DH (On loan from Mr P. Dawe)
Hunslet (On loan from Coal Products, Ness)
Planet and Smith (Bowes Railway Co Ltd)

Stock
20 Ordinary 10-ton wooden hopper wagons (Springwell built)
16 other wooden hopper wagons (of various pedigrees)
2 steel 14-ton hopper wagons
1 steel 21-ton hopper wagon
1 reel bogie (for rope replacement)
1 drift bogie (for shunting by rope)
1 loco coal wagon
7 material wagons
1 tool van
3 brake vans
2 flat wagons
2 wooden hopper wagons (ex-Seaham Harbour)

Stationary haulage
Met-Vick/Wild, 300bhp electric (Blackham's Hill) 1950
BTH/Robey, 500bhp electric (Black Fell) 1950
Clarke Chapman, 22hp electric (Springwell Yard)
14ft Diam, Gravity Dilly Wheel (Springwell)

Committee Secretary, c/o above address or telephone number
Disclaimer: The Bowes Railway Co Ltd wish to point out that all advertised facilities are subject to alteration without prior notice. The company can therefore not be held responsible for any loss or expense incurred

Darlington Railway Centre and Museum   M

Located on the original 1825 route of the Stockton & Darlington Railway, the restored North Road station, dating from 1842, is now a museum which forms the centerpiece of an area devoted to railway history and preservation. The collection includes locomotives, rolling stock and many small exhibits. The site also includes two other historic buildings of the S&DR — the former Goods Shed and the Hopetown Carriage Works. Plans for future development envisage regular operation of restored locomotives. British Rail's 'Heritage Line' provides a link to Darlington's main line station and to Shildon, for the Timothy Hackworth Museum
Location: North Road station, Darlington, County Durham DL3 6ST. Approximately ¾-mile north of town centre, off North Road (A167)
OS reference: NZ 289157

Locomotives

Name	No	Origin	Class	Type	Built
Locomotion	1	S&DR	—	0-4-0	1825
Derwent	25	S&DR	—	0-6-0	1845
—	1463	NER	1463	2-4-0	1885
—	910	NER	901	2-4-0	1875

Industrial locomotives

Name	No	Builder	Type	Built
Met	—	H/Leslie (2800)	0-4-0ST	1909
—	17	Head Wrightson (33)	0-4-0VB	1873
—	—	Bagnall (2898)	0-4-0F	1948
—	39	RSH (6947)	0-6-0T	1938

Stock
1 Stockton & Darlington Rly passenger coach (1846)
1 North Eastern Railway Coach body (c1860)
1 NER 20-ton mineral wagon
1 Chaldron wagon

Telephone: 0325 460532
Car park: At museum site
Access by public transport: BR services to Darlington North Road station. Local bus services along North Road
Catering facilities: Confectionery and drinks. Party catering by arrangement
On site facilities: Souvenir and book shop. Toilets
Public opening: Daily throughout the year 09.30-17.00 (except Christmas/New Year holidays). Last admission 16.30 (times may be subject to amendment)
Special events: Railway Carnival 29/30 September (subject to confirmation)
Facilities for disabled: Access to main museum building for wheelchairs. Disabled persons toilet
Membership details: Friends of Darlington Railway Museum and Darlington Railway Preservation Society, both c/o above address
Note: Additional locomotives and

Owners
Locomotion, Derwent, 1463 and 910 are all on loan from the National Railway Museum

Darlington Railway Preservation Society
Locomotives

Name	No	Origin	Class	Type	Built
—	78018	BR	2MT	2-6-0	1954

Industrial locomotives

Name	No	Builder	Type	Built
—	2	RSH (7925)	0-4-0DM	1959
—	1	Peckett (2142)	0-4-0ST	1953
David Payne	185	Fowler (4110006)	0-4-0DM	1950
Smiths Dock Co Ltd	—	Fowler (4200018)	0-4-0DM	1947
—	—	GEC	4wE	1928
—	—	R/Hornsby (279591)	0-4-0DM	1949

Stock
Various wagons, steam and diesel cranes

rolling stock are in store, for future display. Restoration work is being undertaken by the Darlington Railway Preservation Society in the former goods shed, adjacent to the main museum building (limited opening to visitors — times vary; groups by arrangement)

Embsay Steam Railway SC

Yorkshire's 'Friendly Line' is wholly operated by volunteers whose whole aim is to reopen the line through to Bolton Abbey. A further extension of the present two-mile line is in progress. An atmosphere of the days of the rural branch line prevails
Location: Embsay station, Embsay, Skipton, Yorkshire BD23 6QX
OS reference: SE 007533
Operating society/organisation: Yorkshire Dales Railway Museum Trust
Telephone: Skipton (0756) 4727. 24hr Answerphone (0756) 5189
Car park: Embsay
Access by public transport: Pennine bus from Skipton
On site facilities: Souvenir shop — specialising in transport and industrial archaeological titles, plus model railway supplies, small museum and lead mining centre
Catering facilities: Buffet and real ale bar on most trains. Buffet on station. Evening catering trains will serve meals on selected dates. Special charters can be arranged. Meals for parties can be arranged on normal service trains (subject to advance booking). Please write for further details
Length of line: 2 miles
Public opening: Trains will run,

Locomotives

Name	No	Origin	Class	Type	Built
—	D2203	BR	04	0-6-0DM	1952
—	NCB 38 (D9513)	BR	14	0-6-0DH	1964

Industrial locomotives

Name	No	Builder	Type	Built
Annie	—	Peckett (1159)	0-4-0ST	1908
Gladiator	—	H/Clarke (1450)	0-6-0ST	1922
Slough Estates No 5	—	H/Clarke (1709)	0-6-0ST	1939
Primrose No 2	—	Hunslet (3715)	0-6-0ST	1952
Ann	—	Sentinel (7232)	4wVB	1927
Beatrice	S119	Hunslet (2705)	0-6-0ST	1945
Airedale	—	Hunslet (1440)	0-6-0ST	1923
City Link	—	Yorkshire (2474)	0-4-0ST	1949
—	140	H/Clarke (1821)	0-6-0T	1948
Spitfire	S112	Hunslet (2414)	0-6-0ST	1942
Wheldale	—	Hunslet (3168)	0-6-0T	1944
—	69	Hunslet (3785)	0-6-0ST	1953
Monkton No 1	—	Hunslet (3785)	0-6-0ST	1953
—	22	Barclay (2320)	0-4-0ST	1952
Thomas	4	RSH (7661)	0-4-0ST	1950
H. W. Robinson	—	Fowler (4100003)	0-4-0DM	1946
—	MDE15	Baguley/Drewry (2136)	4wDM	1938
—	887	R/Hornsby (394009)	4wDM	1955
—	—	Wickham (7610)	2w-2PMR	1957
—	—	Lister (9993)*	4wPM	1938
—	—	Lister (10225)*	4wPM	1938
—	—	R/Hornsby (175418)*	4wDM	1936
—	—	R/Hornsby*	4wDM	—
—	—	M/Rail (8979)*	4wDM	1946
—	—	M/Rail (5213)*	4wDM	1930
—	—	R/Hornsby	4wDM	1957

*2ft gauge

Sundays throughout the year, plus Saturdays in July and August. Tuesdays in July and August. Wednesdays and Thursdays August only. Also all Bank Holiday weekends. Site open all year until dusk. Train times at least hourly 11.00-16.15
Special events: 15/16 April Easter Egg Specials; 7 May and 17 June Kiddie's Day; 15 July Steam Gala; 29 July and 19 August Kiddie's Day; 23 September Period Day; 28 October Halloween Special; 3 November

Stock
11 ex-BR Mk 1 coaches (SK, CK, BCK, 5×TSO, RMB, BSO(T) and SLS)
4 ex-LNER coaches
2 SR parcels vans
Freight stock and service vehicles, SR and GW brakes

Bonfire Night; Sundays 25 November-23 December Santa Trains; 1 January 1991 Family Day
Special notes: Steam rides are on 2-mile line to new halt and picnic area.

Unlimited ride facility. Old Midland Rly buildings, fine collection of industrial locomotives
Membership details: Membership Secretary at above address

Keighley & Worth Valley Railway

The epitome of a volunteer-run railway, a thriving branch line which serves six stations (most of them gas lit) which is host to an extensive and varied collection of locomotives and where everything continues to provide the atmosphere of the days of the steam railway. Immaculate stations, immaculate staff, immaculate trains. Very friendly and very much part of the community
Headquarters: Haworth station, Keighley, West Yorkshire, BD22 8NJ
Telephone: Haworth (0535) 43629 (talking timetable) Haworth (0535) 45214 (other calls)
Main stations: Haworth, Oxenhope, Keighley
Other public stations: Ingrow West, Damems, Oakworth
OS reference: SE 034371
Car parks: Free at Keighley, Ingrow West, Oakworth, Oxenhope. Limited parking at Haworth (pay). *Coaches* at Ingrow West and Oxenhope only
Access by public transport: British Rail through services from Carlisle, Morecambe, Lancaster, Leeds, Bradford to Keighley station for Worth Valley trains. (Change to platform 4). Also from Preston, Blackburn, Accrington, Burnley, Manchester, Rochdale, Todmorden to Hebden Bridge Station for connection via bus service 500 to Oxenhope. (Operates Saturdays throughout the year, Sundays May to September, Monday to Friday July and August only. Tel: Wakefield (0924) 375555 for timings.) A large number of bus services serve Keighley including from Burnley; Burnley & Pendle/Keighley & District Service 25 to Keighley bus station. From Bradford Interchange: services 663/664/665/666/667/668/669/699. From Leeds: service 760. From Huddersfield and Halifax: service 502 via Denholme to Ingrow West.

Locomotives

Name	No	Origin	Class	Type	Built
—	41241	LMS	2MT	2-6-2T	1949
—	43924	MR	4F	0-6-0	1920
—	42765	LMS	5P4F	2-6-0	1927
—	45212	LMS	5MT	4-6-0	1935
—	8431	LMS	8F	2-8-0	1944
—	47279	LMS	3F	0-6-0T	1925
City of Wells	34092	SR	WC	4-6-2	1949
—	80002	BR	4MT	2-6-4T	1952
—	75078	BR	4MT	4-6-0	1956
—	78022	BR	2MT	2-6-0	1953
—	30072	SR	USA	0-6-0T	1943
—	5775	GWR	5700	0-6-0PT	1929
—	52044	L&Y	2F	0-6-0	1887
—	19	L&Y	Pug	0-4-0ST	1910
—	51218	L&Y	Pug	0-4-0ST	1901
—	752	L&Y	—	0-6-0ST	1881
—	85	TVR	02	0-6-2T	1899
—	5820	USA TC	S160	2-8-0	1945
—	1931	MoS	WD	2-8-0	1945
—	68077	LNER	J94	0-6-0ST	1947
—	D226	BR	—	0-6-0DE	1956
—	D2511	BR	—	0-6-0DM	1961
—	D3336	BR	08	0-6-0DE	1954
—	D5209	BR	25/1	Bo-Bo	1963

Industrial locomotives

Name	No	Builder	Type	Built
Bellerophon	—	Haydock Foundry (C)	0-6-0WT	1874
Sir Berkeley	—	M/Wardle (1210)	0-6-0ST	1890
Lord Mayor	—	H/Clarke (402)	0-4-0ST	1893
Hamburg	31	H/Clarke (697)	0-6-0T	1903
—	67	H/Clarke (1369)	0-6-0T	1919
Brussels	118	H/Clarke (1782)	0-6-0ST	1945
Fred	—	RSH (7289)	0-6-0ST	1945
—	57	RSH (7668)	0-6-0ST	1950
—	63	RSH (7761)	0-6-0ST	1954
—	2226	Barclay (2226)	0-4-0ST	1946
Merlin	231	H/Clarke (D761)	0-6-0DM	1951
Austins No1	—	Peckett (5003)	0-4-0DM	1961
—	MDHB No 32	Hunslet (2699)	0-6-0DM	1944

Stock
2 ex-BR German-built Waggon und Maschinenbau diesel railbuses
30 coaches including examples of pre-Grouping types, BR Mk 1 stock and a Pullman car

National Coach services Nos 281/2/5/9, 291, 307/8, 318 all serve Keighley from various parts of the country
Refreshment facilities: Buffet restaurant at Oxenhope. Buffet bar at Keighley station. All normally open when steam trains are operating. Buffet car on some trains. Wine and Dine by prior booking only — the 'White Rose Pullman'
Souvenir shops: Haworth, Oxenhope, Keighley
Museums: Oxenhope (open when trains run)
Depots: Carriage and wagon — Oxenhope; Motive power/loco works — Haworth and Ingrow West
Length of line: 4¾ miles
Passenger trains: Steam-hauled services from Oxenhope-Keighley. Some off-peak and local shoppers' services worked by diesel railbus
Period of public operation: Winter diesel railbus service Saturdays

Owners
19, 752 and 51218 (L&Y Saddletanks)
43924 (the Midland 4F Preservation Society)
47279 (South Yorkshire 3F Fund)
75078 and 78022 (the Standard 4 Preservation Society)
42765 (A. Wilson Esq)
Bellerophon and *Sir Berkeley* (the Vintage Carriages Trust)

November-February (Keighley-Oxenhope). Winter steam service Sundays November, January and February (Keighley-Oxenhope); December — Santa Specials only from Haworth and Oxenhope only (pre-booked). Steam/diesel service Saturdays and Sundays March-October. Daily steam service throughout July and August, Easter week and Spring Bank Holiday week.
Special events: Enthusiasts'/Modern Traction Weekends
Facilities for disabled: Toilet on Haworth station forecourt.

Wheelchairs accommodated in guard's compartments on trains. Please advise before visit to the Advanced Bookings Manager c/o Haworth station
Special notes: Accompanied children under 5 years of age free. Children 5-15 and Senior Citizens at 50% discount. BR Family Railcard holders 10% discount
Membership details: Membership Secretary c/o above address
Feature article references: RW September 1988, p458 (locomotive 43924); RW February 1989, p78

Leeds Industrial Museum M

Location: The Leeds Industrial Museum, Armley Mills, Canal Road, Leeds LS12 2QF
OS reference: SE 275342
Operating society/organisation: Leeds City Council, Department of Leisure Services, 19 Wellington Street, Leeds 1
Telephone: (0532) 637861
Car park: Cark park adjacent to the Museum

Access by public transport: Nos 5 or 5A from City Square, Leeds (outside the railway station)
Public opening: April-September: Tuesdays-Saturdays 10.00-18.00, Sundays 14.00-18.00. October-March: Tuesdays-Saturdays 10.00-17.00, Sundays 14.00-17.00. Closed Mondays (except Bank Holidays)
On site facilities: Museum shop, refreshments (vending machines)

Special notes: Facilities for the disabled (toilets, etc), lifts. Museum can be viewed by visitors in wheelchairs (most areas are accessible)
Details of locomotive and rolling stock: Locomotive collection includes steam, diesel, mines locomotives and a narrow gauge railway and engines

Middleton Railway SC

This is a preserved section of one of the world's oldest railways, authorised by Act of Parliament in 1758, and also the first to be re-opened by volunteers
Headquarters: Middleton Railway Trust Ltd, Moor Road, Leeds LS10 2JQ
Telephone: (0532) 710320 (Ansaphone)
Main station: Moor Road, Hunslet
OS reference: SE 302309
Car parks: Tunstall Road/Moor Road (free)
Access by public transport: Bus No 61 from Park Row to MRT (every 10min); Bus 59 from Corn Exchange to Moor Road, ½-hourly on Saturday or hourly on Sundays; Bus 76 from Park Row (opposite City station) to Station

Locomotives

Name	No	Origin	Class	Type	Built
—	1310	NER	Y7	0-4-0T	1891
—	54	LNER	Y1	0-4-0VB	1933
—	385	DSB	HsII	0-4-0WT	1893
—	7401	LMS	—	0-6-0DM	1932

Industrial locomotives

Name	No	Builder	Type	Built
John Blenkinsop	—	Peckett (2003)	0-4-0ST	1941
Henry de Lacy II	—	H/Clarke (1309)	0-4-0ST	1917
Mirvale	—	H/Clarke (1882)	0-4-0ST	1955
Windle	—	Borrows (53)	0-4-0WT	1909
Matthew Murray	—	Bagnall (2702)	0-4-0ST	1943
—	—*	Brush (91)	0-4-0DE	1958
—	No 6	H/Leslie (3860)	0-4-0ST	1935
Carroll	—	H/Clarke (D631)	0-4-0DM	1946

Hotel, Hilledge Road. From bus stop, walk past Station pub, and across railway bridge. Follow footpath alongside dual carriageway and under roundabout. Moor Road station is just in front of you. Bus details correct at time of writing but due to changes taking place every few months, passengers are advised to check details on arrival in Leeds

Refreshment facilities: Moor Road, tea, coffee, snacks. Also café in Middleton Park (300yd)

Souvenir shop: Moor Road

Museum: Depot now open 10.00 to 18.00 during season (10.00 to 16.00 during winter). There is no charge for admission to site

Length of line: 1¼ miles

Passenger trains: Sunday trains all steam operated. Saturday services may be diesel hauled. Special trains operate on request, contact V. Smith, Tel: 0532 528021

Period of public operation: Every Saturday, Sunday and Bank Holiday Monday from 1 April to end of September. Also Easter Tuesday. Normal Sunday timetable; 13.00 then ½-hourly until 16.30. Normal Saturday timetable; 13.30 then every 45min until 16.30

Special events: 31 March Footplate Competition; 13-17 April Easter Train Service; 5-7 May May Day Holiday Trains; 16-17 May Schoolday Trains;

Name	No	Builder	Type	Built
—	—	Hunslet (1786)	4wD	1935
Mary	—	H/Clarke (D577)	0-4-0DM	1932
—	—	Fowler (3900002)	0-4-0DM	1945
Lord Mayor†	—	H/Clarke (402)	0-4-0ST	1893
—	—	Fowler (4200038)	0-4-0DH	1966
—	—	Thomas Hill (138C)	0-4-0DH	1963
Rowntrees No 3‡	—	R/Hornsby (441934)	4wDM	1960

*On loan from BSC Orb Works, Newport
†On loan to Keighley & Worth Valley Railway
‡On loan from North Yorkshire Moors Railway

Stock
2 CCTs converted for passenger use Nos 1867 and 2048
CCT as stores van No 2073
Norwegian brake coach
Various goods vehicles
5-ton Booth rail crane
1 3-ton Smith steam crane
1 3-ton Isles steam crane

Owners
1310, 385 (the Steam Power Trust)

26-28 May Spring Bank Holiday Trains; 16/17 June 30th Anniversary Weekend; 19/20 June Schoolday Trains; 1 July Little Engines Day; 5 August Tank Engine Day; 25-27 August Bank Holiday Trains; 23 September Gala Day; 1/2, 8/9, 15/16, 22/23 December Santa Trains

Facilities for disabled: Access very good

Special notes: It was the first standard gauge railway to be opened by volunteers, in June 1960. The railway terminates in a large car park and a nature trail has been provided by the local council

Feature article reference: RW May 1989, p268

Museum of Army Transport   M

Operating a substantial network of railways in wartime the Army is still responsible for military trains in Germany and railways feeding MoD depots in this country. Not only does the Museum hold extensive archives and display some fascinating maps, drawings and photographs, it contains some very interesting stock from the former military railways

Location: Museum of Army Transport, Flemingate, Beverley

OS reference: TA 041392

Operated by: The Museum of Army Transport Ltd (Charitable Status Company)

Telephone: Hull (0482) 860445

Car park: Yes, 1¼ acres

Access by public transport: Rail: 10min walk from Beverley station. Bus: served by East Yorks Motor Service

On site facilities: Restaurant, Beverley Bar (licensed). Museum, The Royal Corps of Transport Collection of

Industrial locomotives

Name	No	Builder	Type	Built
Gazelle	—	Dodman	0-4-2WT	1893
Woolmer	—	Avonside (1572)	0-6-0ST	1910
Waggoner	92	Hunslet (3792)	0-6-0ST	1953
Rorke's Drift	—	Drewry (2047)	0-4-0DM	1934
—	110	R/Hornsby (411319)	4wDM	1958
—	1035	Wickham Rail Car	4w	1958
—	3282*	Wickham Target Trolley	4w	1943
—	WD2182†	M/Rail (461)	4wDM	1917
—	LOD 758228†	M/Rail (8667)	4wDM	1941
—	LOD 758208†	M/Rail (8855)	4wDM	1943
—	LOD 758208	M/Rail	4wPM	1918

*2ft 6in gauge
†2ft gauge

Rolling stock
Various collection of goods stock including a World War 1 Armoured Train gun truck and a World War 2 ramp wagon

Owners
Gazelle (the National Railway Museum)

road, rail, sea, air and movement control artefacts. Shop in building. Lavatories, including special for handicapped

Facilities for disabled: The Museum is on one floor. This allows viewing of all vehicles. Access is available by ramp into the Armoured Train. Access is not possible into the Beverley Bar (first floor), the Beverley aircraft, the railway locos and the signalbox frame

Public opening: 10.00-17.00 every day

A 2ft gauge system based on the ADLR of World War 1, some 200yd long, and worked by World War 2 Simplex rail tractors operated by volunteers, on Saturday and Sunday afternoons and at other times as advertised locally during the summer. Intending travellers should check the line is operating.

except 24-26 December and Mondays in January, February, November and December

Special notes: Please bear in mind that while what is reported here deals

with railways, other parts of this extensive museum cover movement by road, sea and air

Feature article reference: RW November 1988, p690

National Railway Museum M

Location: National Railway Museum, Leeman Road, York YO2 4XJ

OS reference: SE 594519

Operating society/organisation: Part of the National Museum of Science and Industry

Telephone: York 621261 (STD Code 0904)

Car park: Limited parking for cars and pre-booked coaches at the Museum. York City's Leeman Road car park for cars and coaches visiting the NRM adjoins the main entrance

Access by public transport: The Museum is within a few minutes' walking distance of the railway and bus stations in York. The York City and District Bus Service operates to the door

On site facilities: Museum shop, restaurant and toilets, reference Library (free by appointment)

Public opening: Daily, weekdays 10.00-18.00. Sundays 11.00-18.00. Closed on New Years' Day, Christmas Eve, Christmas Day and Boxing Day

Facilities for disabled: All areas of the museum are accessible by the disabled

Special notes: The Museum has been open since 1975 and has welcomed over 15 million visitors.

A completely new and thematic exhibition, The Great Railway Show, opens on 1 March 1990 in the former York Goods Depot on the Museum's extensive 16-acre site. During the currency of the Show the Museum's Main Hall display area will be re-roofed.

The Great Railway Show illustrates the concept of travel by train — for passengers and freight. Short but representative trains will be drawn up at platforms and some locomotive footplates and carriages will be open to visitors. Outside in the yard there will be a regular programme of working locomotives — together with

rides and footplate visits. A temporary display building will house a rotating exhibition of famous locomotives under the general title of 'Record Breakers and Workhorses'. Finally, the 'Magician's Road', an interactive educational exhibition, will provide booked school parties, and other visitors out of school hours, with 'hands-on' experience of various aspects of railway operation. Table 1 lists the locomotives expected to be on display during the Great Railway Show. A second major exhibition of National Railway Collection items will open at Swindon in April 1990 as the NRM on Tour. The locomotives intended to be displayed at Swindon are listed in Table 3. With this exhibition — which is open daily until the autumn — and the Great Railway Show in York, more of the Collection will be on public display than ever before. Inevitably, however, some items will remain in store and, for completeness, they are listed in Table 2. It must be emphasised that the appearance of any particular item on public display cannot be guaranteed. If it is vital to discover the

exact whereabouts of a specific exhibit enquirers should contact the Museum in York *before* making a visit.

For the first time, *Railways Restored* includes — in Table 4 — a list of National Railway Collection items on loan to other organisations. The list was correct in October 1989 but some changes may have occurred since.

The Museum is now open for evening-hire for private viewings and celebrations. the Great Railway Show offers unique opportunities for corporate hire; menu and details are available on request.

Feature article references: RW August 1988, p486 (Locomotive 4468); RW September 1989 pp524-527 (The NRM's Development Project).

Membership details: Friends of the National Railway Museum c/o above address

Below:
NER No 1275, seen here at Darlington North Road Museum, will be one of the exhibits at Swindon during 1990. *R. R. Darsley*

TABLE 1

Exhibits at Great Railway Show, York

Locomotives

Name	No	Origin	Builder	Class	Type	Built
—	1	GNR	Doncaster	—	4-2-2	1870*
Boxhill	82	LB&SCR	Brighton	A1	0-6-0T	1880
Hardwicke	790	LNWR	Crewe	—	2-4-0	1892
—	1621	NER	Gateshead	M	4-4-0	1893
—	245	LSWR	Nine Elms	M7	0-4-4T	1897
—	673	MR	Derby	—	4-2-2	1899
—	1247	GNR	S/Stewart (4492)	J52	0-6-0ST	1899
—	737	SECR	Ashford	D	4-4-0	1901
—	1000	MR	Derby	4	4-4-0	1902
—	2818	GWR	Swindon	2800	2-8-0	1905*
—	1217	GER	Stratford	J17	0-6-0	1905
Cheltenham	925	SR	Eastleigh	V	4-4-0	1934
Rocket (replica)	—	Sectioned	R. Stephenson	—	0-2-2	1935
Green Arrow	4771	LNER	Doncaster	V2	2-6-2	1936*
Duchess of Hamilton	46229	LMS	Crewe	'Coronation'	4-6-2	1938*†
Mallard	4468	LNER	Doncaster	A4	4-6-2	1938*†
Eustace Forth	—	CEGB	RSH (7063)	—	0-4-0ST	1942
—	D8000	BR	E/Electric	20	Bo-Bo	1957
—	D200	BR	E/Electric	40	1Co-Co1	1958*
—	E5001	BR	Doncaster	71	Bo-Bo	1958
—	84001	BR	N/British	84	Bo-Bo	1960
The King's Own Yorkshire Light Infantry	55002	BR	E/Electric	55	Co-Co	1961*
Rocket (replica)	—	—	Loco Enterprises	—	0-2-2	1979
Iron Duke (broad gauge replica)	—	GWR	RESCO	—	4-2-2	1985

*To be displayed in rotation
†Will visit NRM on Tour exhibition, Swindon during 1990

Rolling Stock

Carriages

1869	LNWR Queen Victoria's Saloon
1885	MR 6-wheel composite brake No 901
1885	WCJS 8-wheel TPO No 186
1887	GNR 6-wheel brake No 948
1898	ECJS 3rd class No 12
1902	LNWR King Edward's saloon No 800
1902	LNWR Queen Alexandra's saloon No 801
1903	LSWR Tricomposite brake No 3598
1905	LNWR Royal service brake No 5154
1908	ECJS Royal Saloon No 395
1913	Pullman Car Co 1st class parlour car *Topaz*
1914	MR Dining car No 3463
1930	L&MR 1st class and 3rd class replicas
1936	CIWL Night Ferry sleeping car No 3792
1937	LNER Buffet Car No 9135
1985	GWR broad gauge carriage replica

Departmental stock

1906	NER Dynamometer car No 902502
1907	NER steam breakdown crane No CME 13
1949	BR (GWR design) inspection saloon No 80790

Wagons

c1826	Chaldron wagon
1925	Dandy cart replica of original c1828
c1870	Seaham Harbour chaldron wagon No 31
1908	LNWR open carriage truck No 11275
1914	LNWR van
1931	GWR Mink G Van No 112884
1931	Stanton Iron Works Wagon
1933	LMS 20-ton goods brake van No 295987
1935	PLM train ferry van No 475014
1936	LMS 3-plank open wagon No 472867
1936	GWR ballast wagon No 80659
1937	LMS/United Dairies 6-wheel milk tank No 44057
1950	BR 12-ton cattle wagon No B892156
1950	BR 20-ton Weltrol wagon No B900805
1954	BR 20-ton iron ore tippler No B383560
1960	BR banana van No B882593

TABLE 2

In store at the National Railway Museum, York
Locomotives

Name	No	Origin	Builder	Class	Type	Built
—	3	FR	Bury Curtis & Kennedy	—	0-4-0	1846
Wren	—	LYR	B/Peacock	—	0-4-0ST	1887
Henry Oakley	990	GNR	Doncaster	C2	4-4-2	1898
—	75S	W&CR	Siemens (6)	—	Bo electric	1898
—	87	GER	Stratford	J69	0-6-0T	1904
—	—	WD	Simplex (60cm gauge)	—	0-4-0	1918
—	—	Berry Wiggins & Co	Simplex	—	0-4-0	1931
—	KF7	Chinese Govt Rlys	Vulcan (4674)	KF	4-8-4	1935
—	—	Yorks Water Auth	R/Hornsby (2ft gauge)	—	0-4-0	1937
Winston Churchill	34051	SR	Brighton	BB	4-6-2	1946
Ellerman Lines	35029	SR	Eastleigh	MN	4-6-2	1949
Respite	—	NCB	Hunslet	—	0-6-0ST	1950
Mine loco (3ft gauge)	—	NCB	H/Clarke (3ft gauge)	—	0-6-0 DM	1950
—	08064	BR	Darlington	08	0-6-0 DE	1953
—	3	CEGB	RSH (7746)	—	0-6-0 DM	1954
—	03090	BR	Swindon	03	0-6-0 DM	1960
—	D2860	BR	YEC	02	0-4-0 DH	1960

NRM Store

Powered Units

1931	GPO Post Office Railway Car No 809
1972	BR APT-E prototype experimental Advanced Passenger Train
1977	Leyland Motors LEV-1 experimental railbus

Departmental Stock

c1890	GNR Loco tender No 1002
1891	NER Snow plough No DE 900566
1899	GWR Hand crane No 537
1904	MR Officers' saloon No 2234
1931	LNER Petrol-driven platelayers' trolley No 960209
1932	LMS Ballast plough brake van No 197266
1938	LMS Mobile test unit No 1, No 45053
1949	BR(LMS) Dynamometer car No 3, No 45049
1957	BR Track recording trolley No DX 50002
1974	BR Matisa tamping machine No 74/007
Uncertain	LNWR Tender/water carrier

Passenger Stock

1834	B&WR 1st & 2nd composite
1834	B&WR 2nd class
1834	B&WR 3rd class
1851	ECR 1st class No 1
1895	Cambrian luggage composite No 238
1896	Glasgow Subway Car No 7
1897	Lynton & Barnstaple Rly brake composite No 6992
1925	LMS 3rd class vestibule No 7828
1925	LMS 3rd class vestibule No 7863
1927	LMS 3rd class vestibule No 8207
1936	LNER 3rd class open No 13251
1936	LNER 3rd class open No 13254
1950	BR(LMS) Corridor 3rd class brake No 27093
1955	BR Lavatory composite No E43046
1956	BR 2nd class open No E4286
1960	BR Griddle car No Sc1100
1960	Pullman Car Co 1st class Kitchen car No 311 *Eagle*
1960	Pullman Car Co 1st class Parlour car No 326 *Emerald*
1962	BR Prototype Mk II 1st class corridor No 13252

Freight & non-passenger carrying stock

1797	Peak Forest Canal quarry truck
1816	Grantham Canal Tramway truck
1828	Two replica chaldron wagons
1838	GJR replica TPO
1850	South Hetton Colliery chaldron wagon No 1155
1889	Shell-Mex oil tank wagon No 512
1894	LSWR Brake van No 99
1895	LSWR Open carriage truck No 5830
1902	NER 20-ton wooden hopper wagon
c1900	CR Bogie trolley wagon No 300041
?	GCR Single bolster wagon No 110
?	GCR Double bolster wagon No 111
1912	LB&SCR Open wagon No 27884
1912	LSWR Gunpowder van No KDS61209
1912	NER Sand wagon No DE14974
1912	GNR 8-ton van No E432764
1914	GWR Shunters' truck No W94988
1917	Shell tank wagon No 3171 (precise identity not known)
1917	MR 8-ton open wagon (precise identity not known)
1917	GCR Van (precise identity not known)
1917	NER Van (precise identity not known)
1924	LMS Van
1924	LNER Fitted tube wagon No 181358
1926	GWR Fitted open wagon No 108246
1928	ICI Nitric acid tank wagon No 14
c1933	LMS Gunpowder van No 288824
1935	SR Bogie goods brake van No 56297
1935	GWR Motor car van No 126438
1936	LNER 20-ton goods brake van No 187774
1936	LMS Tube wagon No 499254

1937	GWR Siphon bogie milk van No 2775	1951	BR(SR) Show cattle wagon No S3733S
1938	LMS Single bolster wagon No 722702	1951	BR 8-ton cattle wagon No B893343
1940	WD Warflat No 161042	1952	BR 30-ton bogie bolster wagon No B943139
1944	LMS Lowmac No M700728	1954	National Benzole oil tank wagon No 2022
1944	GWR 13-ton open wagon No DW143698	1955	BR 16-ton mineral wagon No B234830
1945	GWR Loriat P No 42367	1955	BR 16-ton mineral wagon No B227009
1946	SNCF 16-ton mineral wagon No ADB192437	1957	BR Horse box No S96369
1946	LMS Bogie trolley wagon No 300041	1959	BR Fish van No B87905
1946	LNER 20-ton hopper wagon No E270919	1959	BR Conflat No B737725
1948	BR(SR) 12-ton shock absorbing wagon No 14036	1960	BR 25-ton Weltrol WP No ADB 900916
1949	BR 40-ton Gain-A No DB996724	1961	BR Presflo cement wagon No B873368
1949	BR Bogie bolster D No B941000	1962	BR Speedfreight container No BA 4324B
1950	BR 22-ton iron ore hopper wagon No B436275	1970	Phillips Petroleum 100-ton GLW tank wagon No PP85209
1951	ICI Liquid chlorine tank wagon No 47484	?	Yorkshire Water Authority two tip wagons (2ft gauge)

TABLE 3

Exhibits at Swindon

Locomotives

Name	No	Origin	Builder	Class	Type	Built
Puffing Billy	—	Wylam Colliery	—	—	0-4-0	1813
—	1868	LNWR	Crewe	—	2-2-2	1845
—	1439	LNWR	Crewe	—	0-4-0ST	1865
Aerolite	66	NER	Gateshead	X1 (LNER)	2-2-4T	1969
—	1275	NER	Dubs & Co	—	0-6-0	1874
Gladstone	214	LB&SCR	Brighton	B1	0-4-2	1882
Livingstone Thompson	—	FR	Boston Lodge	—	0-4-4-0T	1885
—	1008	LYR	Horwich	—	2-4-2T	1889
—	563	LSWR	Nine Elms	T3	4-4-0	1893
—	1	NER	BTH	—	Bo-Bo electric	1902
—	251	GNR	Doncaster	C1	4-4-2	1902
City of Truro	3440	GWR	Swindon	'City'	4-4-0	1903
—	K1	TGR	B/Peacock	—	0-4-0+0-4-0	1909
—	1	NSR	Stoke	—	0-4-0	1917
—	2700	LMS	Horwich	5P4F	2-6-0	1926
King George V	6000	GWR	Swindon	'King'	4-6-0	1927
—	26020	BR	Gorton/ Metrovick	76	Bo-Bo electric	1951
—	—	Imperial Paper Mills	Barclay	—	0-4-0F	1956
—	—	Tees-Side Bridge & Engineering Co	Sentinel	—	4wTG	1957
Evening Star	92220	BR	Swindon	9F	2-10-0	1960
—	41001	BR	Crewe	Prototype HST	Bo-Bo	1972

Rolling Stock

1842	L&BR Queen Adelaide's saloon
1845	SDR Composite
1861	NBR Horsedrawn Dandy
1872	NLR Directors' saloon
1887	GWR 6-wheel tricomposite No 870
1899	LNWR Duke of Sutherland's saloon
1900	LNWR Royal dining car No 76
1905	LNWR Royal service brake No 5155
1908	ECJS Royal service brake No 109
1911	GWR 'Whitewash' (track testing) coach
1925	SR 4-SUB electric motor car No 8143
1928	LMS 3rd class sleeping car No 14241
1934	GWR Special buffet car No 9631
1935	SR 2-BIL electric unit Nos 10656/12123
1937	SR 4-COR electric motor car No 11179
1941	LMS Royal saloon No 799
1945	GWR Royal saloons Nos 9006/7

TABLE 4
Items on Loan from the NRM

Locomotives

Original type/No/Name	Location	Builder	Built
Hetton Colliery 0-4-0	Beamish	G. Stephenson	1822
SDR 0-4-0 *Locomotion*	Darlington	R. Stephenson & Co	1825
Shutt End Colliery 0-4-0 *Agenoria*	Science Mus	Foster Raistrick	1829
L&MR 0-2-2 *Rocket*	Science Mus	R. Stephenson & Co	1829
L&MR 0-4-0 *Sans Pareil*	Science Mus	T. Hackworth	1829
L&MR 0-2-2 *Novelty*	Greater Manchester Museum of Science & Technology	Braithwaite & Ericsson	1829
GWR 2-2-2 *North Star*	Swindon GWR Mus	R. Stephenson	1837
SDR 0-6-0 No 24 *Derwent*	Darlington Nth Rd Mus	A. Kitching	1845
LNWR 2-2-2 No 3020 *Cornwall*	Birmingham Rly Mus	Crewe	1847
Wantage Tramway 0-4-0WT No 5 *Shannon*	Didcot Rly Ctr	G. England	1857
LNWR 0-4-0ST *Pet*	Towyn NG Museum	Crewe	1865
MR 2-4-0 No 158A	Midland Rly Ctr	Derby	1866
South Devon Rly 0-4-0WT *Tiny*	Dart Valley Rly	Sara	1868
LSWR 2-4-0WT No 0298	Dart Valley Rly	B/Peacock	1874
Hebburn Works 0-4-0ST No 2 *Bauxite*	Science Mus	B/Hawthorn	1874
NER 2-4-0 No 910	Darlington Nth Rd Mus	Gateshead	1875
NER 2-4-0 No 1463	Darlington Nth Rd Mus	Gateshead	1885
? 0-4-0 Tram loco No 84	Dinting Rly Ctr	B/Peacock	1886
C&SL Bo electric No 1	Science Mus	B/Peacock	1890
S&MR 0-4-2WT *Gazelle*	Mus of Army Transport, Beverley	Dodman	1893
GER 2-4-0 No 490	Bressingham	Stratford	1894
GWR 0-6-0 No 2516	Swindon GWR Mus	Swindon	1897
TVR 0-6-2T No 28	Caerphilly Rly Soc	TVR	1897
LSWR 4-4-0 No 120	Mid-Hants Rly	Nine Elms	1899
GWR 4-6-0 No 4003 *Lode Star*	Swindon GWR Mus	Swindon	1907
LT&SR 4-4-2T No 80 *Thundersley*	Bressingham	R. Stephenson	1909
GCR 2-8-0 No 102	Dinting Rly Ctr	Gorton	1911
Nord (France) 4-6-0 No 3.628	Nene Valley Rly	Henschel	1911
NER 0-8-0 No 901	North York Moors Rly	Darlington	1919
GCR 4-4-0 No 506 *Butler Henderson*	Great Central Rly	Gorton	1920
LNWR 0-8-0 No 485	B'ham Rly Mus	Crewe	1921
GWR 4-6-0 No 4073 *Caerphilly Castle*	Science Mus	Swindon	1923
LMS 0-6-0 No 4027	Midland Rly Ctr	Derby	1924
SR 4-6-0 No 777 *Sir Lamiel*	Humberside Loco Preservation Group, Hull	N/British	1925
SR 4-6-0 No 850 *Lord Nelson*	Steamtown	Eastleigh	1926
LMS 2-6-4T No 2500	Bressingham	Derby	1934
LMS 4-6-0 No 5000	Severn Valley Rly	Crewe	1935
SR 0-6-0 No C1	Bluebell Rly	Eastleigh	1942
GWR 0-6-0PT No 9400	Swindon GWR Mus	Swindon	1947
BR 4-6-2 No 70013 *Oliver Cromwell*	Bressingham	Crewe	1951
English Electric Co-Co DE *Deltic*	Science Mus	E/Electric	1955
BR A1A-A1A No 5500	Steamtown	Brush Traction	1957
BR C-C DH No D1023 *Western Fusilier*	Dart Valley Rly	Swindon	1963

Powered Units

NER electric parcels van No 3267, Tyne & Wear Mus
LPTB driving motor car No 3327, Science Mus
GWR diesel railcar No 4, Swindon GWR Mus
LMS electric motor brake 2nd No 28361, Southport Transport Mus
LMS electric driving trailer composite No 29896, Southport Transport Mus
BR APT-P pre-production Advanced Passenger Train, Crewe Heritage Ctr

Departmental Stock

LNWR Match truck No 284235, Steamtown
LNWR Steam breakdown crane No 2987, Steamtown

Passenger Stock

SDR 1st & 2nd composite No 31, Darlington Nth Rd Mus
SDR 3rd No 179, Timothy Hackworth Mus, Shildon
ECJS Royal saloon No 396, Bressingham

1910 GCR Open 3rd class No 666, Great Central Railway
1925 GWR 3rd class dining car No 9653, Severn Valley Rly
1925 GWR 3rd class dining car No 9654, Severn Valley Rly
1928 Nord (France) 2nd class corridor No 7122, Nene Valley Rly
1930 GWR composite dining car No 9605, Science Mus (Wroughton)
1930 L&MR replica 1st class *Experience*, Liverpool Mus
1930 L&MR replica 2nd class, Liverpool Mus
1937 SR buffet car No S125295, Nene Valley Rly
1937 LMS corridor 3rd class brake No 5987, Steamtown
1941 LMS Royal saloon No 798, Glasgow Museum of Transport
1947 SR 3rd class open No 1456, Bluebell Rly

Freight & non-passenger carrying stock

1907 NER bogie van No 041273, Humberside Loco Preservation Group
1917 GWR Hydra-D No 42193, Didcot Railway Ctr
1922 LB&SCR cattle truck No 7116, Isle of Wight Steam Rly
1939 SR postal sorting van No 4920, Nene Valley Rly
1947 GWR Motorcar van No 65814, Bristol Industrial Mus
1949 BR(LMS) Postal sorting van No M30272M Birmingham Rly Mus

North Yorkshire Moors Railway

This 18-mile line runs through the picturesque North York Moors National Park and is host to an extensive collection of main line locomotives

Headquarters: Pickering station, Pickering, North Yorkshire

Telephone: Pickering (0751) 72508 or 73535

Main station: Pickering

Other public stations: Grosmont, Goathland, Newtondale Halt, Levisham

OS reference: Pickering NZ 797842, Levisham NZ 818909, Goathland NZ 836013, Grosmont NZ 828053

Car parks: Grosmont, Goathland, Levisham, Pickering

Access by public transport: BR service to Grosmont from Whitby and Middlesbrough. Bus services Malton-Pickering, York or Scarborough-Pickering and Whitby-Goathland and Pickering

Refreshment facilities: Available on most trains and at Grosmont, Goathland and Pickering

Souvenir shops: Pickering, Goathland, Grosmont

Museum: Situated within gallery of locomotive depot at Grosmont

Depot: Grosmont

Length of line: 18 miles

Passenger trains: Mainly steam-hauled services Grosmont and Pickering. The 'North Yorkshireman' runs regularly. A GWR saloon is also available for special occasions (eg wedding parties, conferences etc)

Period of public operation: Most days from Easter to October. Santa specials, weekends before Christmas

Locomotives

Name	No	Origin	Class	Type	Built
Eric Treacy	45428	LMS	5MT	4-6-0	1937
George Stephenson	44767	LMS	5MT	4-6-0	1947
—	2238	NER	T2	0-8-0	1918
—	2392	NER	P3	0-6-0	1923
*Bittern**	19	LNER	A4	4-6-2	1937
*Blue Peter**	60532	LNER	A2/3	4-6-2	1948
—	2005	LNER	K1	2-6-0	1949
—	63460	NER	T3	0-8-0	1919
—	69023	LNER	J72	0-6-0T	1951
—	3814	GWR	2884	2-8-0	1940
—	6619	GWR	5600	0-6-2T	1928
—	841	SR	S15	4-6-0	1936
Repton	926	SR	V	4-4-0	1934
—	75014	BR	4MT	4-6-0	1951
—	80135	BR	4MT	2-6-4T	1956
—*	92134	BR	9F	2-10-0	1957
Dame Vera Lynn	3672	MoS	WD	2-10-0	1943
Greyhound	D821	BR	42	B-B	1960
Western Champion†	D1015	BR	52	C-C	1962
—	D2207	BR	03	0-6-0DM	1953
—	D5032	BR	24	Bo-Bo	1959
—	D7029	BR	35	B-B	1962
—	D8568	BR	17	Bo-Bo	1963
—	25191	BR	25	Bo-Bo	1965
—	25278	BR	25	Bo-Bo	1965
Alycidon	55009	BR	55	Co-Co	1961

*Not on site
†Not on site, stored at Swindon

Industrial locomotives

Name	No	Builder	Type	Built
—	29	Kitson (4263)	0-6-2T	1904
—	5	R/Stephenson (3377)	0-6-2T	1909
Stanton No 44	—	Yorkshire (2622)	0-4-0DE	1956
No 21	—	Fowler (4210094)	0-4-0DH	1954
Antwerp	—	Hunslet (3180)	0-6-0ST	1944
—	12139	E/Electric (1553)	0-6-0DE	1948
—	16	Drewry	0-4-0DM	—

Facilities for disabled: The NYMR welcomes visitors who may be suffering from a disability and special attention will gladly be provided if advanced notice is given

Special notes: Operates through North York Moors National Park. Information office at Pickering station.

Name	No	Builder	Type	Built
—	1	R/Hornsby (421419)	4wDM	—
—	2*	R/Hornsby (441934)	4wDM	1960
—	1	Vanguard (129V)	0-4-0DM	1963
—	2	Vanguard (131V)	0-4-0DM	1963

*On loan to Middleton Railway

Stock

There are 56 coaching stock vehicles on the line comprising 32 Mk 1s, 3 Pullmans and the remainder of 'vintage' category. The 7 pre-Grouping vehicles include NER, H&BR, GNR and GCR examples. There are 14 LNER vehicles including 7 of Edward Thompson design — the largest collection in the country of this CM&EE. The 38 freight vehicles are on the NYMR include several rare or unique examples, including complete breakdown train.

Owners

841 (Essex Locomotive Society)
2005, 2238, 2392, 69023 (the North Eastern Locomotive Preservation Group)
19 and 60532 (on loan to the North Eastern Locomotive Preservation Group)
63460 (on loan from the National Railway Museum)
75014 (75014 Locomotive Operators Group)
92134 (the Standard Nine Loco Group)
Antwerp (the National Coal Board)
D821, D1015, D7029, D8568 (Diesel Traction Group)
55009 (the Deltic Preservation Society)
21, 44 (British Steel Corporation)
29 (Lambton 29 Syndicate)
926, 3814 and 80135 (private)

Below:
Owned by the North Eastern Locomotive Preservation Group, LNER No 2005 is seen in action on its home line. No 2005 is at the head of the line's prestige 'North Yorkshireman' Wine and Dine service at Levisham. *John Hunt*

South Yorkshire Railway   SC

Location: Barrow Road Railway Sidings, Barrow Road, Meadowhall, Wincobank, Sheffield S9 1LA
OS Reference: SK389922
Operating Society: South Yorkshire Railway
Telephone: 0742 424405
Car Park: Car parking facilities available, more facilities being developed nearby
Access by public transport: From

Locomotives

Name	No	Origin	Class	Type	Built
—	D2953	BR	01	0-4-0DM	1956
—	D2854	BR	02	0-4-0DH	1960
—	D2199	BR	03	0-6-0DM	1961
—	D2284	BR	04	0-6-0DM	1960
—	D2334	BR	04	0-6-0DM	1961
Dorothy	D2337	BR	04	0-6-0DM	1961
—	D2420	BR	06	0-4-0DM	1958
—	07001	BR	07	0-6-0DE	1962

Sheffield: By bus, No 93 Firth Park, alight at the top of Barrow Road, and follow the signposts.
From Rotherham, Doncaster and Sheffield No X77 bus alighting on Barrow Road.
By rail: Brightside Station which is approximately 1-mile south of Meadowhall. (Note: In Autumn 1990 a new railway station is to open at Meadowhall which is adjacent to the railway)
Refreshment facilities: Light refreshments available
Other on site facilities: Small shop
Length of line: 3½ miles in total, although only ¾-mile is currently occupied
Public opening: Every weekend and Bank Holiday throughout the year
Period of public operation: Not operating a service as yet
Journey time: See above
Special events: It is hoped to have a diesel gala, on August Bank Holiday 1990, and the service which it is hoped will be inaugurated in 1990
Facilities for the disabled: Paths and ramps, designed for wheelchair access, on to the railway
Membership details: c/o above address

Name	No	Origin	Class	Type	Built
—	D3452	BR	10	0-6-0DE	1957
Christine	D4092	BR	10	0-6-0DE	1962
—	12074	BR	11	0-6-0DE	1950
—	12088	BR	11	0-6-0DE	1951
Andania	40013	BR	40	1Co-Co1	1959

Industrial locomotives

Name	No	Builder	Type	Built
—	2	Hunslet (3183)	0-6-0ST	1944
—	8	Hunslet (3192)	0-6-0ST	1944
—	7	H/Clarke (1689)	0-4-0ST	1937
Cathyrn	—	H/Clarke (1884)	0-4-0ST	1955
George	—	Sentinel (9596)	4wVBT	1955
Bigga	—	Fowler (4200019)	0-4-0DH	1947
Rotherham	2	YEC (2480)	0-4-0DE	1950
—	—	Hibbard (3817)	0-4-0DM	1956
Speedy	—	Barclay (361)	0-4-0DM	1942
Hotwheels	—	Barclay (422)	0-6-0DM	1958
Toffo	2	R/Hornsby (432479)	4wDM	1959
BP21	—	H/Clarke (D707)	0-6-0DM	1950
Enterprise	—	H/Clarke (D810)	0-6-0DM	1953
—	406	NBL (277427)	0-4-0DH	1955

Rolling stock
2 diesel-electric cranes
4 Mk 1 coaches
6 Mk 1 General Utility Vehicles
1 Mk 1 bogie van
1 Covered Carriage Truck
4 LNER brake vans
Several other wagons

Stephenson Rly Museum & North Tyneside Steam Rly M

A display in buildings which began life as the Tyne-Wear Metro Test Centre now features locomotives and exhibitions which illustrate railway development from waggonways to the present day
Location: Middle Engine Lane, North Tyneside
OS reference: NZ 396576
Operating society/organisation: North Tyneside Steam Railway Association c/o Stephenson Railway Museum, Middle Engine Lane, West Chirton, North Tyneside NE29 8DX
Car park: On site
Length of line: North Tyneside Steam Railway, 1¾ miles, Stephenson Railway Museum to Percy Main
Access by public transport: Tyne & Wear Metro to Percy Main when North Tyneside Steam Railway is in operation. Bus routes 300/307 (operated by Go-Ahead Northern Co) from Newcastle (Eldon Square or Worswick Street) to North Shields, Tynemouth, Whitley Bay, stops at Museum

Locomotives

Name	No	Origin	Class	Type	Built
—	03078	BR	03	0-6-0DM	1959
—	12098	BR	11	0-6-0DE	1951
Bittern*	4464	LNER	A4	4-6-2	1937

*Externally restored as 2509 *Silver Link* of 1935

Industrial locomotives

Name	No	Builder	Type	Built
Billy	A4	Killingworth or RS & Co (1)	0-4-0	1816-26
—	A5	Kitson (2509)	0-6-0PT	1883
—	E4	Siemens	Bo-BoE	1909
Vulcan	—	Bagnall (2994)	0-6-0ST	1950
—	10	Consett (10)	0-6-0DM	1958

Stock
1 NER electric parcels van
1 LNER Gresley BFK
3 BR non-gangwayed coaches

Owners
12098 (private)
Bittern (on loan from NELPG)
NER van (National Railway Museum)

Public opening: North Tyneside Steam Railway to open Easter 1990 operating Sundays 13.00-17.00 until September. Stephenson Railway Museum displays open Tues to Sun, Easter to end of October. See Press or Tel 091 259 0944 or 091 2622627 for details of train service on North Tyneside Steam Railway

Special notes: Stephenson Railway Museum and North Tyneside Steam Railway share facilities in buildings owned by North Tyneside Council at Middle Engine Lane. North Tyneside Steam Railway Association operates and maintains exhibits from the Museum Collection

Facilities for disabled: Access for wheelchairs to Museum building at Middle Engine Lane

Tanfield Railway

The oldest railway in the world, having opened in 1725, the site maintains its basic appearance of an industrial railway but contains an unusual assortment of stock as well as the Tyneside Locomotive Collection

Location: Off the A6076 Sunniside to Stanley road

OS reference: NZ 207573

Operating society/organisation: The Tanfield Railway, Marley Hill Engine Shed, Sunniside, Gateshead, Tyne & Wear. Postal address: 33 Stocksfield Avenue, Newcastle-upon-Tyne NE5 2DX

Telephone: Newcastle (091) 2742002 (evenings)

Car park: Marley Hill Engine Shed

Access by public transport: Nearest bus stop is Sunniside, 1-mile from shed; buses 644/705/706/707/708/771/ 772/X11/X30/X36 from Newcastle. Summer Sundays X75 direct to Marley Hill, alight at Andrewshouse

Catering facilities: Basic refreshment facilities available on operating days

On site facilities: Shop and toilets

Length of line: 1-mile with construction of a 1-mile extension in progress

Public opening: Marley Hill Engine Shed now open daily throughout the year for viewing, except Christmas and New Years day. Steam trains run bank holiday Sundays and Mondays Easter through to August. Also every Sunday in June, July, August and September. Restricted diesel service other Sundays. Santa steam trains, Saturdays and Sundays in December, up to Christmas and Boxing Day. Additional services will run in 1990 in conjunction with the Gateshead National Garden Festival on

Industrial locomotives

Name	No	Builder	Type	Built
—	9	AEG (1565)	4w-4wE	1913
Gamma	—	Bagnall (2779)	0-6-0ST	1945
Horden	—	Barclay (1015)	0-6-0ST	1904
—	6	Barclay (1193)	0-4-2ST	1910
—	17	Barclay (1338)	0-6-0T	1913
—	32	Barclay (1659)	0-4-0ST	1920
—	3	E. Borrows (37)	0-4-0WT	1898
Wellington	—	B/Hawthorn (266)	0-4-0ST	1873
Enterprise	—	R&W Hawthorn (2009)	0-4-0ST	1884
Cyclops	—	H/Leslie (2711)	0-4-0ST	1907
—	2	H/Leslie (2859)	0-4-0ST	1911
Stagshaw	—	H/Leslie (3513)	0-6-0ST	1923
—	3	H/Leslie (3575)	0-6-0ST	1923
—	3	H/Leslie (3746)	0-6-0F	1929
Irwell	—	H/Clarke (1672)	0-4-0ST	1937
—	38	H/Clarke (1823)	0-6-0T	1949
—	4	Sentinel (9559)	0-4-0T	1953
—	169	RSH (6980)	0-4-0DM	1940
Hendon	—	RSH (7007)	0-4-0CT	1940
—	62	RSH (7035)	0-6-0ST	1940

Right:
Viewed from the Tanfield Railway's new signalbox, Hawthorn Leslie-built 0-4-0ST No 2 storms under Gibraltar Bridge with an Andrewshouse-Sunniside service on 28 September 1989.
A. R. Thompson

Thursdays and Saturdays. Please ring for details
Special events: Please see press for details
Facilities for disabled: Good access to stations and coaches
Special notes: The railway is extending its line back to East Tanfield, and also features the Tyneside Locomotive Collection. Andrewshouse station brought into use in 1989 for special events
Membership details: A. Beeton, 5 Shipley Road, North Shields, Tyne & Wear

Name	No	Builder	Type	Built
—	3	RSH (7078)	4w-4wE	1940
—	49	RSH (7098)	0-6-0ST	1943
Progress	—	RSH (7298)	0-6-0ST	1946
Cochrane	—	RSH (7409)	0-4-0ST	1948
—	44	RSH (7760)	0-6-0ST	1953
—	38	RSH (7763)	0-6-0ST	1954
—	21	RSH (7796)	0-4-0ST	1954
—	47	RSH (7800)	0-6-0ST	1954
—	1	RSH (7901)	0-4-0DM	1958
—	16	RSH (7944)	0-6-0ST	1957
FGF	—	Barclay (D592)	0-4-0DH	1969
—	2	A/Whitworth (D22)	0-4-0DE	1933
Escucha	11	B/Hawthorn (748)	0-4-0ST	1883*

*600mm gauge

Stock
13 4-wheel carriages
2 6-wheel carriage
1 6-wheel van
12 hopper wagons
9 contractors bogies
3 brake vans

3 steam cranes
7 covered wagons
4 open wagons
4 black wagons
1 6-wheel chassis (ex-crane runner)
4 flat wagons
2 4-wheel chassis (ex-PMVs)

West Yorkshire Transport Museum   M

The West Yorkshire Transport Museum's collection consists of some 70 items, of which 13 are rail or tramway vehicles. It is hoped to progressively reopen the Spen Valley Railway, commencing at Low Moor. The railway would be all electric, traction being by integral battery, or overhead electric supply.

Two locomotives and five trams are to be seen at the Ludlam Street Depot. Also stored at Ludlam Street are about 50 road vehicles, mostly motorbuses, but including five tolleybuses and service vehicles.

Recently approved plans will see the opening of the West Yorkshire Transport Centre at Low Moor, Bradford, in the spring of 1992. Proposed attractions include the operation of trams, trolleybuses and rail vehicles backed by extensive interpretation of the West Yorkshire Transport story
Location: Ludlam Street Depot, Mill Lane, off Manchester Road, Bradford, 400yd south of Bradford Interchange, just off A641
OS reference: SE 164322
Operating society/organisation: West Yorkshire Transport Museum Trust Ltd
Telephone: Bradford (0274) 736006
Car park: Yes, free
Access by public transport: Rail/road: 10min walk from Bradford Interchange station, 2min walk from nearest Manchester Road bus stops

Locomotives

Name	No	Origin	Class	Type	Built
Electra	27000	BR	EM2	Co-Co	1953

Industrial locomotives (all electric)

Name	No	Builder	Type	Built
—	10	Siemens	Bo	1913
—	1	E/Electric	Bo	1935

Stock
Derby 'Lightweight' Battery Electric unit Sc79998/9 (on loan to East Lancashire Railway)
Class 506 Electric Unit — 59404/504/604 (on loan to Midland Railway Centre)
1 Blackpool tram 663
1 Rotterdam tram 408
2 Budapest trams 2576/2577
1 Brussels trams 96
Various tram bodies

On site facilities: Viewing of motorbuses, trolleybuses and trams at Ludlam Street; rides on preserved motorbuses are available; souvenir shop and light refreshments available. Special events as advertised
Public opening: Ludlam Street is open every month, from 11.00-17.00. Parties welcome by prior arrangement. Details of opening times, etc, may be obtained by telephoning the museum.
Facilities for disabled: No special toilet facilities, but all parts of museum accessible by wheelchairs
Membership details: The West Yorkshire Transport Museum Society provides volunteers who support the project in many ways, including the restoration of Trust-owned exhibits. Telephone the museum for details

Scotland

Bo'ness & Kinneil Railway — SC

A few miles west of Edinburgh, this railway has won several awards, particularly for its recreated station buildings — the entire railway has been constructed on a 'green field site'. Achieved in 1989 was the extension of the operating line inland to Birkhill where the railway provides access to a new attraction, the Birkhill Clay Mine
Location: Scottish Railway Preservation Society, Bo'ness Station, Union Street, Bo'ness, West Lothian, EH51 0AD
Access by public transport: Nearest BR stations — Falkirk Grahamston, Linlithgow, Dalmeny
OS reference: NT 003817
Telephone: Bo'ness (0506) 822298
Main station: Bo'ness
Car park: At the site (free)
Refreshment facilities: Bo'ness 'Bufferstop' cafe with snacks, unlicensed
Souvenir shop: Bo'ness
Depot: Bo'ness
Length of line: The line was extended to 3½ miles (to Birkhill) from Easter 1989
Passenger trains: Trains run at 11.00 (July and August), 12.10, 13.15, 14.20, 15.25 and 16.30 in season on Saturdays and Sundays
Period of public operation: 14 April-end September, also first two Sundays in October. Bank holiday Mondays 16 April, 7, 28 May, 16 July. Daily (Mondays excepted) 14 July-19 August. Schools services 30 May-1 June and 6-8 June. Pre Christmas
Special events: Santa Specials 8/9, 15/16, 22/23 December
Facilities for disabled: At Bo'ness for shop and cafeteria
Feature article reference: RW September 1989, p528

Locomotives

Name	No	Origin	Class	Type	Built
—	419	CR	439	0-4-4T	1908
—	1313	SJ	B	4-6-0	1917
Morayshire	246	LNER	D49	4-4-0	1928
Maude	673	NBR	—	0-6-0	1891
—	80105	BR	4MT	2-6-4T	1955
—	8(D9524)	BR	14	0-6-0DH	1964
—	D5351	BR	27	Bo-Bo	1961

Industrial locomotives

Name	No	Builder	Type	Built
—	3	Barclay (1937)	0-4-0ST	1928
—	3	Barclay (2046)	0-4-0ST	1937
—	24	Barclay (2335)	0-6-0T	1953
Texaco	—	Fowler (4210140)	0-4-0DM	1958
Sir John King	—	H/Leslie (3640)	0-4-0ST	1926
—	19	Hunslet (3818)	0-6-0ST	1954
DS3	—	R/Hornsby (275883)	4wDM	1949
DS4	P6687	R/Hornsby (312984)	0-4-0DE	1951
(Ranald)	—	Sentinel (9627)	4wVBT	1957
—	970214	Wickham (6050)	2w-2PMR	c1951
—	—	Matisa (48626)	—	—
—	5	Hunslet (3837)	0-6-0ST	1955
—	7	Bagnall (2777)	0-6-0ST	1945
Borrowstounness	—*	Barclay (840)	0-4-0T	1899
—	—*	M/Rail (110U082)	4wDH	1970
—	—	Wickham (10482)	2w-2PMR	1970
—	(17)	Hunslet (2880)	0-6-0ST	1943
—	970213	Wickham (6049)	2w-2PMR	c1951
—	17	Barclay (2296)	0-4-0ST	1952
Lady Victoria	3	Barclay (1458)	0-6-0ST	1916
The Wemyss Coal Co Ltd	20	Barclay (2068)	0-6-0T	1939
—	(6)	Barclay (2127)	0-4-0CT	1942
—	DS1	Barclay (343)	0-6-0DM	1941
City of Aberdeen	—	B/Hawthorn (912)	0-4-0ST	1887
F82 (Fairfield)	—	E/Electric (1131)	4wBE	1940
(Ellesmere)	—	Hawthorns (Leith) (244)	0-4-0WT	1861
Kelton Fell	13	Neilson (2203)	0-4-0ST	1876
—	(1)	Neilson Reid (5710)	0-6-0T	1902
Kilbagie	DS2	R/Hornsby (262998)	4wDM	1949
DS6	(1)	R/Hornsby (421439)	0-4-0DE	1958
St Mirren	(3)	R/Hornsby (423658)	0-4-0DE	1958
—	D88/003	R/Hornsby (506500)	4wDM	1965

Name	No	Builder	Type	Built
—	(DS5)	R/Hornsby (423662)	0-4-0DE	1958
—	—	BTH	4wE	1908
Oakbank Oil Co Ltd No 2	—†	Baldwin (20587)	4wE	1902
(Denis)	—	Sentinel (9631)	4wVBT	1958
—	—	Arrols (Glasgow)	2w-2DM	c1966

*3ft 0in gauge
†2ft 6in gauge

Stock
A large selection of coaching stock, many built by Scottish pre-Grouping companies, and an appropriate collection of early freight vehicles

Owners
80105 and (Denis) (owned by Scottish Locomotive Owners Group)
246, Oakbank Oil Co Ltd No 2 and 24 (owned by Royal Museum of Scotland)

Caledonian Railway (Brechin)   SC

Headquarters: Caledonian Railway (Brechin) Ltd, The Station, 2 Park Road, Brechin, Angus DD9 7AF
Telephone: (0334) 55965, after 4pm Mon-Fri or (03562) 4562
Main station: Brechin
Other public stations: Bridge of Dun
OS reference: NO 603603
Car park: Brechin, Bridge of Dun
Access by public transport: Nearest BR station — Montrose, 8 miles. Buses — hourly from Montrose, Strathtay Scottish
Refreshment facilities: Light cooked meals and refreshments, available during steamdays at Brechin
Souvenir shop: Brechin
Museum: Brechin
Length of line: 4 miles
Passenger trains: Temporary working — Brechin station area shuttle pending opening of full service to Bridge of Dun
Period of public operation: Easter Sunday 15 April; 6/7 May; last Sunday in June; every Sunday in July; first two Sundays in August; Halloween Specials 29 October; Santa Specials 9, 16, 23 December; Boxing Day 26 December
Special events: Gala Day 22 July

Locomotives
Name	No	Origin	Class	Type	Built
—	46464	LMS	2MT	2-6-0	1950
—	D2866	BR	02	0-4-0DM	1961
Brechin City	D3059	BR	08	0-6-0DE	1954
—	27001	BR	27	Bo-Bo	1961

Industrial locomotives
Name	No	Builder	Type	Built
—	6	Bagnall (2749)	0-6-0ST	1944
Bon Accord	2	Barclay (807)	0-4-0ST	1897
—	1	Barclay (1863)	0-4-0ST	1926
—	1	Hunslet (2897)	0-6-0ST	1943
Yard No DY326	—	Planet (3743)	4wDM	1955
—	2/88	R/Hornsby (275880)	4wDM	1949
—	6	R/Hornsby (421700)	4wDM	1959
—	7	R/Hornsby (449747)	4wDE	1960

Stock
3-car Class 126 diesel multiple-unit, Nos 51017, 51043, 59404
3 ex-BR Mk 1 TSOs
1 ex-BR Mk 1 BSK
1 ex-BR Suburban
1 ex-BR Engineers Inspection Saloon
1 ex-BR Mk 1 sleeping car
1 ex-BR Full Kitchen Car
Various items of freight stock

Facilities for disabled: Easy access to both stations, access to toilets and shop, passengers can be assisted on and off trains

Glasgow Museum of Transport   M

Glasgow's magnificent railway collection represents one of the best efforts by a municipal authority to preserve a representative collection of

Locomotives
Name	No	Origin	Class	Type	Built
—	123	CR	123	4-2-2	1886

items appropriate to the 'locomotive builders to the Empire'. In 1989 the collection opened to view once again in its new setting at the former Kelvin Hall

Access by public transport: Strathclyde PTE Underground Kelvinhall: Strathclyde Buses 6, 6A, 8, 8A, 9, 9A, 16, 42, 42A, 44A, 57, 57A, 62, 62A, 62B, 64; Kelvin Scottish Buses 5, 5A; Clydeside Scottish Buses 17

Operating society/organisation: Glasgow City Council, Museums & Art Galleries Department

Location: Museum of Transport, Kelvin Hall, 1 Bunhouse Road, Glasgow G3 8DP

Telephone: 041-357-3929

Car park: Opposite Museum entrance

On site facilities: Toilets, cafeteria, shop and public telephone

Public opening: Monday-Saturday 10.00-17.00; Sunday 14.00-17.00. Closed

Name	No	Origin	Class	Type	Built
—	9	G&SWR	5	0-6-0T	1917
—	103	HR	—	4-6-0	1894
Glen Douglas	256	NBR	K	4-4-0	1913
Gordon Highlander	49	GNSR	F	4-4-0	1920

Industrial locomotives

Name	No	Builder	Type	Built
—	1	Barclay (1571)	0-6-0F	1917
—	—	Chaplin (2368)	0-4-0TG	1888
—	—	BEV (583)	B	1927

Stock
Glasgow District Subway car 39T
Glasgow Corporation Underground cars 1 and 4
LMS King George VI's saloon 498 of 1941

1 January and 25 December only. For extended 1990 opening hours see press

Facilities for disabled: Access to all areas but entry via separate entrance — enquire at main door

Feature article reference: RW March 1989, p155 (locomotive 123)

Lochty Railway   SC

Headquarters: Balbuthie, Leven, Fife
OD reference: NO 522080
Telephone: St Monans (033 37) 210
Main station: Lochty
Car park: Lochty
Access by public transport: Nearest bus service St Andrews-Anstruther service (1¾-mile walk)
Souvenir shop: Lochty
Passenger trains: Steam-hauled from Lochty through the estate of J. B. Cameron (1½ miles)
Period of public operation: Operates only on Sundays from 14.00. Mid-June till first Sunday in September
Special notes: This line operates entirely through the property of J. B. Cameron and no statutory authority was required in order to permit commencement of services in 1967
Membership details: Mr P. Westwater, 5 Sauchenbush Road, Kirkcaldy, Fife

Locomotives

Name	No	Origin	Class	Type	Built
Union of South Africa	60009	LNER	A4	4-6-2	1937

Industrial locomotives

Name	No	Builder	Type	Built
—	1	Peckett (1376)	0-4-0ST	1915
—	16	Bagnall (2759)	0-6-0ST	1944
—	—	R/Hornsby (421415)	4wDM	1958
—	NCB 21	Barclay (2292)	0-4-0ST	1951
—	SGB 10	Barclay (1890)	0-4-0ST	1926
—	BSC 16	YEC (2623)	0-6-0DE	1956

Locomotive notes: SGB 10 is the usual service locomotive.

Note: No 60009 *Union of South Africa* is stored at Markinch station for main line use on railtours.

Stock
3 ex-BR Mk 1 coaches
1 LNER observation coach
1 ex-NBR 8-ton box van (built 1901)
13 assorted private owner wagons
2 flat wagons

Paddle Steamer Preservation Society

The PS *Waverley* was built to the order of the London & North Eastern Railway in 1946; she replaced a vessel of the same name which was sunk off Dunkirk during May 1940. Sold to the PSPS in 1974 she now offers cruises around the coast of the United Kingdom in company with MV *Balmoral*. Also in the 'fleet' is PS *Kingswear Castle* which cruises on the Thames and Medway

Headquarters: Waverley Excursions Ltd, Waverley Terminal, Anderston Quay, Glasgow G3 8HA
Telephone: 041 221 8162

Scottish Industrial Railway Centre   SC

The Scottish Industrial Railway Centre is based on part of the former Dalmellington Iron Co railway system which was one of the best known industrial railway networks in Britain. Steam worked up until 1978 when the system closed and it is the aim of the centre to recreate part of the railway. The Ayrshire Railway Preservation Group also own the former G&SWR station at Waterside, 2 miles from the centre, and have access to the former NCB locomotive shed and wagon workshops at Waterside. These locations are not yet open to the general public. Working in conjunction with the Dalmellington & District Conservation Trust it is hoped to create an industrial heritage centre at Waterside based on the iron, coal and brick making industries

Location: Scottish Industrial Railway Centre, Minnivey Colliery, Dalmellington, Ayrshire
OS reference: NS 476074
Operating society/organisation: Ayrshire Railway Preservation Group
Telephone: The Secretary (0292) 313579
Access by public transport: Nearest BR station, Ayr (14 miles). Western Scottish bus service from Ayr, Nos 52/53. Tel: (0292) 264643
On site facilities: Guided tours of centre, museum of railway relics and photographs, souvenir shop and buffet
Public opening: Open for static display with limited facilities every Saturday, June to end September
Special events: Steam Days 1990: 27 May; 23/24* June; 28/29* July; 25/26

Locomotives

Name	No	Origin	Class	Type	Built
—	MP228 (12052)	BR	11	0-6-0DE	1949
—	MP229 (12093)	BR	11	0-6-0DE	1951

Industrial locomotives

Name	No	Builder	Type	Built
—	16	A/Barclay (1116)	0-4-0ST	1910
—	8	A/Barclay (1296)	0-6-0T	1912
—	19	A/Barclay (1614)	0-4-0ST	1918
Aberdeen Corporation Gas Works	3	A/Barclay (1889)	0-4-0ST	1926
—	8	A/Barclay (1952)	0-4-0F	1928
—	10	A/Barclay (2244)	0-4-0ST	1947
—	25	A/Barclay (2358)	0-6-0ST	1954
—	1	A/Barclay (2368)	0-4-0ST	1955
—	118	A/Barclay (366)	0-4-0DM	1940
—	7	A/Barclay (399)	0-4-0DM	1956
Lily of the Valley	—	Fowler (22888)	0-4-0DM	1943
Blinkin Bess	—	R/Hornsby (284839)	4wDM	1950
Johnnie Walker	—	R/Hornsby (417890)	4wDM	1959
—	—	R/Hornsby (421697)	0-4-0DM	1959
—	107	Hunslet (3132)	0-4-0DM	1944
—	—	Sentinel (10012)	4wDM	1959
—	—	Donnelli (163)	4wDMR	1979

(3ft gauge)

Name	No	Builder	Type	Built
—	—	R/Hornsby (256273)	4wDM	1949
—	—	Hunslet (8816)	4wDH	1981

(2ft 6in gauge)

Name	No	Builder	Type	Built
—	2	R/Hornsby (183749)	4wDM	1937
—	3	R/Hornsby (210959)	4wDM	1941
—	1	R/Hornsby (211681)	4wDM	1942

August; 30 September. *Fireless locomotive expected to be in steam.
Opening times: 11.00-16.00
Membership details: Mr Frank Beattie, 8 Bentick Street, Kilmarnock, Ayrshire KA1 4AS

Stock
2 Wickham trolleys
1 steam crane
Various other items

Scottish Mining Museum — Prestongrange   SC

Location: On the B1348 between Musselburgh and Prestonpans.
OS reference: NT 734737
Operating society/organisation: Scottish Mining Museum Trust, Lady Victoria Colliery, Newtongrange, Midlothian EH22 4QN
Telephone: 031-663-7519
Car park: On site

Industrial locomotives

Name	No	Builder	Type	Built
—	6	A/Barclay (2043)	0-4-0ST	1937
—	17	A/Barclay (2219)	0-4-0ST	1946
Prestongrange	7	G/Ritchie (536)	0-4-2ST	1914
Tomatin	1	M/Rail (9925)	4wDM	1963
—	—*	Hunslet (4440)	4wDM	1952
—	32	R/Hornsby	4wDM	
—	33	R/Hornsby	4wDM	

*2ft gauge

On site facilities: Visitor Centre, Machine Exhibition Hall, Cornish beam engine installed in 1874. Toilets
Refreshment facilities: Available
Public opening: Tuesday-Friday 10.00-16.30, Saturday/Sunday 12.00-17.00
Length of line: 400m (standard gauge)
Facilities for disabled: Access and

Locomotive notes: *Prestongrange* is expected to be out of service during 1990, 6 to be available for passenger trains

toilet at Visitor Centre and footpaths along site
Special events: Steam during summer months — date to be confirmed
Special notes: Locomotive in steam

first Sunday of month April-October, passenger rides available. Advance notice is required for large parties
Membership details: Friends of the Scottish Mining Museum, Elaine Carmichael

Strathspey Railway

Scotland's steam railway in the highlands connects the busy tourist resort at Aviemore to the more traditional highland village of Boat of Garten, famed as one of the few nesting places of the osprey (viewing site 1½ miles from station). A feature of the railway is the special evening dinner and Sunday lunch trains. The former operating during June/August, the latter throughout the season
Headquarters: The Station, Boat of Garten, Inverness-shire PH24 3BH
Telephone: 047 983 692
Main station: Aviemore (Speyside)
Other public stations: Boat of Garten
OS reference: Aviemore NH 898131, Boat of Garten NH 943789
Car parks: Aviemore and Boat of Garten
Access by public transport: BR services and express bus to Aviemore. Highland buses local service to Boat of Garten
Refreshment facilities: On train buffet car or facilities on most trains. Evening and Sunday lunch time diner trains — booking advised — Tel: 047 983 258 for details/bookings
Souvenir shop: Boat of Garten and Aviemore (Speyside)
Museum: Boat of Garten
Depot: Aviemore (not open to public)
Length of line: 5 miles
Journey time: 17min, return within the hour possible on most services
Passenger trains: Steam- and some diesel-hauled services. Boat of Garten-Aviemore
Period of public operation: Please contact for details
Facilities for disabled: Access possible at Boat of Garten and Aviemore (Speyside). Please contact in advance for directions and if a party involved
Special notes: First and third class travel available on most trains. Family fares available for third class travel. Special rates/arrangements for parties.

Locomotives

Name	No	Origin	Class	Type	Built
—	5025	LMS	5MT	4-6-0	1934
—	46512	LMS	2MT	2-6-0	1952
—	828	CR	812	0-6-0	1899
—	08490	BR	08	0-6-0DE	1958
—	D5394	BR	27	Bo-Bo	1962

Locomotive notes: In service 5025, D5394. Under restoration 46512, 828. Under repair 08490.

Industrial locomotives

Name	No	Builder	Type	Built
—	48	Hunslet (2864)	0-6-0ST	1943
Cairngorm	9	RSH (7097)	0-6-0ST	1943
—	60	Hunslet (3686)	0-6-0ST	1948
Victor	2996	Bagnall (2996)	0-6-0ST	1951
Niddrie	6	Barclay (1833)	0-6-0ST	1924
Forth*	10	Barclay (1890)	0-4-0ST	1926
Dailuaine	1	Barclay (2073)	0-4-0ST	1939
Balmenach	2	Barclay (2020)	0-4-0ST	1936
—	7	Barclay (2017)	0-6-0T	1935
Clyde	3	Barclay (2315)	0-4-0ST	1951
Inveresk	14	R/Hornsby (260756)	0-4-0DM	1950
Inverdon	15	Simplex (5763)	4wDM	1957
—	16	North British (27549)	0-4-0DM	1951
Queen Anne	20	R/Hornsby (265618)	4wDM	1948

Locomotive notes: In service 3, 60, 2996.

Stock
14 ex-BR coaches
5 ex-LMS coaches
1 Pullman coach
3 ex-LMS sleeping cars
1 ex-LNER sleeping car
1 ex-LNWR coach
1 ex-HR coach
1 ex-NBR coach
2 ex-GNSR coaches
Numerous examples of rolling stock
*Not on site

Owners
46512 (the Highland Locomotive Co Ltd)
828 (the Scottish Locomotive Preservation Trust Fund)

Membership details: Strathspey Railway Association at above address

Ireland

Downpatrick Railway Project

Location: Downpatrick Station, Market Street, Downpatrick, Co Down
OS reference: J483444
Operating society/organisation: Downpatrick & Ardglass Railway Co Ltd, with the support of the Downpatrick Railway Society
Telephone: (0232) 776608 or 643830, (0396) 830141
Car park: Available adjacent to station in Downpatrick
Access by public transport: A regular service is operated by Ulsterbus from Belfast Tel: (0232) 320011
Refreshment facilities: Buffet carriage open on operating days
On site facilities: Souvenir shop, toilets
Length of line: ½-mile
Public opening: St Patricks Day (17 March); Easter Monday and Tuesday; Saturdays and Sundays in July and August, and in December
Period of public operation: 14.00-17.00
Journey time: 30min return journey to Quoile marshes
Special events: Gala Day 26 August, Easter Egg and Santa Specials
Facilities for disabled: All station facilities at Downpatrick have facilities for disabled
Membership details: Peter King, Secretary, Downpatrick Railway Society, 15 Ravensdene Park, Belfast BT6 0DA, Northern Ireland. (0232) 643830

Locomotives

Name	No	Origin	Class	Type	Built
—	E421	CIE	421	C	1962
—	E432	CIE	421	C	1962
—	G613	CIE	611	B	1962

Industrial locomotives

Name	No	Builder	Type	Built
Guinness	3BG	H/Clarke (1152)	0-4-0ST	1919
—	1	O&K (12475)	0-4-0T	1934
—	3	O&K (12662)	0-4-0T	1935

Rolling stock
1 CIE Brake open standard
1 CIE Brake open standard generating steam van
1 CIE Buffet open standard
2 NCC parcels vans
1 NCC open wagon
1 GNR(I) brake van
1 CIE closed van
1 GS&WR ballast hopper
1 GSR ballast hopper
Belfast & County Down Railway 'Royal Saloon' No 153
1 B&CDR 1st/2nd composite (No 152)
1 B&CDR 3rd open (ex-railmotor)
1 B&CDR 6 wheeled brake 3rd (No 39)
1 B&CDR 6 wheeled 2nd (No 154)
1 GS&WR 3rd open (No 836)
1 GNR(I) 6 wheeled saloon (No unknown)

Owners
1 and 3 (the Irish Sugar Locomotive Group)
G613 (on loan from Westrail [Taum] Ltd)
3BG (on loan from the Railway Preservation Society of Ireland)

Irish Steam Preservation Society   M

Location: Stradbally Hall, eight miles from Athy, six miles from Portlaoise.
Telephone: (0502) 25136
Access by public transport: Irish

Industrial locomotives

Name	No	Builder	Type	Built
—	2	Barclay (2264)	0-4-0WT	1949

Rail train to Athy or Portlaoise.
Kavanagh's Bus Portlaoise-
Stradbally-Athy (daily Monday-
Saturday)
On site facilities: 3ft gauge railway.
Museum in nearby town
Catering facilities: None on site but
town centre ¼-mile away
Length of line: 1km
Public opening: Public open days
Easter 15/16 April; June Bank Holiday
3/4 June; 5/6 August (National Steam
Rally); 16 September; 28/29 October.
14.30-17.00 each day (noon-18.30,
5/6 August)

Name	No	Builder	Type	Built
—	—	Hunslet (2281)	4wDM	1941
Nippy	—	Planet (2014)	4wDM	1936
—	4	R/Hornsby (326052)	4wDM	1952

Stock
1 Passenger coach
2 Ballast wagons
1 Brake van

Railway Preservation Society of Ireland SC

The RPSI is more famed for its
activities elsewhere in Ireland than for
its line based at Whitehead and
Mullingar. The Society enjoys
excellent co-operation from the
national railway system of both parts
of Ireland and its spring 'Three-Day
Railtour' (which normally provides up
to five days of activities) has become
renowned world-wide and regularly
sells out well in advance. Numerous
other day excursions are operated
throughout the year for those unable
to participate in the spring weekend
tour. Short steam train rides are also
provided on certain dates at the main
depot at Whitehead which is well
worth a visit to view the Society's
extensive collection
Location: Whitehead Excursion
station
Operating society: Railway
Preservation Society of Ireland
Telephone: Whitehead (09603) 78567
Car park: At the site
Access by public transport:
Northern Ireland Railways services
from Belfast (York Road) or Larne
Harbour: Ulster Bus service
On site facilities: Souvenir shop,
refreshments in dining car, open on
Sundays during, July and August
Public opening: Easter Sunday,
Monday and Tuesday; Sundays during
July and August for steam train rides
and for Santa services on December
Sundays before 25 December

Right:
**The 08.14 Portadown-Belfast
service on 10 August 1989 was
worked by GNR(I) No 85** *Merlin.*
**This was one of the highlights of
'Ulster 150' week, during which a
number of commuter specials were
worked by steam.** *Charles P. Freil*

Special notes: The RPSI is noted for its main line railtours operated each year using its own rolling stock and coaches. For details telephone above number and leave name and address

Steam train rides, Sundays in July and August 14.00-17.00 at Whitehead **Special excursions:** Easter Bunny train rides at Whitehead 15, 16, 17 April; Comeragh Railtour 12, May (Dublin-Limerick) 13 May (Limerick-Athenry-Dublin-Belfast) 14 May (Belfast Central-Belfast York Road-Whitehead; Portrush Flyer. 12 July, 4, 18 August (Belfast-Portrush and return); Steam Enterprise 1, 15, 22 September (Belfast-Dublin and return); Santa train rides at Whitehead 2, 9, 15, 16 December.

1990 Dublin-based events: Dublin-Maynooth shuttle 26 May; Dublin-Galway and return 22 June; Dublin-Arklow (or Dundalk) 28 July; Greystones-Dublin-Malahide shuttle 18 August; Dublin-Rosslare and return 8 September
Feature article references: RW August 1988, p454; RW October 1989, p594 (1989 Mount Brandon railtour)

Locomotives

Name	No	Origin	Class	Type	Built
Merlin	85*	GNR (I)	V	4-4-0	1932
Slieve Gullion	171	GNR (I)	S	4-4-0	1913
—	4	LMS (NCC)	WT	2-6-4T	1947
—	184†	GS&WR	J15	0-6-0	1880
—	186	GS&WR	J15	0-6-0	1879
—	461	D&SER	K2	2-6-0	1922
Lough Erne	27	SL&NCR	Z	0-6-4T	1949

Industrial locomotives

Name	No	Builder	Type	Built
Guinness	3‡	H/Clarke (1152)	0-4-0ST	1919
R. H. Smyth	3	Avonside (2021)	0-6-0ST	1928
—	23	Planet (3509)	0-4-0DM	1951

*On loan from Ulster Folk & Transport Museum
†Normally based in the Republic of Ireland
‡On loan to Downpatrick & Ardglass Railway Society

Stock
The Society also owns some 20 coaches, normally resident at Whitehead, where a small number of freight wagons are also preserved

Shanes Castle Railway   SC

A 3ft gauge line runs from the Lodge Gates to the Old Castle ruins through the park and along the shore of Loch Neagh and runs through Lord O'Neill's nature reserve
Headquarters: Antrim station, Shanes Castle Estate, Co Antrim, Northern Ireland
Telephone: Antrim (084 94) 63380/62216
Main station: Antrim (SCR)
Car parks: Shanes Castle Estate, Antrim
Access by public transport: By Ulsterbus from several centres. By NI Railways to Antrim station
Refreshment facilities: Shanes Castle station
Length of line: 1½ miles, 3ft gauge
Souvenir shop: Antrim station
Passenger trains: Steam and diesel-hauled trains from Antrim station through the Shanes Castle estate. Diesel service only on Saturdays in May, June and September
Period of public operation: Sundays and Bank Holidays April; Saturdays, Sundays and Bank Holidays in May and September; Wednesday, weekends and Bank Holidays in June, Tuesday, Wednesday, Thursdays and weekends July-August; Sundays in September. Opening times 12.30-18.30
Special events: Events scheduled for steam working 7 May; Car Rally 10 June; Steam Rally 13/14 July
Facilities for disabled: Limited, no toilets, ramps available
Special notes: Railway serves visitors to the Shanes Castle estate of Lord O'Neill which includes an extensive nature reserve

Locomotives

Name	No	Builder	Type	Built
Tyrone	1	Peckett (1026)	0-4-0T	1904
—	2	Simplex (11039)	0-4-0DM	1956
Shane	3	Barclay (2265)	0-4-0WT	1949
Blue Circle	4	Simplex (102T016)	0-4-0DH	1976
Nancy	5	Avonside (1547)	0-6-0T	1908
Rory	6	Simplex (102TO07)	0-4-0DH	1974

Stock
12 4-wheel carriages
3 4-wheel Tram cars
2 ex-Londonderry & Lough Swilly Railway wagons
1 ex-Belfast & Northern Counties Railway wagon

This former weaving machinery manufacturer's premises has all the atmosphere of an early Victorian railway terminus with the trains waiting in the platforms. A real Aladdin's cave and alone would justify a visit to the province

Location: Witham Street, Belfast

Operating organisation: Ulster Folk & Transport Museum, Cultra Manor, Holywood, Co Down

Telephone: Belfast (0232) 451519

Access by public transport: Citybus routes 16, 21, 24, 25, 76 and 77 to Rope Works

Car park: No facilities

On site facilities: Shop, toilets. 7¼in line (at Cultra)

Public opening: Daily (except Sunday) 10.00 to 17.00

Locomotives (5ft 3in)

Name	No	Origin	Class	Type	Built
—	93	GNR(I)	JT	2-4-2T	1895
—	30	BCDR	I	4-4-2T	1901
Dunluce Caste	74	LMS(NCC)	U2	4-4-0	1924
Maeve	800	GSR	B1A	4-6-0	1939
—	1	R/Stephenson (2738)	—	0-6-0T	1891
Merlin	85*	GNR(I)	V	4-4-0	1932

Locomotives (narrow gauge)

Name	No	Origin	Class	Type	Built
Kathleen	2	CLR	—	4-4-0T	1887
Blanche	2†	CDJRC	—	2-6-4T	1912
Phoenix	11	CVR	—	4wD	1928
—	2	Industrial	—	0-4-0	1956
—	20	Industrial	—	0-4-0	1905

*On loan to RPSI for operational use
†On loan to Derby Railway Heritage Centre

Stock
1 Dublin, Wicklow & Wexford Railway coach
1 Dundalk, Newry & Greenore Railway coach
1 Midland & Great Western Railway director's saloon (ex-private vehicle)
1 Electric tramcar of Bessbrook-Newry Tramway, bodywork from a Dublin & Lucan Railway car
1 Covered 'toastrack' of Giant's Causeway, Portrush and Bush Valley Railway & Tramway Co
1 Caven-Leitrim Railway coach
1 County Donegal Railway railcar
1 County Donegal Railway director's coach

Westrail

Location: Tuam, Co Galway, Ireland

OS Reference: Lat 42, Long 52

Operating society/organisation: Westrail (Tuam) Ltd, The Railway Station, Vicar Street, Tuam, Co Galway

Telephone: (093) 24200, (091) 91039, (091) 65269. **Fax:** (091) 65384

Car park: On site

Access by public transport: Irish Rail — Athenry. Bus Eireann — Tuam

Catering facilities: On train, licensed snack bar. Platform shops at Athenry

Length of line: Athenry-Tuam, 15 miles

Period of public operation: Weekends June-August — please check for specific details

Journey time: 1-3hr return (see timetable for details)

Memberships details: Contact above address for details

Locomotives

Name	No	Origin	Class	Type	Built
—	90	GSWR	J30	0-6-0T	1875
—	E428	CIE	421	C	1962
—	G613*	CIE	611	B	1962
—	3	CSET	—	0-4-0DM	1960
—	B104	CIE	101	A1A-A1A	1956
—	B113	CIE	113	Bo-Bo	1951

*On loan to Downpatrick & Ardglass Railway

Rolling stock
3 ex-CIE coaches

Right:
On 1 July 1989 Westrail's ex-CIE shunter, No E428, rejoins the head of its train at Athenry main line station during the inaugural service from Tuam. *Shane G. McQuillan*

Alderney Railway

Location: Alderney, Channel Islands
Operating society/organisation:
Alderney Railway Society, PO Box 75,
Alderney, Channel Islands
Telephone: 0481-82 3534 (Operations
Manager)
Car park: Yes
Access by public transport: Aurigny
Air Services from Southampton and
Bournemouth. Weymouth Maritime
Services from Weymouth. Torbay
Seaways from Torquay
On site facilities: Shop at Braye
Road, refreshments nearby
Public opening: Weekends and Bank
Holidays, Easter to October
Special events: Alderney Week

Industrial locomotives

Name	No	Builder	Type	Built
J. T. Daly	3	Bagnall (2450)	0-4-0ST	1931
Elizabeth	D100	Vulcan (D100)	0-4-0DM	1949

Stock

3 Wickham trolleys run as multiple-unit
2 Goods wagons
2 ex-London Underground 1938 Stock tube cars (locomotive-hauled)
2 Wickham Flats

4-12 August. Easter Egg Specials on
Easter Saturday. Santa Specials,
Saturday before Christmas

Length of line: 2 miles
Facilities for disabled: By prior
arrangement

Groudle Glen Railway

SC

Location: Groudle Glen Railway, Isle
of Man
Operating company: Groudle Glen
Railway Ltd (managed by the Isle of
Man Steam Railway Supporters'
Association) of 19 Ballabrooie Grove,
Douglas, Isle of Man
Telephone: 0624 22138 (evenings)
Car park: Yes
Access by public transport: Manx
Electric Railway
On site facilities: Sales shop
Length of line: ½-mile, 2ft gauge
Public opening: Sundays and Bank
Holidays May to September with some
Wednesday evening services in July
and August; Santa Trains in December
Facilities for disabled: Due to the
line's location, those who are disabled
will have some difficulty. It is
suggested that they telephone for
advice
**Further information and
membership details:** From above
address

Locomotives

Name	No	Builder	Type	Built
Dolphin	1	H/Hunslet (4394)	4wDM	1952
Walrus	2	H/Hunslet (4395)	4wDM	1952
Sea Lion	—	Bagnall (1484)	2-4-0T	1896

Below:
Llen Coan on 2 July 1989 with Bagnall 2-4-0T *Sea Lion* running round its train. *Mike Jones*

Isle of Man Railway

The 3ft gauge Isle of Man Railway is a survivor of a system which covered the whole island. Almost continuous operation since 1874 makes it one of the oldest preserved railways in the British Isles. The railway has changed little since the turn of the century and retains much of its Edwardian atmosphere. It runs for 15 miles between Douglas and Port Erin through the island's rolling southern countryside. One of the original locomotives built in 1874 is still in daily service making it one of the oldest operational steam locomotives in the British Isles

Headquarters: Isle of Man Railways, Strathallan Crescent, Douglas, Isle of Man
Telephone: Douglas (0624) 74549
Main station: Douglas
Other public stations: Port Soderick, Santon, Castletown, Port Erin, Ballasalla, Port St Mary
Car parks: Douglas, Ballasalla, Castletown, Port Erin
Access by public transport: Isle of Man Transport buses to main centres
Refreshment facilities: Port Erin and Douglas
Souvenir shops: Douglas and Port Erin
Museum: Port Erin
Depot: Douglas
Length of line: 15¼ miles, 3ft gauge
Passenger trains: Douglas-Port Erin
Period of public operation: Daily

Locomotives

Name	No	Builder	Type	Built
Loch	4*	B/Peacock (1416)	2-4-0T	1874
G. H. Wood	10	B/Peacock (4662)	2-4-0T	1905
Maitland	11*	B/Peacock (4663)	2-4-0T	1905
Hutchinson	12*	B/Peacock (5126)	2-4-0T	1908
Kissack	13*	B/Peacock (5382)	2-4-0T	1910
—	19*	Walker (GNR (I))	diesel railcar	1950
—	20*	Walker (GNR (I))	diesel railcar	1951

*Operational, No 10 is stored out of use, not on display.

On display in museum at Port Erin

Name	No	Builder	Type	Built
Sutherland	1	B/Peacock (1253)	2-4-0T	1873
Caledonia	15	Dubs & Co (2178)	0-6-0T	1885
Mannin	16	B/Peacock (6296)	2-4-0T	1926

Owned by Isle of Man Railway Society (not on display)

Name	No	Builder	Type	Built
Mona	5	B/Peacock (1417)	2-4-0T	1874
Tynwald*	7	B/Peacock (2038)	2-4-0T	1880
Fenella	8	B/Peacock (3610)	2-4-0T	1894
Douglas	9	B/Peacock (3815)	2-4-0T	1896

*Chassis only

13-20 April and 7 May-29 September 1990
Facilities for disabled: Level access throughout Douglas and Port Erin stations including snack bar. Carriages able to carry wheelchairs, ramps provided. Advance notice helpful

Manx Electric Railway

The 3ft gauge Manx Electric Railway is a unique survivor of Victorian high technology. A mixture of railway and tramway practice, it was built in 1893 and was a pioneer in the use of electric traction. Two of the original cars are still in service making them the oldest tramcars still in operation in the British Isles. After leaving Douglas, the railway passes the newly opened Groudle Glen Railway before reaching the charming village of Laxey, home of the Snaefell Mountain Railway. The line continues over some of the most breathtaking coastal scenery in the island before reaching its terminus at Ramsey nearly 18 miles from Douglas

Motor Cars

Nos	Type	Seats	Body	Built
1, 2	Unvestibuled saloon	34	Milnes	1893
5, 6, 7, 9	Vestibuled saloon	32	Milnes	1894
14, 15, 17, 18	Cross-bench open	56	Milnes	1898
16	Cross-bench open	56	Milnes	1898
19-22	Winter saloon	48	Milnes	1899
23	Centre-cab locomotive	—	IOMT & EP	1900
25-27	Cross-bench open	56	Milnes	1898
28-31	Cross-bench open	56	ERTCW	1904
32, 33	Cross-bench open	56	UEC	1906

Trailers

	Type	Seats	Body	Built
13	Cross-bench open	44	Milnes	1893
36, 37	Cross-bench open	44	Milnes	1894
40, 41, 44	Cross-bench open	44	EE Co	1930

Headquarters: Isle of Man Railways, Strathallan Crescent, Douglas, Isle of Man
Telephone: Douglas (0624) 74549
Main station: Douglas (Derby Castle)
Other public stations: Laxey, Ramsey
Car parks: Douglas, Laxey, Ramsey nearby
Access by public transport: Isle of Man Transport buses to main centres
Depots: Douglas, Laxey, Ramsey
Refreshment facilities: Laxey
Museum and souvenirs: Ramsey

42, 43	Cross-bench open	44	Milnes	1903
45-48	Cross-bench open	44	Milnes	1899
49-50, 53, 54	Cross-bench open	44	Milnes	1893
52	pw flatcar (ex trailer)	—	Milnes	1893
55, 56	Cross-bench open	44	ERTCW	1904
57, 58	Saloon	32	ERTCW	1904
59	Special Saloon	18	Milnes	1895
60	Cross-bench open	44	Milnes	1896
61, 62	Cross-bench open	44	UEC	1906

Length of line: 17 miles, 3ft gauge
Passenger service: Douglas-Ramsey
Period of public operations: Daily 9 April-29 September 1990

Special notes: Folded wheelchairs can be carried. Please notify in advance

Ramsey Electric Railway Museum M

Location: Manx Electric Railway Station, Parsonage Road, Ramsey, Isle of Man
Operating society/organisation: (General enquiries) Isle of Man Railway Society, 4 Clifton Road, Rugby, Warwickshire
(Applications for special opening) c/o Isle of Man Railways, Douglas, IoM
Telephone: (General enquiries) 0788 543026
Car parks: Locally in nearby street
Access by public transport: Manx Electric Railway station adjoins museum; Douglas-Laxey-Ramsey buses pass within a few yards, alight at Parsonage Road
On site facilities: Museum shop, toilets in MER station
Public opening: Monday to Friday

No	Origin/Type	Built
	Manx Electric Railway	
23	MER Bo-Bo electric loco	1900
26	MER Bogie freight car	1895
	Douglas Horse Tramway	
11	Douglas, open toastrack	1886
47	Douglas, bulkhead car	1911
49	Douglas, convertible car	1935
—	Horse tram transporter wagon	c1930
	Queens Pier Tramway	
—	Hibberd 'Planet' 4WPM (2037)	1937
—	Hibberd-PRV bogie trailer (2038)	1937
—	4w Skip, ex-Ballajora Quarry	
—	4w Skip, ex-Poortown Quarry	

only; late May to mid-September 11.00-15.45
Special notes: For parties travelling by MER, opening outside normal hours may sometimes be possible

Snaefell Mountain Railway

The 3ft 6in gauge Snaefell Mountain Railway is unique. It is the only electrically-driven mountain railway in the British Isles. Almost all the rolling stock is original and dates back to 1895. The railway begins its journey at the picturesque village of Laxey where its terminus is shared with the Manx Electric Railway. The climb to the summit of Snaefell (2,036ft) is a steep one and the cars travel unassisted up gradients as steep as 1 in 12. From the summit, the views extend to Wales, Scotland, England and Ireland
Headquarters: Isle of Man Railways, Strathallan Crescent, Douglas, Isle of Man

Nos	Type	Seats	Body	Built
1-4, 6	Vestibuled saloon	48	Milnes	1895
5 (rebuild)	Vestibuled saloon	48	MER/Kinnin	1971

Telephone: Douglas (0624) 74549
Main station: Laxey
Other public stations: Bungalow, Summit
Car parks: Laxey, Bungalow (nearby)
Access by public transport: Manx Electric Railway or Isle of Man Transport bus to Laxey
Refreshment facilities: Laxey, Summit
Museum: Ramsey
Souvenirs: Summit
Length of line: 5 miles, 3ft 6in gauge
Passenger service: Laxey-Snaefell summit
Period of public operation: Daily 6 May-29 September 1990
Special notes: No special facilities for disabled

Miniature Railway Section

Audley End Railway
Audley End House, Saffron Walden, Essex. Tel:
(0799) 22345 or 27956
Opening details: Daily — Easter week, summer
half-term, summer school holidays and Sundays and
bank holidays April-October (from 14.00)
10¼in gauge; 1½-miles long; 4 steam, 2 diesel
locomotives
Public access: BR Audley End (1 mile), free car park
Site facilities: Light refreshments, toilets
Note: (Postal address) Estate Office, Audley End,
Saffron Walden, Essex CB11 4JG

Great Cockcrow Railway
Hardwick Lane, Lyne, Chertsey, Surrey. Tel: Mon-Fri
(0932) 228950; Sun (0932) 565474
Opening details: Every Sunday May to October
inclusive, 14.15-17.30
7¼in gauge; normal run ⅞-mile; 14 steam locomotives,
1 electric, 1 petrol (nine normally in service)
Public access: BR Chertsey (1¼-miles); Green Line 716
Holloway Hill (½-mile), free car park
Site facilities: Toilet

Lightwater Valley Theme Park
North Stainley, Nr Ripon, North Yorkshire. Tel: (0765)
85368
Opening details: 24hr answer phone on above number
15in gauge; 1-mile long; 4 steam, 1 diesel, 1 petrol
locomotives
Public access: BR Harrogate (12 miles), free car park
Site facilities: Restaurant, food bar, coffee shop,
museum, toilets (including disabled), shops

Moors Valley Railway
Horton Road, Ashley Heath, Nr Ringwood, Dorset.
Tel: (0425) 471415
Opening details: Open every weekend throughout the
year, plus half-term holidays and daily from Spring
Bank Holiday to end September. Santa Specials in
December
7¼in gauge; 1-mile long; 6 steam locomotives
Public access: BR Christchurch, free car park
Site facilities: Toilets (including disabled), shop

Below:
Audley End Miniature Railway's Curwen-built 2-8-2 is based on an American narrow gauge prototype.
R. E. Ruffell

Association of Railway Preservation Societies Ltd

Company Limited by Guarantee and not having a share capital.

Registered in England No 1222717

(Registered Office: 21 Market Place, Wednesbury, West Midlands WS10 7AY)

Administrative Office: 3 Orchard Close, Watford, Hertfordshire WD1 3DU. Tel: (0923) 221280. Fax: (0923) 241023 (ARPS).

President: Dame Margaret Weston DBE

Vice President: Capt Peter F. Manisty MBE, Royal Navy (Retd) (also Member of Council)

Directors/Council of Management

Chairman and Legal Advisor:
David Morgan, 7 Cheyne Place, London SW3 4HH. Tel: 01-352 6077

Vice Chairman and Meetings Officer:
Peter Ovenstone, 33 Palmerston Place, Edinburgh EH12 5AU. Tel: 031-225 1486 (answerphone).

Company Secretary/Treasurer:
Robert Yates FCA, 21 Market Place, Wednesbury, West Midlands WS10 7AY. Tel: (Office) 021-556 1084.

General Administrator:
Douglas Whittle, 3 Orchard Close, Watford, Hertfordshire WD1 3DU. Tel: (0923) 221280. Fax: (0923) 241023 (ARPS).

Technical Officer:
David Madden, The Station, Sheringham, Norfolk NR26 8RA. Tel: (0263) 822045.

Press Officer:
John Jeffery, 42 North Street, Oundle, Peterborough PE8 4AL. Tel: (Office) (0733) 67474, ext 2129, (Home) (0832) 73010.

Annual Award:
John Ransom, Woodside, Craggan, Lochearnhead, Perthshire FK19 8QD.

Coaching Stock:
Chris Smyth, 7 Woodside, Knutsford, Cheshire WA16 8BX.

Minutes Secretary and Overseas Liaison:
Richard Tapper, 39 Grange Court, Boundary Road, Newbury, Berkshire RG14 7PH. Tel: (0635) 30464.

Journal Editor:
Stephen Broadbent, 11 Kings Walk, Whitchurch, Hampshire. Tel: (Home) (0256) 892798, (Office) (0256) 63111. Fax: (0256) 840149.

Membership Secretary (Corporate):
David Woodhouse, c/o Talyllyn Railway, Wharf Station, Tywyn, Gwynedd LL36 9EY. Tel: (0654) 710472.

Officers and Advisors

Membership Secretary (Private):
Arthur Harding, 6 Ullswater Grove, Alresford, Hants SO24 9RP. Tel: (0962) 733327.

Sales Officer:
Edward Boxell, 17 Azalea Close, Uxbridge Road, Hanwell, London W7 3QA. Tel: 01-840 2917.

Information Papers Officer:
Revd Eric Buck, 40 Chapel Lane, Wymondham, Norfolk NR18 0DL. Tel: (0953) 602153.

Railway Heritage Awards:
Gordon Biddle, The Crossings, Levens, Kendal, Cumbria. Tel: (05395) 60993.

Historical Adviser:
Dick Riley, 115 Albemarle Road, Beckenham, Kent BR3 2HS.

Diesel/Electrical Adviser:
John Crane, 7 Robert Close, Potters Bar, Herts. Tel: (0707) 43568.

Publications Adviser:
Roger Cromblehome, 140 New Road, Netherton, Dudley, West Midlands DY2 6AY.

Railway Operating Adviser:
Allan Garraway MBE, Coedwig, Nethybridge Road, Boat of Garten, Invernesshire PH24 3BQ. Tel: 047-983 303.

Railtours Adviser:
Malcolm Burton, 85 Balmoral Road, Gillingham, Kent.

Special Projects Adviser:
Andrew Roberts, 2 Litchfield Close, Frog Hall, Brixworth, Northampton NN6 9BP.

Technical Adviser:
John Snell, RH&DR Head Office, New Romney, Kent TN28 8PL.

Magazine Competition Organiser:
Post vacant.

Chairman Irish Branch:
John Lockett, 21 Knollwood Road, Branbridge, County Down BT32 4PE.

Late Information

Harry (Barclay 1823 of 1924) has been transferred from Peak Rail to the Middleton Railway.

A 2ft gauge rack locomotive built by Ornstein & Kopple has been donated to Railworld, Peterborough (Nene Valley Railway).

Peak Rail's Class 25, No D7615 is now located at Matlock.

Didcot Railway Centre's No 6106 is expected to be on loan to the Gloucestershire Warwickshire Railway for the season.

Members of the Association of Railway Preservation Societies

Full Members

Bitton Railway Co Ltd: Mr G. Clark, 12 Cranwell Grove, Whitchurch, Bristol BS14 9QR

Bluebell Railway Preservation Society: Mr P. Thomas, 'Grey Friars', Gravelye Lane, Lindfield, Haywards Heath, Sussex

Bowes Railway Co Ltd: 112 Donvale Road, Donwell, Washington, Tyne & Wear NE37 1DN

The Bulleid Society Ltd: Mr D. A. Foale, 'Namron', South Chailey, Lewes, East Sussex BN8 4AD

Cambrian Railways Society Ltd: Mr J. L. D. Price, 'Delamere', Old Chirk Road, Gobowen, Oswestry, Salop SY11 1PE

Chasewater Light Railway & Museum Co: Mr B. Bull, Brownhills West Station, Hednesford Road, Brownhills West, Walsall WS8 7LT

Cholsey & Wallingford RPS: Mr D. Button, 1 Warwick Close, Abingdon, Oxford OC10 0NF

Colne Valley Railway Co Ltd: Mr J. R. Hymas, Castle Hedingham Station, Yeldham Road, Castle Hedingham, Halstead, Essex CO9 3DZ

Corris Railway Society: Mr A. H. Lawson, 165 Gynsill Lane, Anstey, Leicester LE7 7AN

Darlington Railway Preservation Society: S&DR Goods Depot, Station Road, Hopetown, Darlington DL3 6ST

Dart Valley Railway Association: Mr M. Webb, 7 The Orchard, Corn Park Road, Abbotskerwell, Devon TQ12 5QE

Dean Forest Railway Society Ltd: Mr C. A. Bladon, Laurel Cottage, Northwood Green, Westbury-on-Severn, Gloucestershire

Dinting Railway Centre Ltd (Bahamas Locomotive Society): Mr K. J. Tait, 73 Derby Road, Heaton Moor, Stockport, Cheshire SK4 4NG

East Lancashire Railway Preservation Society: Mr H. Hatcher, Bury Transport Museum, Castlecroft Road, Bury, Lancashire BL9 0LN

East Somerset Railway Co Ltd: Mr B. Buckfield, The Railway Station, West Cranmore, Shepton Mallet, Somerset

Festiniog Railway Society Ltd;: Mr D. Gordon, 72 West Street, Comberton, Cambridge CB3 7DS

Foxfield Light Railway Society Ltd: Mrs L. Reed, 63 Maythorne Road, Blurton, Stoke-on-Trent ST3 3AE

Friends of the National Railway Museum: Mr J. Spencer Gilks, c/o The National Railway Museum, Leeman Road, York YO2 4XJ

Great Central Railway Co: The Chairman, Loughborough Central Station, PO Box 33, Loughborough, Leicestershire LE11 1RW

Great Western Society Ltd: Mr J. B. O'Hagen, GWS, Didcot Railway Centre, Didcot, Oxon OX11 7NJ

Gwili Railway Co Ltd: The Chairman, 49 Gabalfa Road, Sketty, Swansea SA2 8NA

H Class Trust: Mr E. R. C. Oades, 5 Senlac Way, St Leonards-on-Sea, Sussex

Irish Steam Preservation Society Ltd: Mr F. C. Flewitt, 6 Waterloo Avenue, Dublin 3, Ireland

Keighley & Worth Valley Preservation Society: Mr R. G. Mitchell, 1 Smithy Row, Hurst Green, Blackburn, Lancs BB6 9QA

Lakeside Railway Society: Mr T. D. Owen, 83 Camberton Road, Linslade, Leighton Buzzard, Bedfordshire LU7 7UW

Leighton Buzzard Narrow Gauge Railway Society Ltd: Miss J. Churchill, 63 Holmbridge Gardens, Enfield, Middx EN3 7EY

Llangollen Railway Society: Mr A. Terry, 33 Deeside, Ellesmere Port, S. Wirral, Cheshire

Locomotive Club of Great Britain: Mr R. L. Patrick, 8 Wolviston Avenue, Bishopgate, York YO1 3DD

Locomotive Owners Group (Scotland) Ltd: Mr J. L. Stevenson, 4 Queens Road, Blackhall, Edinburgh EH4 2BY

Maid Marian Locomotive Fund: Mr H. Jones, 'Walden', 139 Stoops Lane, Bessacar, Doncaster DN4 7RG

Main Line Steam Trust Ltd: The Chairman, 112 Halstead Road, Mountsorrel, Loughborough LE12 7HG

Merchant Navy Locomotive Preservation Society Ltd: Mr R. Abercrombie, 12 Inglewood Avenue, Heatherside, Camberley, Surrey

Mid-Hants Railway Trust Ltd: Mr R. P. C. Higgs, 18 Barnsford Crescent, West End, Woking, Surrey GU24 9HX

Middleton Railway Trust Ltd: Mr I. Smith, The Station, Moor Road, Leeds LS10 2JQ

Midland & Great Northern Joint Railway Society Ltd: The Librarian, Sheringham Station, Sheringham, Norfolk NR26 8RA

Midland 4F Preservation Society: Mr I. Johnson, 13 Shepley Close, Hazel Grove, Stockport, Cheshire SK7 6JJ

Midland Railway Trust Ltd: Mr R. Clegg, 9 Hawthorn Crescent, Findern, Derby DE6 6AN

Nene Valley International Steam Railway: Wansford Station, Stibbington, Peterborough PE8 6LR

North Eastern Locomotive Preservation Group: Mr D. F. Martin, 21 Grassington Avenue, Northallerton, North Yorkshire DL7 8SY

North Gloucestershire Railway Co Ltd: Mr R. H. Wales, 7 Lypiatt Street, Tivoli, Cheltenham, Gloucestershire GL50 2UA

North York Moors Historical Railway Trust: Mr J. H. Meredith, 11 College Road, Copmanthorpe, York YO2 3US

Railway Preservation Society of Ireland: Mr R. Morton, 13 Sharman, Belfast BT9 5HE

Ravenglass & Eskdale Railway Preservation Society Ltd: Mr D. Pickup, The Retreat, Ravenglass, Cumbria CA18 1SW

Scottish Railway Preservation Society: Dr A. Glen, 21 Monks Road, Airdrie, Lanarkshire ML6 2QW

Severn Valley Railway Co Ltd: Mr M. J. Draper, 'Dyniatts', The Hill, Abberley, Worcester WR6 6BZ

Shackerstone Railway Society Ltd: Mr R. A. Briggs, 40 Newstead Avenue, Burbage, Hinckley

Sittingbourne & Kemsley Light Railway Ltd: Mr M. Burton, 85 Balmoral Road, Gillingham, Kent ME7 4QE

South Tynedale Railway Preservation Society: The Railway Station, Alston, Cumbria CA9 3JB

Southern Electric Group: Mr J. F. Chapter, 12 Cutter Field, Ashford, Kent TN23 2YU

Stanier 8F Locomotive Society Ltd: Mr D. R. McIntosh, 296 Lower Hillmorton Road, Rugby, Warwickshire CV21 4AE

Steam in Hereford Ltd (6000 Locomotive Association): Mr B. R. Wallis, 8 Little Birch Croft, Whitchurch, Bristol BS14 0JB

Stour Valley Railway Preservation Society: Mr L. Houghton, Old Railway Tavern, Station Road, Wakes Colne, Colchester, Essex CO6 2DS

Strathspey Railway Association: Mr R. Black, 37 Castle Avenue, Balloch, Alexandria, Dunbartonshire G83 8HU

Talyllyn Railway Co Ltd: Wharf Station, Tywyn, Gwynedd LL36 9EY

Tenterden Railway Co Ltd (Kent & East Sussex Railway): The Company Secretary, Tenterden Railway Co Ltd, Tenterden Town Station, Tenterden, Kent TN30 6HE

Vintage Carriages Trust: Mr M. W. Cope, Haworth Station, Keighley, West Yorkshire BD22 8NJ

Wainwright 'C' Preservation Society: Mr I. Demaid, 69 Bromley Gardens, Bromley, Kent BR2 0ES

Welshpool & Llanfair Light Railway Preservation Co Ltd: Llanfair Station, Llanfair Caereinion, Powys

Wight Locomotive Society: The Secretary, Railway Station, Haven Street, Ryde, Isle of Wight PO33 4DS

Yorkshire Dales Railway Museum Trust: Mr M. D. Cleaver, 26 Birch Hall Lane, Earby Colne, Lancashire BB8 6JX

1247 Society: Capt W. G. Smith, 1 Church road, Willington, Bedford MK44 3QD

1708 Locomotive Preservation Trust Ltd: Mr G. W. Kingham, Registered Office, 106 Stanford Road, Luton, Beds LU2 0QA

6201 Princess Elizabeth Society Ltd: E. J. Whitlock, 4 Lypiatt View, Bussage, Stroud, Gloucestershire LG6 8DA

Associate Members

A4 Locomotive Society Ltd: Mr G. R. Pope, Secretary, Keeper's Cottage, Muntham Farm, North End, Findon, Worthing BN14 0RQ

Avonside Steam Preservation Society: B. Barham, The Buffers, High Street, Hinxton, Saffron Walden, Essex

Ayrshire Railway Preservation Group: Mr G. Thompson, 4 Kyle Crescent, Loans, Troon, Ayrshire KA10 7EZ

Battle of Britain Locomotive Preservation Society: Mr R. J. Tanner, 317 Cardington Road, Bedford MK42 0DU

Bodmin & Wenford Railway plc: Mr R. G. Fitzgerald, Bodmin General Station, Bodmin, Cornwall PL31 1AQ

BRC&W Type 3 Preservation Group: Mr I. Simmons, 131 Sompting Road, Worthing, West Sussex BN14 9EX

Brechin Railway Preservation Society: The Station, 2 Park Road, Brechin, Angus DD9 7AF

Brecon Mountain Railway Association: The Chairman, Pant Station, Merthyr Tydfil, Mid Glamorgan

Bressingham Steam Engine Trust: Mr A. Bloom, Bressingham Hall, Bressingham, Diss, Norfolk IP22 2AB

Britannia Locomotive Society: Mr A. A. Lawson, Gaylands, 9 Bennett Drive, Myton Grange, Warwick CV34 6QJ

Butetown Historic Railway Society Ltd: Mr D. J. Morgan, 34 Bryngwyn Road, Cyncoed, Cardiff CF2 6PG

Cadeby Light Railway: Mrs A. Boston, Cadeby Rectory, Cadeby, Hinckley, Nuneaton, Warwickshire

Caerphilly Railway Society Ltd: Mr A. Smith, 51 Worcester Crescent, Newport, Gwent

Camelot Locomotive Society: Mr P. W. Gibbs, 3 Garden Close, Northolt, Middx UB5 5ND

Cholsey & Wallingford Railway Preservation Society: Mr D. Button, 1 Warwick Close, Abingdon, Oxon

Conwy Valley Railway Museum Ltd: c/o Burtons of Walsall Ltd, 65 Bradford Street, Walsall, West Midlands WS1 3QD

Cornish Steam Locomotive Preservation Society Ltd: Mr M. Orme, 3 Jubilee Terrace, Goonhavern, Truro, Cornwall TR4 9JY

Cotswold Steam Preservation Ltd: Mr J. M. Colley, Birchwood Farm, Bridgnorth Road, Shatterford, Nr Bewdley, Worcs DX12 1TP

Derwent Railway Society: Mr R. K. Demain, 1st Floor, 28 Main Street, Keswick, Cumbria CA12 5JH

Diesel and Electric Group: Mr J. M. Crane, 7 Robert Close, Potters Bar, Hertfordshire EN6 2DH

Dyfed Railway Co Ltd: The Chairman, Henllan Station, Llandyssul, Dyfed

Eastleigh Railway Preservation Society: Mr D. B. Smith, 17 Twiggs End Close, Locksheath, Southampton, Hants SO3 6ET

Fairbourne & Barmouth Railway: Mr J. Ellerton, Plas Gwyntog, Rhoslefain, Tonwy, Gwynedd LL37

Forest Pannier Tank Fund: Mr J. S. Metherall, 15 Sudbrook Way, Gloucester

Forest Prairie Fund: Mr J. Harris, 52 Rockfield Road, Hereford HR1 2UA

Foxcote Manor Society: Mr I. N. Travers, 5 Harlow Avenue, Upton-by-Chester, Cheshire CH2 1NQ

Gloucestershire Warwickshire Steam Railway PLC: Toddington Station, Toddington, Cheltenham, Gloucestershire GL54 5DT

Gravesend Railway Enthusiasts Society: Mr D. Hanger, 47 Lower Range Road, Gravesend, Kent DA12 2QL

Great Central Railway Coach Group: Mr K. H. Brooker, Manor Road, Sulgrave, Banbury, Oxon OX17 2RY

Great Western Preservations Ltd: Mr A. R. Machon, 15 Calder Close, Maidenhead, Berkshire SL6 7RS

The Gresley Society: Mr P. Holmes, Argyll Cottage, Thurgarton Quarters, Oxton Road, Southwell, Nottinghamshire NG25 0RW

GWR 813 Preservation Fund: Mr P. Goss, 23 Hatchmere, Thornbury, Bristol BS12 3EU

Hexham Rolling Stock Group: Mr G. Hall, 21 Birkdene, Stocksfield, Northumberland NE43 7EN

Hull & Barnsley Railway Stock Fund: Mr A. Halman, 6 Chequerfield Court, Chequerfield Avenue, Pontefract, West Yorkshire WP8 2TQ

Ivatt Locomotive Trust: Mr R. B. Miller, 'Ducal', 25 Loudham Road, Little Chalfont, Amersham, Buckinghamshire

Lambton No 29 Syndicate: Mr J. M. Richardson, 5 Ravine Hill, Filey, North Yorkshire YO14 9EU

Lancashire & Yorkshire Railway Preservation Society: Mr A. Cox, 3 Bastwell House, Blackburn, Lancashire BB1 9TY

Leicester Industrial Locomotive Group: Mr J. P. Bailey, 414 Hinckley Road, Leicester LE3 0WA

Lincolnshire Coast Light Railway: Mr H. L. Goy, 12 Giles Street, Cleethorpes DN35 8AE

Liverpool Locomotive Preservation Group: Mr K. Soper, 90 Brick Kiln Lane, Rufford, Lancs L40 1SY

Lloyds Railway Society: Hon Secretary, Lloyds, Lime Street, London EC3

LM 2MT 46464 Trust: Mr I. N. Fraser, Palace Gates, Viewfield Road, Arbroath, Angus DD11 2BS

London & North Western Society: Mr J. C. James, 'Solaby', 4 Longview Drive, Huyton, Liverpool L36 6EE

Lowthers Railway Society Ltd: Mr D. Lappin, 44 Lednock Road, Stepps, Glasgow G33 6LU

Manchester Rail Travel Society: Mr F. G. Cronin, 12 Chiltern Road, Ramsbottom, Lancashire

Manston Locomotive Preservation Society: T. L. Mann, 41 Crow Hill Road, Garlinge, Margate, Kent CT19 5PF

Maunsell Locomotive Society: Mr R. Packham, Chairman, 132 Church Road, Swanscombe, Kent DA10 0PH

North Staffordshire Railway Co Ltd: Mr A. Dale, The Railway Station, Cheedleton, Staffs ST13 7EE

North Tyneside Steam Railway Association: Mr R. J. Maughan, Stephenson Railway Museum Project, Middle Engine Lane, W. Chirton, N. Shields, Tyne & Wear

Peak Rail Ltd: Mr R. Raynor, 2A Avenue Road, Forest Gate, London E7 0LD

Plym Valley Railway Association: Mr B. Mills, 11 Hill View, Buckland, Monachorum, Yelverton, Devon PL20 7ND

Pontypool & Blaenavon Railway Society: Mr P. Powell, Haul-y-Bryn, Church Road, Abersychan, Gwent

Quainton Railway Society Ltd: Mr R. B. Miller, 'Ducal', 25 Loudham Road, Little Chalfont, Amersham, Buckinghamshire

Railway Club of Wales: Mr P. Trotter, 14 Lon Masarn, Tycoch, Swansea SA2 9EL

Railway Vehicle Preservation Ltd: Mr G. E. Maslin, 25 Peterborough Road, Farcet, Peterborough PE7 3BH

Redditch Steam Locomotive Preservation Society: Mr A. Marsden, 72 Longhurst Croft, West Heath, Birmingham B31 4SQ

Rheilffordd Llyn Tegid Ltd (Bala Lake Railway): Mr G. H. Barnes, 'Yr Orsaf', Llanuwchllyn, Bala, Gwynedd

Romney, Hythe & Dymchurch Railway Association: Mr A. Goyns, 9 Oak Farm Gardens, Headcorn, Ashford, Kent TN22 9TZ

Ruislip Lido Railway Society: Mr P. R. Shafe, 3 Oxleay Road, Rayners Lane, Harrow, Middx HA2 9UZ

Rutland Railway Museum: Mr G. E. Kobish, 9 The Knoll, Great Gonerby, Grantham, Lincolnshire NG31 8JY

Salisbury Steam Locomotive Preservation Trust: Mr E. J. Roper, 33 Victoria Road, Wilton, Salisbury, Wiltshire SP2 0OZ

Somerset & Dorset Railway Trust: M. J. Palmer, The Haven, Chandlers Lane, Edington, Bridgwater, Somerset

Southern Steam Trust: Mr M. L. Norris, The Station, Swanage, Dorset

South Western Circle: Mr D. E. S. Hill, 19 Cobton Drive, Hove, Sussex BN3 6WF

South Yorkshire Railway Preservation Society: Mr J. Wade, 138 Newman Road, Wincobank, Sheffield S9 1LS

Stanier Black Five Locomotive Preservation Society: Mr D. J. Porter, 29 High Street, Shoreham Village, Kent

Steamport Southport: Mr H. J. M. Royden, 35 Argameols Road, Freshfield, Crosby, Merseyside L37 7BY

Steam Power Trust '65: Mr K. H. Cockerill, 30 Hartburn Lane, Stockton-on-Tees TS18 3QH

Swindon & Cricklade Railway Society: Mr J. Larkin, Boscreeg, Church Lane, Fernham, Faringdon, Oxon

Telford Horsehay Steam Trust: Mr P. M. Davis, 23 Strutfield Road, Aqueduct, Telford TF4 3RS

Tunbridge Wells & Eridge RPS: Mr F. Wallace, The Old Dairy, Snatts Lane, Uckfield, East Sussex TN22 2AL

Thompson B1 Locomotive Trust: Mr J. G. Gwnett, 11 Valance End, Dunstable LU6 3LP

Underground Railway Rolling Stock Trust: Mr D. C. Alexander, 13 Irvine Drive, Stoke Mandeville HP22 5UN

Urie Locomotive Society: Mr A. Ball, 'Lavenham', Adams Lane, Selbourne, Atlton, Hants GU34 3LJ

Wells & Walsingham Light Railway: Mr R. W. Francis, Wells-next-the-Sea, Norfolk

Welsh Highland Light Railway 1964 Ltd: Mr W. J. Jones, Avalon, Llanfrothen, Gwynedd LL48 6LJ

Welsh Industrial and Maritime Museum: Dr E. S. Owen-Jones, Bute Street, Docks, Cardiff CF1 6AN

West Somerset Railway Co: The Railway Station, Minehead, Somerset

Western Locomotive Association: Mr A. M. Clarke, 6 Greatly, Welwyn Garden City, Herts AL7 4TS

Winchcombe Railway Museum Association: Mr T. R. Petchey, 23 Gloucester Street, Winchcombe, Gloucestershire GL54 5LX

Worcester Locomotive Society Ltd: Mr N. Powles, Station House, Station Road, Lower Heyford, Oxon OX5 3PD

1857 Society: Mr K. R. Bowen, 18 Lochmore Close, Hollycroft, Hinckley, Leicestershire

4247 Preservation Society: Mr N. Bilton, 41 Papist Way, Cholsey, Oxon OX10 9LL

6024 Preservation Society Ltd: Mr E. F. W. Ives, 63 Georges Hill, Widmer End, High Wycombe, Buckinghamshire HP15 6BH

9462 Preservation Group: Mr W. L. Jones, 74 Coychurch Road, Bridgend, Glamorgan CF31 2AP

45428 Stanier Class Five Locomotive Society Ltd: Mr J. B. Hollingsworth, 'Creua', Llanfrothen, Penrhyndeudraeth, Gwynedd LL48 6SH

71000 Duke of Gloucester Steam Locomotive Trust Ltd: Mr J. Shuttleworth, 55A Parma Crescent, Clapham, London SW11 1LU

Affiliate Members

ABAC: Dr J. Brenot, Boite No 1, 33034 Cedex Bordeaux, France

ABPF: The Chairman, Caixa Postal 6501 01051, São Paulo, Brazil

AECFM: M J. David, President, Marcilly-sur-Maulne, 37330 Chateau-la-Valliee, France

APPEVA: M Jacques Pradaro, 21 Rue Gueneguard, 75006 Paris 6, France

Berliner Eisenbahn Freunde: Herr Rudiger Reich, Stresemanstrasse 30, 1000, Berlin, Germany

CFM Blonay-Chamby: Mr J. F. Andrist, PO Box 366 CH 1001, Lausanne, Switzerland

Glasgow Museum of Transport: Mr J. Clayson, c/o Art Gallery & Museum, Kelvingrove, Glasgow G3 8AG

Great Western Railway Museum: Mr T. F. Bryan, Faringdon Road, Swindon, Wilts SN1 5BG

Guild of Railway Artists: Mr F. P. Hodges, 45 Dickens Road, Warwick CV34 5NS

Ian Allan Group: Chairman, Mr Ian Allan, Clock House, Station Approach, Shepperton TW17 8AS

Jarrold Colour Publications: The Chairman, Barrack Street, Norwich, Norfolk NR3 1TR

Leicester University Library: Periodicals Department, University Road, Leicester LE1 7RH

London Transport Museum Library: Mrs M. A. Fletcher, 39 Wellington Street, Covent Garden, London WC2E 7BB

Monkswearmouth Station Museum: The Curator, North Bridge Street, Sunderland

Museum Buurt Spoorweg: M. Livius Kooy, Vincentstraat 15 7481, LB-Haaksbergn, Netherlands

Narrow Gauge Railways of Wales: Mr D. Woodhouse, Wharf Station, Tywny, Gwynedd LL36 9EY

National Federation of Rail Societies: Mr K. Henderson, PO Box 2429, Auckland, New Zealand

National Museum of Science & Technology: The Librarian, PO Box 9724, Terminal T, Ottawa, Ontario K1G 5A3, Canada

National Railway Historic Society: Mr V. A. Vaughan, 320 Wisconsin Avenue, Oak Park, Illinois 60302, USA

National Tramway Museum Society: The Chairman, Crich, Matlock, Derbyshire DE4 5DP

National Trust Industrial Railway Museum: Mr I. W. Jones, Penrhyn Castle, Bangor, Gwynedd LL57 4AH

Pacific Vapeur Club: M Henri Williaume, Boite Postale 115 76303, Sotteville-le-Rouen, France

Railway Associations in London: Mr J. Heinemann, 43 Barn Rise, Wembley Park, Harrow, Middlesex HA9 9NT

Smalsparet Vajo-H-Vastervik: Philip Groves, WHVJ-Sec, Box 64 14600, Tullinge, Sweden

Stichting Brabant Rail: Mr J. E. F. L. Simons, Karel Dormanlaan 14, 4B19 BK Breda, Netherlands

Stoomscentrum Maldegem: Rik Degruyter, De Streep 19, B-B340 Damme-Sysele, Belgium

Stoomtram Goes Borsele: Mr J. P. Wijtenburg, Postbus 250 4460, AR Goes, Netherlands

Stoomtram Hoon-Medemblik: Mr Peter Scholten, PO Box 137, 1620-AC Hoorn, Netherlands

Transport Ticket Society: Mr A. Fairholm, 16 Blake Road, Seafar, Cumbernauld, Glasgow

Transport Trust: Mr D. Muirhead, Room 131, Melbury Houseice, Marylebone, London NW1 6JU

Ulster Folk & Transport Museum: Mr J. S. Moore, Cultra Manor, Hollywood, Co Down, Northern Ireland BT18 0EU

Westinghouse Signals: Mr H. R. Preater, PO Box 79, Pew Hill, Chippenham, Wiltshire SN15 1ND

To a person actively interested in nationwide railway preservation as opposed to one particular preservation scheme, PRIVATE MEMBERSHIP of the ASSOCIATION OF RAILWAY PRESERVATION SOCIETIES LTD offer many advantages. Three major meetings are organised annually, often at the railway site of a leading Member Society. Here one can meet well known personalities in the railway preservation world, and the host society invariably lays on a full day's programme which is both stimulating and enjoyable.

The ARPS Journal is sent to members, containing mostly the latest news of member societies' activities but also full of interesting titbits such as lists of steam locomotives for sale.

Railways Restored and other publications by Ian Allan in conjunction with ARPS are made available at reduced prices.

Private Membership Application Form (1990)

To: Membership Secretary, ARPS, 6 Ullswater Grove, Alresford, Hants SO24 9NP

Name...
(BLOCK LETTERS PLEASE)

Address...

....

Post Code.. Telephone.

Subscription enclosed .... Donation enclosed.

Private membership costs: 1 April-31 March (12 months) £10; 1 January-31 March (15 months) £12; Life membership £100.

Index